D1545974

MOTOR DEVELOPMENT

Current Selected Research
Volume 1

MOTOR DEVELOPMENT

Current Selected Research
Volume 1

Edited by

Jane E. Clark *and* James H. Humphrey
UNIVERSITY OF MARYLAND

PRINCETON BOOK COMPANY, PUBLISHERS

About the Editors

JANE E. CLARK, Assistant Professor of Physical Education at the University of Maryland, conducts and directs research in motor development. Her major research interest is in the area of motor control and coordination. Currently she is focusing on the development of certain locomotor skills.

JAMES H. HUMPHREY, Professor Emeritus at the University of Maryland, is perhaps best known for his work in child learning through motor activity. In recent years he has been exploring the area of stress in childhood with reference to its influence on child development.

Library of Congress Catalog Card Number 85-060703
ISBN-916622-35-5

Printed in the United States of America
Design by Bruce Campbell
Typesetting by Delmas

Board of Reviewers

Suzette Blanchard
University of Maryland
College Park, Maryland

David H. Clarke
University of Maryland
College Park, Maryland

Marguerite A. Clifton
California State University
Long Beach, California

Charles Corbin
Arizona State University
Tempe, Arizona

Walter Davis
Kent State University
Kent, Ohio

Patrick DiRocco
University of Maryland
College Park, Maryland

Charles O. Dotson
University of Maryland
College Park, Maryland

Gail Dummer
Indiana University
Bloomington, Indiana

Helen M. Eckert
University of California
Berkeley, California

Sarah Erbaugh
California State University
Long Beach, California

Martha Ewing
Michigan State University
East Lansing, Michigan

Trent Gabert
University of Oklahoma
Norman, Oklahoma

Jere P. Gallagher
University of Pittsburgh
Pittsburgh, Pennsylvania

David Gallahue
Indiana University
Bloomington, Indiana

Gladys Garrett
University of Connecticut
Storrs, Connecticut

David Goodman
Simon Fraser University
Vancouver, B.C., Canada

Susan Greendorfer
University of Illinois
Champaign/Urbana, Illinois

Lolas A. Halverson
University of Wisconsin
Madison, Wisconsin

Kathleen Haywood
University of Missouri
St. Louis, Missouri

Christine MacKenzie
University of Waterloo
Waterloo, Ont., Canada

Robert Malina
University of Texas
Austin, Texas

Hugh McCracken
Northeastern University
Boston, Massachusetts

Ricardo Petersen
University of Maryland
College Park, Maryland

G. Lawrence Rarick
University of California
Berkeley, California

Greg Reid
McGill University
Montreal, Que., Canada

Marcella Ridenour
Temple University
Philadelphia, Pennsylvania

Contents

Contents (Continued)

Introduction

This first volume of *Motor Development: Current Selected Research* presents original research and reviews on contemporary problems of interest to motor development scientists. Papers investigating motor control, motor skills, sociocultural considerations, and developmental delay make up this volume. With the exception of the Reviews section, all papers represent original research. For this volume the Reviews section includes symposium papers presented at the 16th Gatlinburg Conference on Mental Retardation and Developmental Disabilities, Gatlinburg, Tennessee, March 16-18, 1983.

It is the intention of the editors and Princeton Book Company, Publishers to provide motor development researchers with a periodic series reporting original research that investigates issues in motor development. The volumes should supplement and support journals and annual reviews reporting on similar topics. However, to the best knowledge of the editors, this is the only publication devoted specifically to research in motor development as such.

Motor development has evolved into a complicated and complex subject and involves, among others, biological, behavioral, and biomechanical considerations. The scholarly researchers who have contributed to this first volume represent the field well, and we extend our gratitude to them for their contributions. In addition, we wish to thank the members of the board of reviewers for giving of their time and talent in evaluating the papers.

A volume of this nature could serve as a basic and/or supplementary text in motor development courses. It could also serve as a reference for motor development specialist as well as for scientists investigating similar topics.

J.E.C.
J.H.H.

Coincidence-Anticipation Behavior of Children

ROBERT E. STADULIS
Kent State University

To examine the effects of age (7-, 9-, and 11-year-olds), gender, rate of stimulus display speed (from slow = 84cm/s to fast = 270 cm/s), and practice upon coincidence-anticipation performance, two experiments were conducted. In the first experiment, the stimulus display was a projected rolling ball; in the second experiment, the stimulus display was the Bassin Anticipation Timer. Results indicated that coincidence-anticipation accuracy increased over age, especially for boys, with a gender difference evidenced for 11-year-olds. Greatest accuracy for 7-year-olds occurred at the fastest rate of display speed. Responses were early for the projected ball task and late for the Bassin task. Improved performance occurred only over the first block of eight trials; practice increased response accuracy primarily for the slowest rate on the Bassin task. Over all children, for the first eight trials, greatest error was evidenced at the slowest speed. Results are discussed with reference to research findings in the coincidence-anticipation literature.

Within the past 10 years, the motor behavior research literature has reflected a rather consistent focus upon motor tasks that involve the coincidence-anticipation response; that is, the execution of a movement response coincident with the arrival of a moving stimulus at a designated interception point. The label "coincidence-anticipation," coined by Belisle (1963), has been used most frequently, but other terms have been employed to describe the interception task or process. These terms include "transit reaction" (Hick & Bates, 1950; Slater-Hammel, 1960), "prediction motion" (Gottsdanker, 1952), "prediction" in concert with "receptor and effector anticipation" (Poulton, 1957), "perceptual anticipation" (Broadbent, 1958), "visuo-perception" (Williams, 1968), "anticipation and timing" (Schmidt, 1968), "ball skill" (Whiting, 1969),

Data for the initial experiment were collected as part of my doctoral dissertation at Teachers College, Columbia University, under the direction of A.M. Gentile. Appreciation is extended to Richard Flynn for his assistance in conducting the first experiment, and to Herb Goldsmith, David Toothaker, and especially Mary Rydzel for their assistance in conducting the second experiment.

"interception" (Ridenour, 1977), "coincident timing" (Wrisberg & Ragsdale, 1979), " anticipation of coincidence" (Wrisberg & Mead, 1981), and "anticipation time" (Thomas, Gallagher, & Purvis, 1981). Similarly, investigations employing motor skills such as batting (Miller & Shay, 1964; Slater-Hammel & Stumpner, 1950) and catching (Bruce, 1966) have focused upon the coincidence-anticipation process.

The more recent concentration of research investigations that employ the coincidence-anticipation task apparently corresponds to the availability, from the Lafayette Instrument Company, of the Bassin Anticipation Timer since 1976. Pre-1976 research efforts employed coincidence-anticipation tasks that were developed and constructed by the individual researchers, resulting in unique tasks wherein comparisons between data from different studies were difficult. Although some researchers (e.g., Dorfman, 1977; Dunham, 1977) still employed unique tasks, many researchers began to use the Bassin. The development of the Bassin Anticipation Timer thus has made possible more valid comparisons between studies investigating the coincidence-anticipation response.

Within the recent proliferation of coincidence-anticipation studies have been a number of research efforts aimed at describing the developmental aspects of the coincidence-anticipation response. Investigations by Dorfman (1977), Dunham (1977), Haywood (1977, 1980), Wade (1980), Haywood, Greenwald, and Lewis (1981), Bard, Fleury, Carriere, and Bellec (1981), Thomas, Gallagher, and Purvis (1981), Manning (1982), Williams (1982), Hoffman, Imwold, and Koller (1983), and Wrisberg and Mead (1983) have attempted to further the knowledge of how children perform and/or acquire the coincidence-anticipation response and what variables may affect coincidence-anticipation performance and learning. Throughout these investigations, my earlier work (1971) has been cited. However, although a developmental analysis of the coincidence-anticipation process has been presented elsewhere (Stadulis, 1972), the 1971 data remain unpublished. It is the purpose of this report to share these previously unpublished data. Given that the 1971 investigation employed a unique coincidence-anticipation task which I developed and constructed, involving a rolling ball as the stimulus, the design of the original investigation was replicated as nearly as possible using the Bassin Anticipation Timer. The results of this replication attempt are presented here as well.

The design employed in both investigations entailed four factors: age (7-, 9-, and 11-year-olds); gender (boys and girls); rate of the moving (or apparently moving) stimulus (fast, medium fast, medium slow, and slow); and practice (three or four blocks of eight trials each). The movement response required was a key release (rolling ball task) and a key press (Bassin task). Coincidence-anticipation performance accuracy, in both investigations, was the difference in time between the arrival of the moving (or apparently moving) stimulus at a designated intercept point and the child's movement response. The experiments thus examined whether coincidence-anticipation accuracy varied systematically across the ages studied and between genders, and whether practice and the rate of stimulus movement affected coincidence-anticipation performance.

METHOD

Subjects

For both experiments, parental consent was obtained. Other than age, the only selection requirement was that the children not be visually impaired or classified as learning disabled.

Rolling Ball Task Experiment. Volunteer children ($N = 42$) from the Agnes Russell School at Teachers College, Columbia University, served as subjects; there were an equal number of girls and boys ($n = 7$) within each group.

Bassin Anticipation Timer Experiment. Children ($N = 38$) from the Kent State University School volunteered for the study. Although it was planned to replicate the cell sizes of the first experiment, the number of volunteer children available did not match the initial experiment's distribution for age and gender; for 7-year-olds ($n = 14$), 9-year-olds ($n = 12$), and 11-year-olds ($n = 12$), there were eight and six, seven and five, and nine and three boys and girls respectively.

Apparatus

Rolling Ball Task. The coincidence-anticipation task consisted of releasing a standard telegraph key at the same time that a projected steel ball bearing (diameter = 1 in. [2.5 cm]), rolling down a chute, arrived at a designated intercept point. The projecting device[1] was a "pinball machine" plunger; the ball was projected down (2.3° slope toward the child) a 6-foot (183-cm) aluminum "V-beam" chute (the sides of the V-beam were 2 in. (5 cm) high). A solenoid with a heavy release arm was used to vary the pull distance of the plunger setting and thus the rate of ball speed. A hinge mounted at the end of the chute served as the designated intercept point. Children were

[1]I designed the projecting device, which was constructed by the Research Service of the Columbia University School of Engineering. A complete description of the apparatus can be found in my dissertation (Stadulis, 1971).

instructed to release the telegraph key as the ball struck the hinge. The response key was directly in line with the chute and mounted such that the center of the key button was 9 in. (23 cm) from the intercept point. The child performed the coincidence-anticipation task while seated on an adjustable swivel-type stool, and was positioned such that the projected ball rolled directly toward, and perpendicular to, the child's body midline.

A Hunter Repeat Cycle Interval Timer (Model 1245) controlled sequential procedures and time intervals; after a 3-s warning interval, the plunger was released and two Standard Electric Clocks (Type S1-3H-10) were started. The ball travel time clock stopped when the ball broke a photoelectric beam situated at the intercept point; the child's latency clock stopped when the child released the response key.

Bassin Anticipation Timer Task. A Bassin Anticipation Timer (Lafayette Instruments Model 59-575), using a start and a finish runway, was employed; the runways consisted of 32 LED lamps, spaced 4.5 cm apart. Each lamp illuminated sequentially from the start to the finish of the runway, thus simulating a moving stimulus. The movement response required pressing a response button, integral to the runway near the finish lamp, as the last lamp illuminated. The control unit included a digital display which presented the difference in milliseconds between the time of illumination of the last light and the child's button press, as well as whether the response was early or late. The position of the child, with reference to the apparently moving stimulus, was identical to the child's position in the rolling ball task.

Rate of Stimulus Display

In the initial experiment, the rate of projected ball travel (in centimeters per second) down the chute was as follows: slow rate = 84, medium slow rate = 140, medium fast rate = 209, and fast rate = 279. Given Bassin Timer restrictions[2] for speed settings to miles per hour, the nearest available Bassin setting to the rolling ball task's rates were employed: slow = 2 mph (89 cm/s); medium slow = 3 mph (134 cm/s); medium fast = 5 mph (224 cm/s); and fast = 6 mph (268 cm/s). In both experiments, the warning interval between a verbal ready signal (and the amber warning light for the Bassin) and the commencement of stimulus movement (rolling ball task = release of plunger; Bassin = illumination of first red LED) was 3 s.

[2]Subsequent to the data collection for the second experiment, Shea, Krampitz, Northam, and Ashby (1980) modified the Bassin circuitry such that rates between integer miles-per-hour settings are possible.

Procedure

Each child was taken individually, by the experimenter, from his or her physical education class. The apparatus and task were explained; inaccurate (early or late) and accurate responses were demonstrated as the child inspected the apparatus before being seated and positioned. Once positioned, three practice trials were administered, using the fast rate, slow rate, and fast rate again, in the initial experiment. In the second experiment, four practice trials were administered, one trial at each of the four rates. (Although presenting all four rates in the Bassin experiment represented a variation from the practice trials procedure in the rolling ball experiment, the change was considered a necessary improvement to avoid potential confounding effects of practice at only two of the rates.) Corrective feedback concerning task procedures and qualitative knowledge of results (early, late, or accurate, i.e., error = within ± 30 ms) were given after each practice trial to ensure that the children "got the idea" of the task (Gentile, 1972).

Once all questions by the child had been answered and the experimenter judged that the child understood the task, the test trials began. Four blocks of eight trials were employed for the rolling ball experiment; only three blocks of eight trials were administered in the Bassin experiment. (Minimal practice effects after 25 trials have been demonstrated by several researchers, e.g., Stadulis, 1971, and Dorfman, 1977.) Each rate was presented, in random order, twice within each block. No knowledge of results was given during the test trials in either experiment.

Analysis

Coincidence-anticipation performance was measured in terms of absolute error (AE) and constant error (CE); for CE, early responses were assigned a negative value. Scores were the means of the two trials at each rate within each block of trials. Analysis of the resulting AE and CE scores was accomplished using 3 (Age: 7, 9, and 11) × 2 (Gender: boys and girls) × 4 (Rate: slow, medium slow, medium fast, and fast) × 4, or 3 in the Bassin experiment (Practice: trial blocks I, II, III, and IV), ANOVAs, with repeated measures on the last two factors. Analysis for simple effects and the Newman-Keuls procedure were used to further analyze significant effects ($p \leq .05$ was employed for all analyses).

RESULTS

The mean AE and CE for the main effects of age, gender, rate, and practice are presented in Table 1. Overall, children responding to the Bassin Anticipation Timer demonstrated less AE and CE than the

Table 1
Main Effects of Age, Gender, Rate, and Practice: Rolling Ball Task Experiment and Bassin Anticipation Timer Experiment

Variable		Absolute Error (ms)				Constant Error (ms)[a]			
		Rolling Ball Task Experiment		Bassin Task Experiment		Rolling Ball Task Experiment		Bassin Task Experiment	
		M	*SD*	*M*	*SD*	*M*	*SD*	*M*	*SD*
Age	*F(df)*	10.10*	(2,36)	0.33	(2,36)	2.74	(2,36)	2.31	(2,32)
7		166.9	150.3	94.9	80.3	125.2	176.7	40.4	108.4
9		130.0	92.4	94.9	59.0	116.5	10.19	59.1	68.0
11		90.8	69.6	85.4	73.0	78.9	78.7	64.7	84.1
Gender	*F(df)*	0.31	(1,36)	24.62*	(1,32)	0.10	(1,36)	15.18*	(1,32)
Male		133.1	122.5	74.0	63.1	109.6	136.4	34.1	85.0
Female		125.3	104.1	122.5	75.5	104.2	118.4	88.1	96.1
Rate	*F(df)*	24.30*	(3,108)	0.84	(3,96)	28.28*	(3,108)	2.98*	(3,96)
Slow		117.9	136.2	97.0	71.0	98.3	145.9	74.0	85.0
Medium slow		125.7	116.8	93.8	75.5	106.0	128.7	52.2	101.4
Medium fast		179.3	108.9	88.3	80.7	163.4	122.0	42.9	96.9
Fast		93.9	62.7	88.5	58.7	59.8	84.8	46.4	85.6
Practice	*F(df)*	3.01*	(3,108)	1.34	(2,64)	2.71*	(3,108)	4.29*	(2,64)
Block I		152.2	116.4	96.1	72.1	131.6	131.3	63.6	90.4
Block II		126.1	134.9	89.1	79.8	103.9	146.4	37.0	106.0
Block III		121.5	97.9	90.5	62.8	97.5	113.5	60.9	78.8
Block IV		117.1	99.2			94.6	114.1		

[a] Negative (–) constant error = early response.
* $p \leq .05$.

children performing the rolling ball tasks. In addition, whereas children in the initial experiment were consistently early, the Bassin CE indicated late responses on the average.

Using ANOVA, main and interactional effects of the four factors were assessed for AE and CE in each experiment. Each analysis yielded significant main effects (see Table 1); these are presented first, to be followed by the presentation of significant interaction effects.

Main Effects

Age. Analyses for the rolling ball experiment indicated that, for AE, the older the child the more accurate the response. Although it only approached significance ($p = .08$), the CE analysis indicated the same pattern. However, the Bassin results indicated no significant differences for either AE or CE.

Gender. The initial experiment yielded little evidence of any difference in coincidence-anticipation performance between boys and girls. The second experiment, on the other hand, demonstrated gender differences, with boys responding with lower AE and CE than the girls.

Rate of Stimulus Display. For both AE and CE, the rolling ball task demonstrated less coincidence-anticipation accuracy at the medium fast rate and greatest accuracy at the fastest rate of ball projection. Although a nonsignificant difference for rate effects on AE was obtained for the Bassin task, the descriptive statistics indicated greater accuracy at the two faster rates. For CE, a significant effect was obtained in the Bassin experiment, with the slowest rate of the display yielding later responses than the other three rates.

Practice. All analyses, except for the Bassin AE, indicated that greatest error occurred during the first block of eight trials, with subsequent little variation between blocks. Although the Bassin AE F ratio for practice was nonsignificant, descriptively, the greater error did occur in the first block of trials.

Interaction Effects

Age and Gender. The Bassin task AE ANOVA yielded a significant effect due to the interaction of age and gender, $F(2, 32) = 4.20$. Analysis for simple effects indicated that 11-year-old girls had greater AE than 11-year-old boys. As is evident in Figure 1, differences in AE between the girls and boys were minimal at 7 years of age; over age, the differences between the two genders became more pronounced. Thus, the AE for the boys in the second experiment

Figure 1. Bassin Anticipation Timer experiment: Age × Gender interaction for mean absolute error.

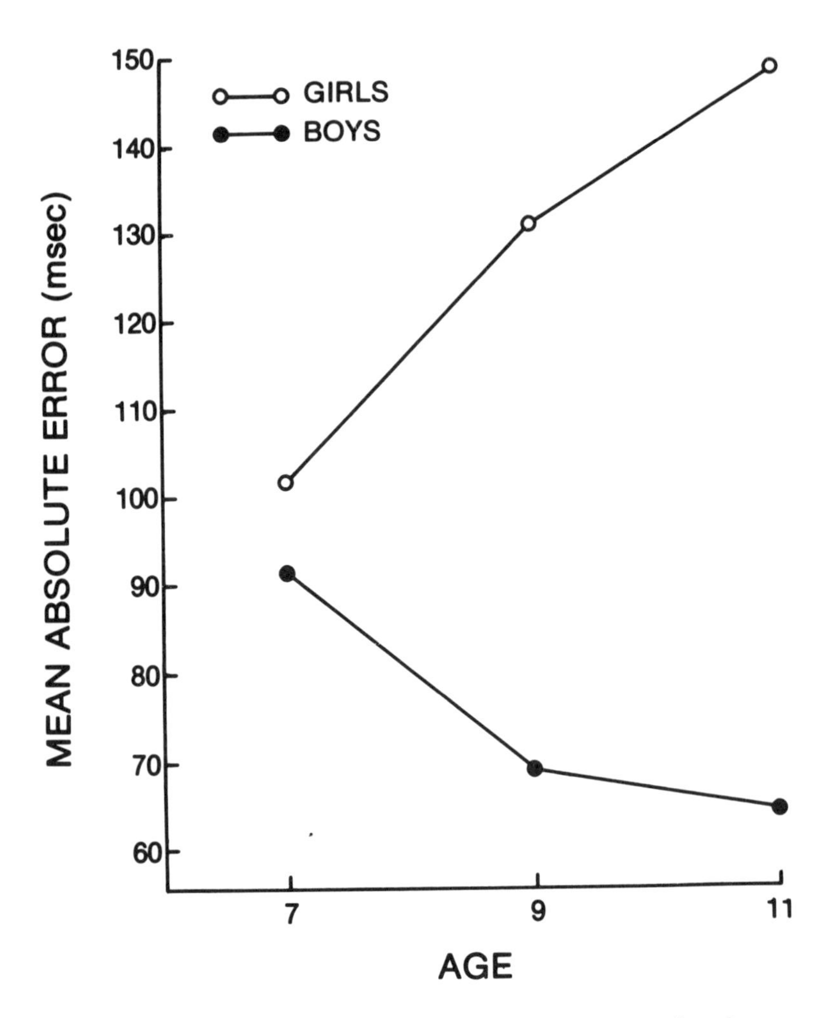

appeared to demonstrate a similar change over age to the change evidenced by *both* girls and boys in the first experiment; that is, the older the child the better the coincidence-anticipation performance. The age by gender interaction must be interpreted with caution, however, because of the small cell size for the 11-year-old girls ($n = 3$).

Age and Rate. For only the rolling ball task, significant effects were obtained for the interaction of the age and rate variables. Subsequent analyses indicated that part of the observed interaction effect was due to an anomaly in the apparatus relative to the medium fast rate of ball projection; these analyses have not been presented here.[3] However, analysis for simple effect, followed by the Newman-Keuls individual comparison procedure, yielded significant differences that were not related to the medium fast rate anomaly; given the similarity in findings for AE and CE, only AE findings have been presented (see Figure 2).

Figure 2. Rolling ball experiment: Age × Rate interaction for mean absolute error.

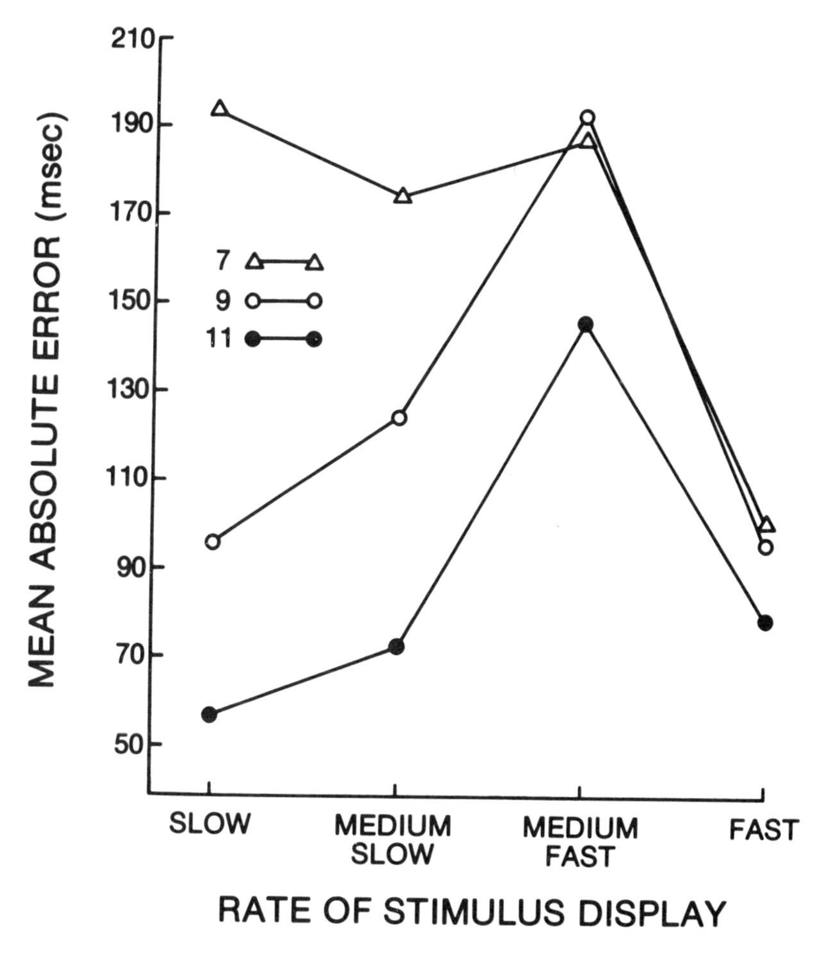

[3]The anomaly was that whereas each of the three other rates demonstrated rather constant speed over the length of the chute, the medium fast rate resulted in a rather pronounced deceleration of the ball over the last 2 ft (61 cm) of travel down the chute. This deceleration resulted in magnifying AE and CE, for all age children, at the medium fast rate; see my dissertation (Stadulis, 1971) for further discussion of the deceleration effect.

With respect to rates over levels of age, 7-year-olds had significantly less AE (and CE) at the fastest rate of stimulus display, with no significant differences obtained for these younger children between the other three rates. All differences for the older children (9s and 11s) were with reference to only the medium fast rate in comparison to the other rates. In examining the effects of age over each rate, both the slow and medium slow rates yielded significant simple effects, $F(2, 36) = 16.95$ and 9.28, respectively. The Newman-Keuls procedure indicated that at both slower rates, 7-year-olds had greater error than either the 9s or 11s. In addition, for the medium slow rate only, 9-year-olds had more error than the 11-year-olds.

Rate and Practice. The initial experiment yielded a significant practice effect without any evidence of an interaction between practice and the other three factors. The Newman-Keuls test indicated that greater error occurred over the first block of eight trials as compared with the other three blocks; there were no differences between the last three blocks of trials. Although similar practice main effects were evident on the Bassin task, significant interactions for practice and rate were demonstrated for both AE and CE, $F(6, 192) =$ 2.92 and 2.52, respectively. Analysis for simple effects of rates over practice levels indicated significant differences between rates at Block I only, $F(3, 111) = 5.80$ (AE) and 6.64 (CE). Individual mean comparisons (Newman-Keuls) yielded significant differences as follows: for AE, greater error occurred at the slow rate than at the medium fast rate; for CE, the slow rate evidenced significantly later responses than within the medium fast or fast rates (see Table 2).

Table 2
Rate and Practice Interaction Effects: Bassin Task for Mean Absolute and Constant Error

	Practice					
	Block I	Block II	Block III	Block I	Block II	Block III
Rate	Absolute Error (ms)			Constant Error (ms)[a]		
Slow	117.0[b1]	77.6[b]	96.5[b]	94.1[c1]	47.1[c]	80.7
Medium slow	92.4	93.6	95.3	70.3[d1]	17.8[d]	68.5
Medium fast	79.0	101.1	84.8	38.5[c]	37.8	52.3
Fast	95.9	84.1	85.3	51.5[c]	45.5	42.1

[a]Positive constant error = late response.
[b]Means significantly different ($p \leq .05$) from Block I slow AE mean ([b1]).
[c]Means significantly different ($p \leq .05$) from Block I slow CE mean ([c1]).
[d]Means significantly different ($p \leq .05$) from Block I medium slow CE mean ([d1]).

When examining the simple effects of practice over rate levels, for AE, a practice effect for the slow rate only was observed, $F(2, 111) = 9.61$. Individual comparisons demonstrated significantly greater AE at the slow rate for Block I when compared to Blocks II and III. For CE, significant practice simple effects were demonstrated for the two slower rates, $F(2, 111) = 6.38$ (slow) and 5.65 (medium slow). For both slower rates, CE during Block I was greater than in Block II.

DISCUSSION

Before comparing the results of my experiments with other coincidence-anticipation research, it is important to note that although the development of the Bassin Anticipation Timer has resulted in greater comparability between different studies, comparisons are still difficult. Some researchers continue to employ "unique" apparatus (e.g., Hoffman et al., 1983; Wade, 1980); others use scores that do not correspond to the scoring procedures employed in the majority of other studies (e.g., Thomas et al., 1981; Wade, 1980). Even more problematic are the variances in procedures between studies employing the Bassin, such as different viewing positions (e.g., side view vs. front view), respondent locations (very near the intercept point, within a few centimeters, to as much as 457 cm away), movement responses (finger press, finger release, foot release, arm movement), length of runway (two, three, or four Bassin sections), and so forth. Although there may be valid reasons for researchers to vary these aspects of the coincidence-anticipation task, it is difficult to generalize without replication of previous variable manipulations, procedures, and tasks.

The developmental pattern of coincidence-anticipation performance, within the age groups studied in the rolling ball experiment, appears to be linear. As confirmed by other studies (e.g., Dorfman, 1977; Haywood, 1977, 1980; Thomas et al., 1981; Wade, 1980), the incremental accuracy of coincidence-anticipation performance appears to continue over childhood, until approximately 11 years of age. At pre-adolescence or early adolescence, performance may be no different than that of the adult (Dorfman, 1977; Haywood, 1980); Williams (1982) even showed little difference between coincidence-anticipation performance between 9-year-olds and adults. However, as indicated by the findings of the present studies, as well as other investigations, gender and the rate of the stimulus display speed may differentially interact with these apparent age-related changes in coincidence-anticipation performance

The first experiment showed little difference between boys and girls, for both AE and CE. On the other hand, the second experiment demonstrated an effect due to gender, with boys showing greater coincidence accuracy than girls. The interaction effects between gender and age (see Figure 1) seemed to clarify the effect; whereas boys demonstrated the expected linear decrease in coincidence-anticipation error, the girls demonstrated a deterioration in performance, culminating in a significant difference between girls and boys at 11 years of age. Of course, the limited number of 11-year-old girls involved tempers possible prediction. Recently, Hoffman et al. (1983) indicated better prediction performance by boys, and especially noted a large decrement in performance by 9-year-old girls. Dorfman (1977) and Thomas et al. (1981) have showed more accurate timing performance by boys, but only at the younger age levels (6–9 years). Some studies have demonstrated consistent gender differences in coincidence-anticipation performance over age (Bard et al., 1981; Dunham, 1977), but others have demonstrated no such differences (Haywood et al., 1981; Manning, 1982; Wrisberg & Mead, 1981).

When discussing an obtained gender difference in adults, Wrisberg, Paul, and Ragsdale (1979) speculated that sociocultural factors caused the female subjects to demonstrate lower levels of coincidence-anticipation performance than the male subjects. In noting the improvement to coincidence-anticipation accuracy over practice by girls (whereas boys did not demonstrate such improvement), Bard et al. (1981) raised similar experiential explanations for the increased performance level. Unfortunately, such explanations remain speculative and await further inspection through empirical methods. Based upon the available research, although the differences in coincidence-anticipation performance between the sexes seem equivocal, it should be noted that no investigation has shown greater coincidence-anticipation accuracy for female as compared to male subjects.

The rolling ball experiment indicated that the change in coincidence-anticipation accuracy over age interacted with the rate of ball projection (see Figure 2). Age differences in performance were especially evident at the two slower rates (84 and 140 cm/s); at the faster rates, no age differences were demonstrated. Additionally, for the 7-year-olds only, performance at the fastest rate was superior to the three slower rates. A variety of other studies have demonstrated similar better performance at the faster rate of stimulus display (Bard et al., 1981; Haywood, 1977, 1983; Manning, 1982; Wrisberg & Mead, 1981, 1983). Explanations for the faster rate accuracy level are varied. Some have proposed that the coincidence-anticipation response, at a fast rate, is actually a reaction time (RT) task, with resulting better performance the result of the fast speed approximating, or highly related to, the respondent's RT (Stadulis, 1971; Thomas et al., 1981;

Williams, 1973; Wrisberg & Mead, 1983). An alternative explanation, but related to the RT hypothesis, is that children, especially the younger ones (e.g., 7s), have great difficulty delaying a planned response (Rothstein, 1970; Stadulis, 1971). These children are characterized by "impulsiveness" (Wade, 1980), the inability to "hold back" a response (Roberton, 1981; Williams, 1967), and the inability to "inhibit an action" (Williams, 1982). Research by Haywood (1977), Thomas et al. (1981), and Stadulis, Manning, and Rydzel (1982) seems to at least partially support the relationship of RT to coincidence-anticipation performance.

Two studies have failed to demonstrate more accurate performance at the faster rate of stimulus display. Dunham (1977) showed no difference in AE as a result of presenting four speeds; however, the fastest speed was well beyond (488 cm/s) most rate ranges employed by other researchers, and the children were responding at a distance of 457 cm from the display (again, well beyond distances used by other researchers). Only one published study has demonstrated greater coincidence-anticipation accuracy under the slowest rate (Ridenour, 1977). The task used in Ridenour's study involved striking rather large-sized balls (15 and 22 cm in diameter) with a paddle. It is likely that a task such as this, which is more ecologically valid than the laboratory coincidence-anticipation task, may offer different response requirements (Wade, 1980). Indeed, Shope (1976) and Katovsky (1978) have demonstrated little, if any, relationship between contrived coincidence-anticipation tasks (projected ball and Bassin Timer, respectively) and actual motor tasks normally performed by individuals (striking activities and tennis, respectively).

With respect to CE, consistent rate effects are not as evident: the first experiment resulted in consistently early responses at all rates, whereas the second experiment yielded late responses. The majority of studies seem to support early responses at the slower rates and late responses at the fast rates (Alderson & Whiting, 1974; Haywood, 1977; Haywood et al., 1981; Manning, 1982; Pavlis, 1972; Wade, 1980; Williams, 1982; Wrisberg & Mead, 1981, 1983), with Haywood (1983) showing the reverse trend and Dunham (1977) finding late responses at all rates. The fairly consistent finding concerning late at fast and early at slow seems to lend further support to the "inability to delay" hypothesis; Haywood et al. (1981) offered additional alternative explanations (i.e., contextual factors: range effects, assimilation effects, and contrast effects). The apparent CE differences between the two experiments presented here might be explained in terms of stimulus display variability between the two tasks. Although speeds between the two tasks were equated approximately, the Bassin runway length was only 81% of the rolling ball chute length (145 vs. 178 cm).[4] Thus, for the second experiment, with less preview of the approaching stimulus available (from 95 to 490 ms depending on the speed), late responses may have resulted. Such an interpretation, however, would predict that with the slower rates there should be a reduction in the lateness of responses; such was not the case (see Table 1). The lack of less positive CE at the slower rates may be a function of the greater difficulty children seem to have when responding to the slow speeds, thus producing an interaction effect. Further research seems necessary to clarify the rate of speed/amount of preview issue.

The failure to demonstrate age differences using the Bassin task may be related to the limited preview available. If such a time factor increased the task difficulty, the children may have more frequently used an RT strategy in responding. If such was the case, younger children would be expected to have slower RTs, which may have benefited their performance; that is, their RTs would be closer to the amount of stimulus display viewing time (e.g., for the fast rate, 541 ms; for the medium fast rate, 647 ms). It is conceivable as well that the younger child uses an RT strategy and then, as a function of development, begins to use different strategies. Thus, if the Bassin task used in the second experiment could be best performed using an RT strategy, the older children may have been at a disadvantage, especially at the faster rates, resulting in the lack of a demonstrated age effect. Such a developmental relationship between RT and performance has been shown by Thomas et al. (1981).

The practice effects demonstrated in both of the experiments presented here have been duplicated repeatedly in other research efforts. It appears that after 5-12 trials, whether the subjects are children or adults, relatively little change in coincidence-anticipation performance occurs (e.g., Dunham, 1977; Manning, 1982; Wrisberg & Mead, 1981, 1983). Even over extended practice (Haywood, 1983), stabilization of coincidence-anticipation performance appears to be rather rapid. Of note is the interaction demonstrated between practice and rate within the Bassin experiment. Differences between rates—i.e., greater error at the slowest speed—occurred during the first eight trials; these differences between the slow rate and the other rates dissipated over the second

[4]Although the second experiment, using the Bassin Anticipation Timer, attempted to replicate the initial experiment, it was decided to use the standard Bassin length, i.e., two modules, to enable comparison to other research efforts that have employed the Bassin. Extending the Bassin to match the length of the rolling ball task (178 cm) would serve as a better replication effort; however, matching the medium fast rate anomaly of the initial experiment seems unlikely. However, if our understanding of the coincidence-anticipation response is to have any utility, findings must be replicated across various tasks.

block of eight trials, with the slow rate showing less late responses over blocks of trials. Hoffman et al. (1983) demonstrated similar practice effects, with the first block of eight trials demonstrating late responses followed by early responses in Block II. Thus, the evidence seems to confirm the apparent difficulty children have in responding accurately to slower rates of stimulus display speed. Whereas performance seems to level off rapidly at faster rates, more practice seems necessary for children to stabilize their performance at the slower rates.

Although the attention to the coincidence-anticipation process has amplified our descriptive understanding of the relationship between such variables as age, gender, rate of stimulus display, and practice, the level of theoretical explanation for the development of the coincidence-anticipation response appears limited. Some preliminary efforts have been made (Kay, 1969; Rothstein, 1977; Stadulis, 1971, 1972; Whiting, 1969), but more work is necessary. The recent attempt by Hoffman et al. (1983) clearly conveys the need to employ theoretical constructs in attempting to understand the development of coincidence-anticipation behaviors.

REFERENCES

Alderson, G.J.K., & Whiting, H.T.A. (1974). Prediction of linear motion. *Human Factors, 16,* 495-502.

Bard, C., Fleury, M., Carriere, L., & Bellec, J. (1981). Components of the coincidence-anticipation behavior of children aged 6 to 11 years. *Perceptual and Motor Skills, 52,* 547-556.

Belisle, J.J. (1963). Accuracy, reliability and refractoriness in a coincidence-anticipation task. *Research Quarterly, 34,* 271-281.

Broadbent, D. E. (1958). *Perception and communication.* London: Pergamon Press.

Bruce, R. (1966). *The effects of variations in ball trajectory upon the catching performance of elementary school children.* Unpublished doctoral dissertation, University of Wisconsin.

Dorfman, P.W. (1977). Timing and anticipation: A developmental perspective. *Journal of Motor Behavior, 9,* 67-79.

Dunham, P., Jr. (1977). Age, sex, speed and practice in coincidence-anticipation performance of children. *Perceptual and Motor Skills, 45,* 187-193.

Gentile, A. M. (1972). A working model of skill acquisition with application to teaching. *Quest, 17,* 3-23.

Gottsdanker, R.M. (1952). The accuracy of prediction motion. *Journal of Experimental Psychology, 43,* 26-36.

Haywood K.M. (1977). Eye movements during coincidence-anticipation performance. *Journal of Motor Behavior, 9,* 313-318.

Haywood, K.M. (1980). Coincidence-anticipation accuracy across the life span. *Experimental Aging Research, 6,* 451-462.

Haywood, K.M. (1983). Responses to speed changes in coincidence-anticipation judgments after extended practice. *Research Quarterly for Exercise and Sport, 54,* 28-32.

Haywood, K.M., Greenwald, G., & Lewis, C. (1981). Contextual factors and age group differences in coincidence-anticipation performance. *Research Quarterly for Exercise and Sport, 52,* 458-464.

Hick, W.E., & Bates, J.A.V. (1950). *The human operator in control mechanisms* (Permanent Records of Research and Development Monograph No. 17-204). London: Ministry of Supply.

Hoffman, S.J., Imwold, C.H., & Koller, J.A. (1983). Accuracy and prediction in throwing: A taxonomic analysis of children's performance. *Research Quarterly for Exercise and Sport, 54,* 33-40.

Katovsky, T.M. (1978). *The relationship of various visual components to tennis skill.* Unpublished master's thesis, Kent State University.

Kay, H. (1969). The development of motor skills from birth to adolescence. In E.A. Bilodeau (Ed.), *Principles of skill acquisition* (pp. 33-51). New York: Academic Press.

Manning, K.M. (1982). *The effects of sex, age and task complexity on the timing measures of learning disabled and non-learning disabled children.* Unpublished doctoral dissertation, University of Toledo.

Miller, R.G., & Shay, C.T. (1964). Relationship of reaction time to speed of a softball. *Research Quarterly, 35,* 433-437.

Pavlis, C.E. (1972). *The coincidence-anticipation ability of children of various ages.* Unpublished master's thesis, Pennsylvania State University.

Poulton, E.C. (1957). On prediction in skilled movements. *Psychological Bulletin, 54,* 467-478.

Ridenour, M. (1977). Influence of object size, speed, direction, height, and distance on interception of a moving object. *Research Quarterly, 48,* 138-143.

Roberton, M.A. (1981, April). *Developmental kinesiology: The childhood years.* Paper presented at the National Convention of the American Alliance for Health, Physical Education, Recreation and Dance, Boston, MA.

Rothstein, A.L. (1970). *Timing behavior in children.* Unpublished doctoral dissertation, Columbia University Teacher's College.

Rothstein, A.L. (1977). Prediction in sport: An information processing approach. In R.E. Stadulis (Ed.), *Research and practice in physical education* (pp. 205-216). Champaign, IL: Human Kinetics.

Schmidt, R.A. (1968). Anticipation and timing in human performance. *Psychological Bulletin, 70,* 631-646.

Shea, C.H., Krampitz, J.B., Northam, C.C., & Ashby, A.A. (1980). *Information processing in coincident timing tasks: A development perspective.* Unpublished manuscript.

Shope, G.N.E. (1976). *Relationships between striking skills and various perceptual components in five-year-old children.* Unpublished master's thesis, Kent State University.

Slater-Hammel, A.T. (1960). Reliability, accuracy and refractoriness of a transit reaction. *Research Quarterly, 31,* 217-228.

Slater-Hammel, A.T., & Stumpner, R.L. (1950). Batting reaction time. *Research Quarterly, 21,* 353-356.

Stadulis, R.E. (1971). *Coincidence-anticipation behavior in children.* Unpublished doctoral dissertation, Columbia University Teacher's College.

Stadulis, R.E. (1972). Motor skill analysis: Coincidence-anticipation. *Quest, 17,* 70-73.

Stadulis, R.E., Manning, K.M., & Rydzel, M. (1982, May). *The relationship of reaction time and amount of display preview to coincidence-anticipation performance.* Paper presented at the Annual Conference of the North American Society for the Psychology of Sport and Physical Activity, College Park, MD.

Thomas, J.R., Gallagher, J.D., & Purvis, G.J. (1981). Reaction time and anticipation time: Effects of development. *Research Quarterly for Exercise and Sport, 52,* 359-367.

Wade, M.G. (1980). Coincidence-anticipation of young normal and handicapped children. *Journal of Motor Behavior, 12,* 103-112.

Whiting, H.T.A. (1969). *Acquiring ball skills: A psychological interpretation.* Philadelphia: Lea & Febiger.

Williams, H.G. (1967). *The perception of moving objects by children.* Unpublished manuscript, University of Toledo.

Williams, H.G. (1968). *The effects of systematic variation of speed and direction of object flight and of skill and age classifications upon visuo-perceptual judgments of moving objects in three-dimensional space* (Office of Education Report No. 6-8102). University of Toledo.

Williams, H.G. (1973). Perceptual-motor development in children. In C.B. Corbin (Ed.), *A textbook of motor development* (pp. 111-148). Dubuque, IA: Brown.

Williams, K. (1982). *Age differences in performance of a coincident anticipation task: Application of a modified information processing model.* Unpublished doctoral dissertation, University of Wisconsin.

Wrisberg, C.A., & Mead, B.J. (1981). Anticipation of coincidence in children: A test of schema theory. *Perceptual and Motor Skills, 52,* 599-606.

Wrisberg, C.A., & Mead, B.J. (1983). Developing coincident timing skill in children: A comparison of training methods. *Research Quarterly for Exercise and Sport, 54,* 67-74.

Wrisberg, C.A., Paul, J.H., & Ragsdale, M.R. (1979). Subject gender, knowledge of results, and receptor anticipation. *Research Quarterly, 59,* 699-708.

Wrisberg, C.A., & Ragsdale, M.R. (1979). Further tests of Schmidt's schema Theory: Development of a schema rule for a coincident timing task. *Journal of Motor Behavior, 11,* 159-166.

2

Contribution of Vision to the Performance and Learning of a Directional Aiming Task in Children Aged 6, 9, and 11

C. Bard
Laval University, Quebec
L. Hay
INP4-CNRS, Marseilles, France
M. Fleury
Laval University, Quebec

In the first study, the contribution of visual feedback to the accuracy of an aiming task, performed at either high or low speed, was investigated in children aged 6, 9, and 11. Regardless of speed, all children were more accurate when they saw the complete arm trajectory or the first part of their movement. Aiming accuracy deteriorated when they worked in an open-loop condition. Speed also affected accuracy: all children were more accurate at low speed, but 6-year-old children were less accurate in their slow aiming movement than the other two groups. In all feedback conditions, independent of age group, aiming accuracy deteriorated with target eccentricity.

In the second experiment, the possible improvement in the ability of open-loop aiming through learning procedure was investigated. The children practiced aiming in closed loop at an approximate speed of either 300 or 650 ms. All children, regardless of speed, improved their aiming accuracy in an open-loop condition after training in closed loop, but the 9-year-olds showed greater improvement after practicing at higher speed.

Findings from these two experiments support the contentions that peripheral vision can be used for correction in very fast aiming and that proprioceptive information is not fully reintegrated in the programming, especially at age 6 when working at a speed of approximately 300 ms and at ages 6, 9, and 11 when working at a speed of approximately 100 ms.

The role of visual information in the control of movement has been a central issue in the study of motor behavior since Woodworth's

---

This research was supported by an FCAC grant, Ministry of Education, Government of Quebec.

initial investigation in 1899. One of the major concerns has been the time required to process visual feedback and the contribution of visual information feedback to the control of movements (Carlton, 1979, 1981; Conti & Beaubaton, 1976; Keele & Posner, 1968; Zelaznik, Hawkins, & Kisselburgh, 1983). However, very few studies have addressed the questions of how children differ from adults in their ability to use visual feedback in the control of their movement and how the contribution of vision to accuracy evolves with the training of the task performed at varying speeds. These questions are addressed with the aiming task used in the present research.

Aiming allows a clear distinction between two mechanisms: triggered and guided (Paillard, 1982; Paillard & Beaubaton, 1978). A preprogram, its precision and the proprioceptive re-afferences contributing to its maintenance, can be set off through the triggered portion. The guided portion, in turn, sets off the assistance of the visual mechanisms in the task accuracy.

As Paillard (1982) suggested, on physical ground, two separate channels may contribute to the visual guidance of movement: one operating mainly in central vision and the other in peripheral vision. These channels are primarily dependent upon a high-pass and a low-pass spatial filter, respectively. From Paillard's studies, it appears that movement cues, processed mainly in the peripheral field, are used to control the direction of the trajectory relative to the direction of the visual axis clamped on the visual target by foveal grasp's mechanism. Therefore, faced with a directional aiming task at high velocity, we might predict that the low-pass filter will prevail to determine the accurate execution of the task. Consequently, feedback delay is expected to be faster (< 100 ms) than the delays required by the terminal feedback procedure studied by Keele and Posner (1968), Conti and Beaubaton (1976), and Carlton (1979, 1981), which originate mainly from central vision.

It must be stressed that the aiming task used in our study differs from pointing tasks often used in visuomotor coordination studies, wherein the subject has to stop on the target, therefore requiring the encoding of both amplitude and direction of the trajectory. Aiming tasks are more like throwing tasks in which most of the segment trajectory is ballistic, and in which peripheral vision is prevalent because the arm movement is mainly seen in peripheral vision (Figure 1).

The assumption that a saccade is taking place during a trial is discarded because (1) a pilot study with adults revealed no vertical eye saccade during the performance of this aiming task; (2) the appearance of a target is known to anchor the eye on the target (Paillard, 1978); and (3) the eye is prevented from moving into the

Figure 1. Hand trajectory according to the visual field. From initial position to target, the hand is seen in peripheral vision for most of the trajectory, which greatly limits the role of central vision in the control of movement.

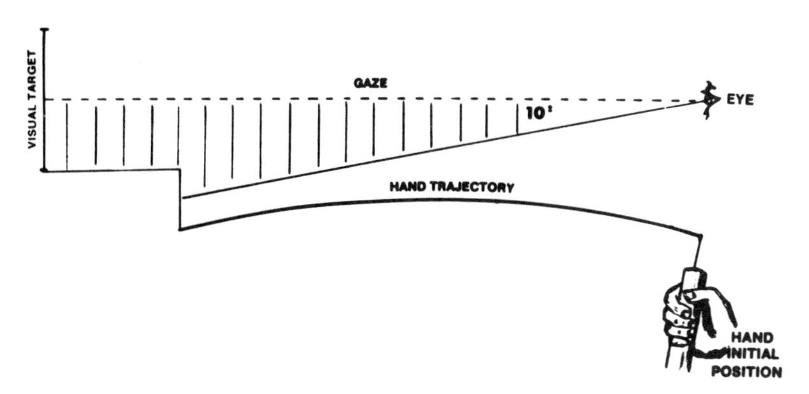

peripheral field by the very nature of the movement performed: a ballistic trajectory of very short duration.

Recent research on eye-hand coordination in infants has been mainly concerned with the distinction of ballistic versus guided approaches to the target. Evidence for a component of reaching has been found as early as 2 months of age (Bower, 1974; Bullinger, 1976). Moreover, successful ballistic movements have been reported at 20 weeks of age, while suppressing light during the approach (Bower & Wishart, 1972). Even if both types of control mode operate early in life (Hofsten, 1979, 1980, 1983; Hofsten & Lindhagen, 1979), they both show important improvement during childhood (Bard & Hay, 1983; Hay, 1978, 1979, in press).

The experiments described in this paper were designed to (1) analyze the behavior of children aged 6, 9, and 11 using visual feedback in the control of an aiming task and (2) determine the contribution of vision to their eye-hand accuracy during the training process.

EXPERIMENT 1

Method

Children were seated in front of a black curved board supporting the targets and shaded by surrounding screens. The targets were a line of vertical pieces of Plexiglas lighted by green diodes 10 cm high × 0.05 cm wide, and set 5° apart. Four targets were used: one in the median plane and three others at 10°, 20°, and 40° in the right hemifield. Aiming movements consisted of horizontal projections of the right arm at full extension toward the target. The directional error of the trajectory was recorded when intersecting the frontal plane of the target display, which was 30 cm away.

To perform the task, the subject held in hand a vertical lever mounted on a double universal joint. Two potentiometers, fixed at the base of the vertical lever, recorded all lever displacements. Times at which the movement was initiated and intersected the target plane were recorded by means of two contacts activated by the lever displacement. Reaction time (RT), intersection (IT), and absolute directional error (ADE, in degrees) were stored and computed on a microprocessor (Data General MP 100—RAM 32K) with 16 bits CPU. The system had an analog-to-digital interface 4223 (resolution 12 bits) and a digital input/output interface 4222. The temporal resolution was ± 1.5 ms. Languages used were Assembler for collecting data and BASIC (single precision floating point) for statistics.

Horizontal screens of different shapes covered either the first part of the arm trajectory (initial feedback condition), the last part (terminal feedback condition), or the complete arm trajectory (open-loop condition). In the closed-loop condition, no screen was present and the subjects could see their entire arm trajectory.

Subjects. Sixty children participated in this experiment. Three groups of ten subjects (five girls and five boys) performed the task at high speed (movement time [MT] between 100 and 130 ms). Three more groups of ten subjects (five girls and five boys) performed the task at low speed (MT between 290 and 350 ms). The mean ages were 6.8, 9.5, and 11.8 years, respectively, with a range of 16, 16, and 8 months.

Procedure. At the beginning of each trial, the subjects held the lever in their hand and close to their chest. As soon as the target lit up, they moved the lever toward the target as accurately as possible and at a speed corresponding to the experimenter's instructions; trials that were performed outside of the required speed range were discarded and subsequently retaken ($n < 5\%$). Subjects were familiarized with the apparatus and the task prior to the experiment (40 trials with temporal knowledge of results). During testing sessions, 20 trials (five repetitions on each of the four targets) were executed with target locations randomly varied.

Analysis. Data were subjected to a five-way (Age × Sex × Speed of Movement × Feedback Condition × Target Eccentricity) analysis of variance (ANOVA), with repeated measures on feedback condition and target eccentricity (BMDP 2V).

Results

The ANOVA conducted on ADE revealed a significant speed effect; $F(1, 48) = 99.30, p < .01$, all subjects being more accurate at low speed than at high speed. The Speed × Age interaction was also significant. Figure 2 shows that in the high-speed condition there is no age difference, but in low speed 6-year-old children are significantly less accurate than the other two groups.

Figure 2. Mean absolute directional error according to age and movement speed.

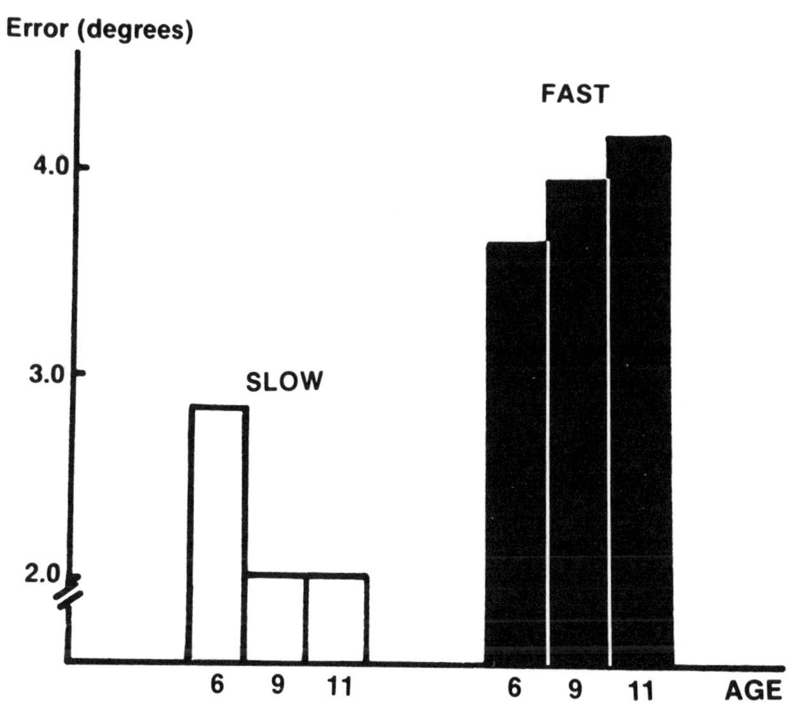

Visual feedback manipulation also revealed a significant difference in ADE; $F(3, 144) = 24.34, p < .01$. Duncan's comparisons demonstrated that there was no significant difference in ADE between the closed-loop and initial feedback conditions, subjects being equally accurate in both situations. Subjects were more accurate in the terminal feedback than in the open-loop condition, but accuracy was less in those two conditions than in the initial feedback and closed-loop conditions. Figure 3 clearly illustrates the deterioration

Figure 3. Mean absolute directional error according to feedback condition and movement speed.

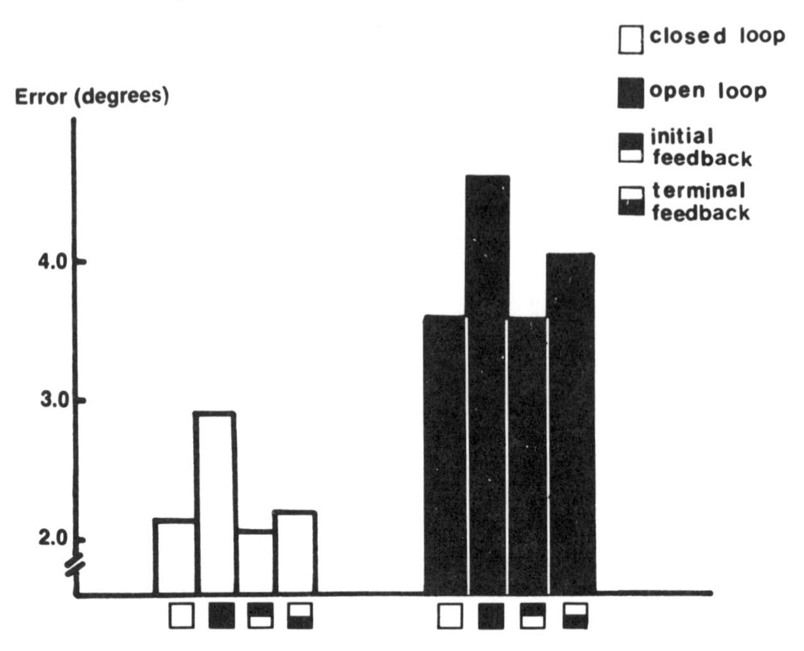

of aiming accuracy in the open-loop condition, independent of the speed of arm movement.

The target eccentricity effect was also significant; $F(3, 144) = 34.80$, $p < .01$. Duncan's comparisons showed no significant difference between accuracy on the central and 10° targets, but accuracy levels at 20° and 40° were significantly different from each other and from both other targets. The Speed × Target interaction was also significant, and Figure 4 shows that accuracy deterioration, according to target eccentricity, was more important when movement was performed at high speed. No significant difference was found for sex on ADE.

ANOVA conducted on RTs showed a significant age effect; $F(2, 48) = 13.10$, $p < .01$, the 6-year-old group being slower than both other age groups. The Speed × Age interaction was also significant. The 6-year-old children showed no RT difference between fast and slow aiming, but the 9- and 11-year-old children had shorter RTs in fast aiming (Figure 5).

The visual manipulation effect was significant; $F(3, 144) = 6.06$, $p < .01$. Duncan's comparisons revealed that RTs were the slowest in the open-loop condition, and initial feedback RTs were the fastest (Figure 6).

Figure 4. Mean absolute directional error according to movement speed and target eccentricity.

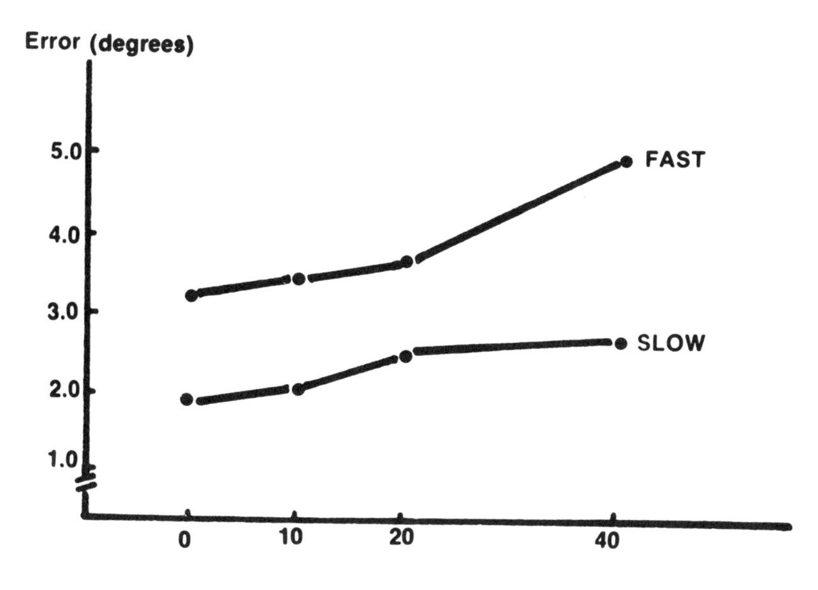

Figure 5. Mean reaction time according to age and movement speed.

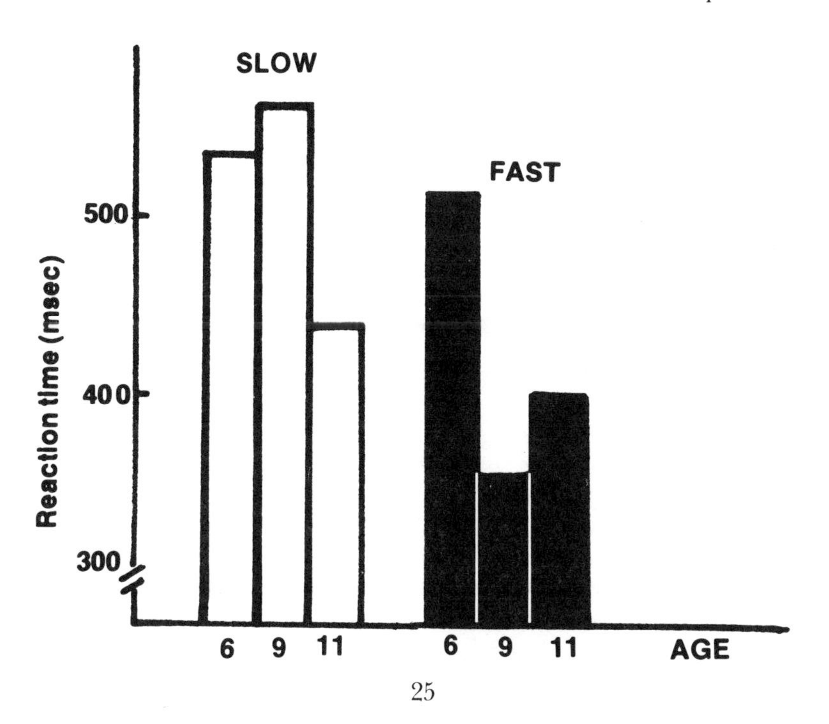

Figure 6. Mean reaction time according to feedback condition.

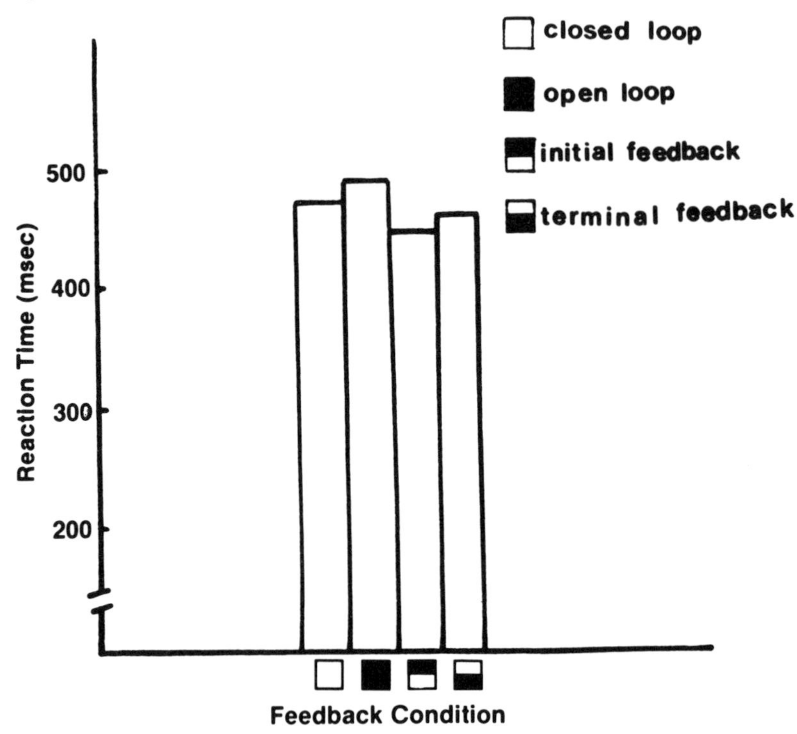

The target eccentricity effect was also significant; $F(3, 244) = 34.93$, $p < .01$. The RTs for 0°, 10°, 20°, and 40° eccentricities were 471, 455, 457, and 492 ms, respectively. Duncan's comparisons revealed significant differences between these RTs. No significant difference was found for sex on RTs.

Discussion

From present data it is clear that the movements of children are less accurate when executed at high speed, whatever the visual condition under which the movement is executed, a result that is also found in adults (speed/accuracy trade-off, Schmidt, Zelaznik, & Frank, 1978). Of interest here is the fact that whatever the age of the subject or the speed of movement execution, a more important deterioration of performance is found when subjects work in an open-loop condition as opposed to any other feedback conditions. This finding supports the hypothesis that given high-speed movements ($MT < 190$ ms), visual corrections are possible. It is interesting to note that in fast aiming there is no difference in accuracy between closed-loop condition and initial feedback condition, but terminal feedback leads to reduced accuracy which is nevertheless more precise than open-loop condition. This result could fit the hypothesis that peripheral vision can extract a directional error signal which allows correction of the trajectory (Paillard, 1980, 1982).

The difference between terminal feedback and open-loop results may be explained on the basis of positional information available at the end of the movement (error signal between target and hand position), whereas the ongoing feedback utilized during the first part of the trajectory would have time to operate. Further investigation of this hypothesis is presently underway using recordings of the trajectory kinematic.

When a movement is performed at lower speed (MT $\simeq$ 300 ms) the accuracy improvement is the same for all feedback conditions, indicating that visual ongoing feedback operates during both the first and second parts of the arm trajectory.

Results in RTs are in general agreement with the literature indicating an improvement with age of information-processing operations (Michalicka, 1966; Wickens, 1974). Moreover, it is interesting to note that when no visual feedback is available, children tend to increase their processing time (RT) for preprogramming; this may suggest a more demanding program elaboration.

In the first experiment, conditions of feedback similarly affected the three age groups studied. The only age-related differences were apparent in the slow movement condition, and only between 6-year-old children and the older subjects. Thus the second experiment concentrated on 6- and 9-year-old children, using a range of lower movement speeds. The goal of this second experiment was to investigate the possible improvement in the ability of open-loop aiming through training procedures in which movement speed was manipulated.

EXPERIMENT 2

Method

The apparatus and the aiming task were the same as those of Experiment 1, except that only three targets were used: one 20° to the left of the median plane, two others at 10° and 30°, respectively, to the right.

Subjects. Two groups of children of 6 and 9 years of age were tested. Each group had 16 subjects, with an equal number of boys and girls. The mean ages were 6.5 and 9.4, with a range of 5 and 10 months, respectively. All children were right-handed. Two control groups were also used: five 6-year-old and five 9-year-old children.

Procedure. The subjects were familiarized with the task. The experiment involved three phases:

1. Pretest—The subject had to perform the movements at a spontaneous speed and without visual feedback (open-loop condition). The three targets were presented five times.
2. Practice session—The horizontal screen was removed so that the subjects could receive visual feedback from their movement. The subjects performed three series of 24 trials each (8 on each target) separated by a resting interval. Two practice conditions were employed: half of the subjects had to execute the movements at a speed of approximately 300 ms, the other half had to execute the movements at a speed of approximately 650 ms.
3. Posttest—After the practice session the screen was fitted and all subjects were tested again in the open-loop condition, using their spontaneous speed.

The control groups were given only the pretest and posttest to control for any possible effect of repeating the test in the open-loop condition.

Analysis. Aiming accuracy was analyzed on the basis of the mean ADE for each subject in each condition. Data were processed separately for open-loop conditions (pre- and posttest) and for the closed-loop condition (practice session).

For the closed-loop condition, data were analyzed by means of a three-way (Age × Movement Speed × Practice Series) ANOVA, with repeated measures on the last factor. For open-loop conditions, various treatments were applied. A three-way (Age × Movement Speed × Test) ANOVA was first conducted. Following this analysis, no difference having been found between pretest conditions, a two-way (Age × Movement Speed) ANOVA was applied in which the pretest conditions were covaried. The specific effect of practice was further analyzed in terms of the rate of improvement between the pre- and posttests by means of a two-way (Age × Movement Speed) ANOVA. The scores of the control groups were analyzed by a two-way (Age × Test) ANOVA. In all ANOVAs the error term for each factor was the Factor × Subjects interaction.

Results

The ANOVA on ADE revealed a significant difference between pre- and posttest in all conditions (age and speed of training); $F(1, 28) = 31.54$, $p < .01$. This effect is also significant for age and speed. Figure 7 illustrates a tendency for the 9-year-old group to improve more than other groups in the condition of rapid movement practice.

Figure 7. Mean absolute directional error according to testing condition, age, and practice session.

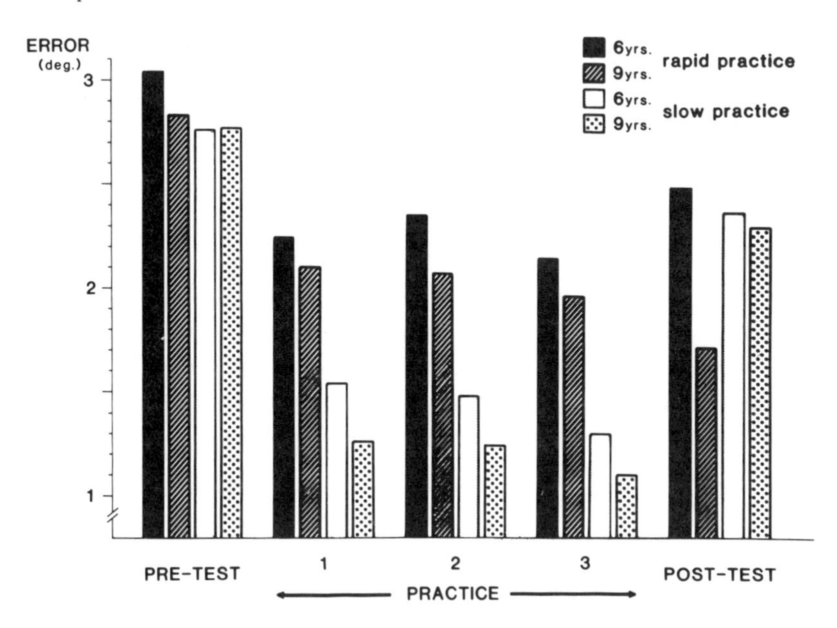

This tendency is supported by a significant age effect; $F(1, 28) = 5.23$, $p < .04$, which holds only for the rapid practice condition in a separate analysis ($p < .05$). It is also supported by a significant practice effect; $F(1, 48) = 4.23$, $p < .05$. The improvement in accuracy between the pre- and posttests can be accounted for by the practice of the task, since an ANOVA on the control groups does not reveal any significant difference between pre- and posttests, for both age groups.

Figure 7 illustrates that accuracy is much higher in practice sessions in the closed- than in both open-loop conditions. Within the practice session, the speed effect is significant; $F(1, 28) \times 23.85$, $p < .01$, which holds for each age group separately. There is no significant age effect, however. There is a significant effect of repetition over the three series; $F(2, 56) = 3.46$, $p < .02$, which holds only for the slow movement condition ($p < .05$). This suggests that, when visual feedback is available, accuracy is greatly improved in all conditions and particularly for slow movements in both age groups. Nevertheless, repetition of the task in the closed-loop condition improves accuracy only in the case of slow movements.

Discussion

When pre- and posttest accuracy are compared in the open-loop condition, an important improvement is found in both training conditions; the speed of movements therefore does not affect the subjects' ability to integrate visual information to correct and improve motor programming. However, the amount of feedback processed might not be the same in both conditions. In the fast training condition, the subject is most probably able to perform a few or even only one correction during the movement; consequently an important contribution to accuracy of movement is left to motor programming. In the slow training condition, MTs allow continuous feedback control such as in ramp trajectories, which greatly reduces the accuracy requirement of initial programming.

In the fast training condition, there may be an adaptation of the motor program on the basis of delayed feedback (from trial to trial) in addition to "on-line" feedback control, which results in a gain in accuracy when testing is done in the open-loop condition, whereas in the slow training condition the extended assistance of feedback control limits the necessity of adapting the motor program. This results in a higher accuracy during closed-loop movements, but also in a lower level of learning when testing is done in an open-loop condition afterward.

A point of interest is the difference in the effect of fast training between 6- and 9-year-old children. According to our previous hypothesis about fast versus slow training, it was suggested that delayed feedback (leading to adaptation of motor program) can be fully integrated into motor programming only after 6 years of age.

A final comment should be made concerning proprioception and particularly the development of its spatial significance. This can be illustrated by experimental results indicating the relationships between accuracy and MT, using a large range of MTs.

Subject aged 6 and 9 performed the same aiming task with movements of various speeds in open-loop conditions. For each child, all trials for this experiment were grouped according to MTs in 100-ms blocks and plotted against the corresponding average error scores (Figure 8). An ANOVA conducted on ADE showed a significant age effect, $F(1, 14) = 8.94$, $p < .01$; feedback, $F(1, 14) = 28.46$, $p < .01$; and speed, $F(6, 84) = 8.15$, $p < .01$, which could have been hypothesized from present knowledge on the topic. The interesting point is the difference found in the slope functions according to MTs. There is no effect of MTs for the 6-year-olds in the open-loop condition, but there is a significant linear component for the other three conditions (closed-loop in the 6-year-olds, and both feedback conditions in the 9-year-olds). The respective F values are CL_6—$F(1, 7) = 16.86$, $p < .01$; OL_9—$F(1, 7) = 68.12$, $p < .01$; OL_9—$F(1, 7) = 24.69$, $p < .01$.

Figure 8. Mean absolute directional error according to movement time, age, and feedback condition.

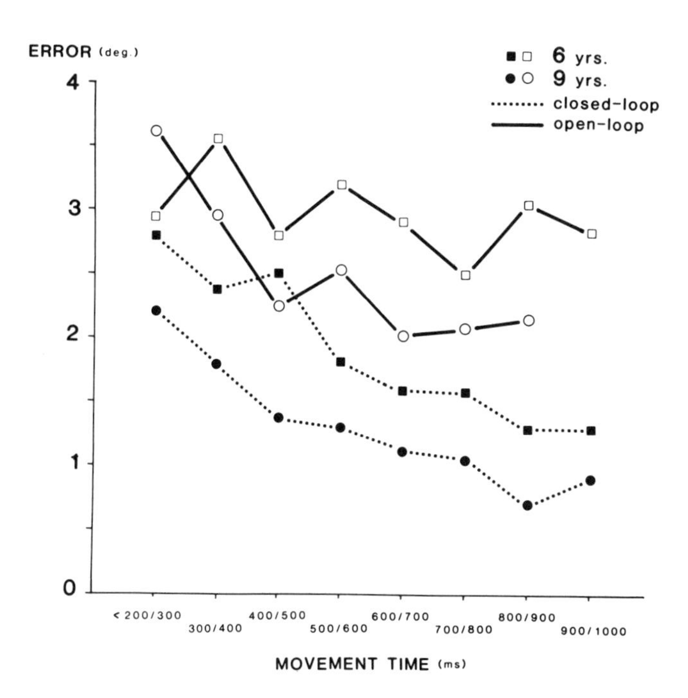

These results suggest that in 6-year-old children proprioceptive feedback does not supply spatial information in the open-loop task, even when time permits, but it does in 9-year-olds. It appears that in 6-year-old children proprioception has not yet acquired its spatial significance and is not efficient in a feedback process involving spatial requirements.

CONCLUSIONS

From the studies presented in this paper, several conclusions can be drawn.

First, aiming tasks performed at high speed (≃ 100 ms) can be assisted by peripheral vision leading to better spatial accuracy than when performed without any visual assistance. It also appears that children are able to adequately use such visual cues as adults normally do.

Second, at high speed the triggered portion of the movement in children, which is preprogrammed, deteriorates with repetition when no visual information is available to recalibrate the system. It appears therefore that high-speed proprioceptive information cannot be adequately analyzed by children, and in adults the triggered portion of movement remains constant over trials.

Third, when aiming is performed at lower speed ($\simeq$300 ms) both visual channels, peripheral and central, may contribute to the guidance of the movement. Here again children perform nearly as well as adults. However, 6-year-olds appear less accurate than the other groups while performing the task and, as mentioned for higher speed, the preprogrammed phase is unstable. This may be due to the fact that a well-documented agonist/antagonist control mechanism is still in a developmental stage.

Finally, practicing with feedback appears to help older children to refine and calibrate their motor programming, leading to better aiming even though visual feedback is withdrawn. In 6-year-olds, visual aids do not appear to be fully reintegrated in the program, resulting in less improvements than in 9-year-olds.

REFERENCES

Bard, C., & Hay, L. (1983). Etude ontogénétique de la coordination visuo-manuelle. *Journal Canadien de Psychologie, 37,* 390–412.

Bower, T.G.R. (1974). *Aspects of development in infancy.* San Francisco: Freeman.

Bower, T.G.R., & Wishart, J.C. (1972). The effects of motor skill on object permanence. *Cognition, 1,* 165–172.

Bullinger, A. (1976). Orientation de la tête du nouveau-né en présence d'un stimulus visuel. *Cahiers de psychologie, 19,* 223.

Carlton, L.G. (1979). Control processes in the production of discrete aiming responses. *Journal of Human Movement Studies, 5,* 115–124.

Carlton, L.G. (1981). Processing visual feedback information for movement control. *Journal of Experimental Psychology: Human Perception and Performance, 7,* 1019–1030.

Conti, P., & Beaubaton, D. (1976). Utilisation des informations visuelles dans le contrôle du mouvement: Étude de la précision des pointages chez l'homme. *Travail Humain, 39,* 19–32.

Hay, L. (1978). Accuracy of children on an open-loop pointing task. *Perceptual and Motor Skills, 47,* 1079–1082.

Hay, L. (1979). Spatial-temporal analysis of movements in children: Motor programs versus feedback in the development of reaching. *Journal of Motor Behavior, 11,* 189–200.

Hay, L. (in press). Discontinuity in the development of motor control in children. In W. Prinz & A.F. Sanders (Eds.), *Cognition and motor processes.* Berlin: Springer-Verlag.

Hofsten, C.V. (1979). Development of visually directed reaching: The approach phase. *Journal of Human Movement Studies, 5,* 160–178.

Hofsten, C.V. (1980). Predictive reaching for moving objects by human infants. *Journal of Experimental Child Psychology, 30,* 369–382.

Hofsten, C.V. (1983). Catching skills in infancy. *Journal of Experimental Psychology: Human Perception and Performance, 9,* 75-85.

Hofsten, C.V., & Lindhagen, K. (1979). Observations on the development of reaching for moving objects. *Journal of Experimental Child Psychology, 28,* 158-173.

Keele, S.W., & Posner, M.I. (1968). Processing of visual feedback in rapid movements. *Journal of Experimental Psychology, 77,* 155-158.

Michalicka, M. (1966). Influence du réglage en retour ("feedback") sur la rapidité de la réaction motrice simple chez les enfants de 7 à 16 ans. *Travail Humain, 29,* 73-83.

Paillard, J. (1980). The multichanneling of visual cues and the organization of a visually guided response. In G.E. Stelmach & J. Requin (Eds.), *Tutorials in motor behavior* (pp. 259-279). Amsterdam: North Holland.

Paillard, J. (1982). The contribution of peripheral and central vision to visually guided reaching. In D.J. Ingle, M.A. Goodale, & D.J.W. Mansfield (Eds.), *Analysis of visual behavior* (pp. 129-151). Cambridge, MA: MIT Press.

Paillard, J., & Beaubaton, D. (1978). De la coordination visuomotrice à l'organisation de la saisie manuelle. In H. Hécaen & M. Jeannerod (Eds.), *Du contrôle moteur à la coordination du geste* (pp. 225-260). Paris: Masson.

Schmidt, R.A., Zelaznik, H.N., & Frank, J.S. (1978). Source of inaccuracy in rapid movement. In G.E. Stelmach (Ed.), *Information processing in motor control and learning* (pp. 183-204). New York: Academic Press.

Wickens, C.D. (1974). Temporal limits of human information processing: A developmental study. *Psychological Bulletin, 81,* 739-755.

Woodworth, R.S. (1899). The accuracy of voluntary movement. *Psychological Review, Monograph Supplement, 3,* 54-59.

Zelaznik, H.N., Hawkins, B., & Kisselburgh, L. (1983). Rapid visual feedback processing in single-aiming movements. *Journal of Motor Behavior, 15,* 217-236.

3

Ball-Catching Proficiency Among 4-, 6-, and 8-Year-Old Girls

Rosa Du Randt
University of Port Elizabeth, Republic of South Africa

The purpose of the study was to determine the success of girls aged 4 (n = 30), 6 (n = 30), and 8 (n = 32) in the task of catching a ball projected over a constant distance of 5 m. Three different ball flight trajectories and two different ball sizes were used. By means of 3 × 2 × 2 × 3 factorial design, a four-way analysis of variance with repeated measures was used to determine the effect of age, surety of which ball flight trajectory to expect, ball size, ball flight trajectory, and the interactions of these factors on the subjects' success rate in this task. The results indicate that age, ball size, and ball flight trajectory; the interaction of age and ball flight trajectory; and the interaction of ball size and ball flight trajectory all significantly influenced ball-catching ability among all three age groups. The implications of these results for teaching young children ball catching are discussed.

The knowledge of what governs a smooth, well-coordinated, and successful movement can lead to more effective teaching strategies in the development of such performances. Obtaining this information, however, is a formidable task, because the understanding of skilled performance is dependent on the study of motor behavior (Keele, 1968).

Catching a ball is an ontogenetic and open skill task. "Ontogenetic" refers to those tasks in which children do not automatically obtain proficiency with age (Lawther, 1977), whereas "open skill" refers to the fact that changing spatial and temporal environmental factors determine the performance of the subject (Gentile, 1972). Ball catching and striking are considered by Halverson (1966) and by Espenschade and Eckert (1980) to be tasks in which children cannot rely on maturation alone to improve their proficiency. They do need guidance to improve effectively. Ball catching is a task that also figures very prominently among the

---

This paper is based on a doctoral dissertation completed under the guidance of Professor Dr. H. Isabel Nel at the University of Stellenbosch, South Africa. The study was financially supported by the Human Sciences Research Council.

physical education activities prescribed for young children. Pederson (1973), who studied the physical education syllabi of the preprimary schools, found that about one third of the activities prescribed in textbooks and curricula guidelines involved games or activities in which a ball is handled, and ball catching was one of the tasks generally occurring in the ball games. The development of this ability is thus very important to the young child.

To plan effective teaching strategies and curricula, a detailed analysis of the children's response strategies while performing this task is necessary. Information about the children's motor response, specifically their reaction to the different spatial and temporal environmental variables, is needed to develop quantitative and descriptive information on the success of the subjects and the phase of progression.

The problem under investigation in this study was the influence of variables such as age, ball size, ball flight trajectory, and predictability of the ball flight trajectory on ball-catching ability of 4-, 6-, and 8-year old girls. The experimental situation used to study the gross motor response was catching a ball projected from a constant distance. The spatial variables of the task were three ball flight trajectories and two ball sizes.

METHOD

Subjects

Three groups of girls—30 aged 4, 30 aged 6, and 32 aged 8—were randomly selected from three nursery and two primary schools in Port Elizabeth, South Africa, to participate in the study. They were familiarized with the testers and the apparatus used at least one day prior to testing.

Task

The task employed consisted of the catching of a ball projected at three trajectories (low, medium, and high) from a set distance of 5 m away from the subject. Two ball sizes were used: 200 mm and 72 mm in diameter, respectively. The ball was always tossed underhand by the same teacher, who was trained for 2 weeks prior to the commencement of the testing to project the ball at the desired trajectories. A second tester was used to evaluate each toss. Each ball flight trajectory had to reach a maximum vertical height at 2.5 m from the tosser. The following range was used for each trajectory: low—1-1.5 m, medium—1.5-2 m, and high—2-3m. If the ball did not reach the height desired at the right time or if the ball did not reach the subject within one step from where she was standing, that particular toss was disregarded and another attempt made. The procedure was repeated until the desired number of tosses of a particular flight trajectory were reached.

A separate tester was used to indicate to the ball tosser the sequence of ball flight trajectory to follow. This tester was also responsible for noting whether or not the subject was successful in catching the ball. A catch was considered to be successful if the subject could control the ball before it reached the ground or was projected away from the subject.

Procedure

To attain the cooperation and interest of the younger subjects, the testing of the 4- and 6-year-olds took place on the playgrounds of the respective nursery schools. Although each subject was tested individually, all volunteers were allowed to participate. Only the results of those subjects whose names were randomly selected prior to the testing were noted. The 8-year-olds were tested after school at the Physical Education Department of the local university. They were organized to report in groups of three. Although only one subject was tested at a time, the other two were allowed to play around the testing area until their turn came.

Each of the 8- and 6-year-olds received 10 balls projected at each flight trajectory. The 4-year-olds only received seven balls at each flight trajectory because of their inability to concentrate for longer periods. During the first part of the testing the subjects were aware of which flight trajectory to expect (sure circumstances). This was followed by unsure circumstances, in which they did not know which trajectory to expect, and each subject received 15 balls—5 balls at each trajectory presented in a "random" order (it appeared random to the recipient but was actually determined beforehand).

The sure and unsure circumstances were blocked and followed one another immediately in the case of the 6- and 8-year-olds. Because of the 4-year-olds' limited concentration span, they were allowed to interrupt the testing between the two parts. The sure and unsure circumstances were employed with both ball sizes. However, all age groups were given a rest period after testing with the large ball, and before the small ball was used.

The dependent measure used was the number of successful catches expressed as a percentage of the total number of balls received by the subject. Using a $3 \times 2 \times 2 \times 3$ factorial design, the data obtained were analyzed by means of a four-way (depending on the number of factors involved) analysis of variance (ANOVA) for repeated measures (Winer, 1971). The arcsine transformation was applied to the data because it is known to stabilize the variance of binomial proportions (percentage measurements) (Snedecor & Cochran, 1980). A study of the standard deviations after transformation, however, showed that in this analysis the transformation did not seem to stabilize the variance in all cases. Hence it was decided to use the original data. The level of significance for the influence of factors such as age, surety of ball flight trajectory, ball size, ball flight trajectory, and the interactions of these factors on ball-catching success was set at 5%.

RESULTS AND DISCUSSION

ANOVA revealed that the catching ability of the subjects used in this study was significantly influenced by factors such as age ($F[3.07] = 153.96$, $p < .001$), ball size ($F[3.92] = 84.41$, $p < .001$), ball flight trajectory ($F[3.00] = 2.73$, $p < .068$), interaction of ball flight trajectory and age ($F[2.37] = 6.83$, $p < .001$), and interaction between ball flight trajectory and ball size [$F[3.00] = 14.13$, $p < .001$). Insufficient evidence was found to indicate that the "sure" factor regarding ball flight trajectory expectation could influence the catching skill ($F[3.92] = 0.00$, $p > .05$).

Table 1 reflects the mean percentage of the two different-sized balls caught successfully by the three different age groups. A post hoc analysis revealed that all means differed significantly ($p < .05$). The fact that catching ability improved with age is in accordance with the findings of many researchers, including Wellman (1937), Gutteridge (1939), Seils (1951), Warner (1952), Victors (1961), Sweeney (1965), and Katzenellenbogen (1976). This is also true for the negative effect that the 72-mm ball had on the success rate of the task, when compared to the larger, 200-mm ball. Researchers such as Warner (1952) and Meyer (1956), who used ball sizes of comparative diameter in their investigations, reported similar effects.

Table 1
Mean Success Rate (%) in Catching Different-Sized Balls

	Age Groups		
Ball Size	4 Years	6 Years	8 Years
Large	25.64	51.22	85.89
Small	13.22	35.07	76.51
Both sizes	19.43	43.17	81.20

Note. All means differ significantly at $p < .05$.

Table 2 gives the mean percentage of balls caught successfully at the three different trajectories. The age groups seem to differ with regard to which ball flight trajectory results in the most success in catching the ball. The 4-year-olds clearly catch the balls of low

Table 2
Mean Success Rate (%) in Catching Balls of Different Trajectories

Trajectory	Age Groups 4 Years	6 Years	8 Years	All Age Groups
Low	24.31	[42.48]	77.19	47.99
Medium	[17.96]	47.29	[83.67]	50.38
High	[16.02]	[39.75]	[82.73]	46.96

Note. All means differ significantly at $p < .05$ except those encased in brackets.

trajectory best, and both the 6- and the 8-year-olds catch the balls of medium trajectory best, although not much difference exists between the medium and high trajectories for the 8-year-olds. The subjects also differ with regard to which trajectory results in the least success. The 4-year-olds find the balls of medium and high trajectories and the 6-year-olds the balls of low and high trajectories significantly more ($p < .05$) difficult to catch, whereas the 8-year-olds have significantly ($p < .05$) more difficulty with the balls of low trajectory. The significant influence of ball trajectory, however, is contrary to the results reported by Bruce (1966), the only researcher known to have studied the effect of ball flight trajectory on ball-catching ability. The subjects participating in Bruce's study were second-, fourth-, and sixth-graders, and it is possible that ball flight trajectory may not influence ball-catching ability after age 8. The decreasing effect of ball flight trajectory, as indicated in Table 2, gives some support to this argument.

One explanation for the success of the 4-year-olds in catching the low trajectory ball is the possibility that they have more reference points within the background (e.g., the tosser, ball, and ground as well as the position of the arms and hands which are held in line with the ball) to aid them in judging the ball's velocity. However, Smith (1970) has indicated that figure-ground ability develops with increasing age and only reaches a plateau at 14–16 years of age, so one would expect this ability to be relatively underdeveloped at the age of 4. A more likely explanation would be that the low trajectory suits the catching response strategy that the 4-year-olds most commonly apply, namely that of a "scoop" action, more than the other two trajectories (Du Randt, 1981).

The 6- and 8-year-olds catch the medium trajectory balls more often, probably because this trajectory ball moves at a lower velocity than the low and high trajectory balls. This stimulation elicits a more mature catching response of "momentum absorption," as is also the case with the high trajectory ball. Because the subjects are not very experienced in this response, and as a result of the higher vertical velocity of the high trajectory and horizontal velocity of the low trajectory, they are more successful with the medium than with the high or low trajectory balls.

The 4- and 6-year-olds are least successful with the high ball flight trajectory, probably because of the velocity of the ball and the response strategy they employ, as well as the fact that they have fewer reference points in the environment to aid their judgment of the ball's velocity. These subjects probably lose sight of the tosser and their own hands, particularly in the first half of the ball's movement, resulting in the effect described. The 8-year-olds are least successful with the low trajectory ball, probably because of the horizontal velocity of the ball or the relatively shorter viewing time, as well as the fact that they do not need to use head movements to track the ball and thereby reduce proprioceptive feedback, which could have aided in velocity anticipation.

One factor that has not been studied to determine its effect on catching ability is the surety of knowing which ball flight trajectory to expect. My investigation failed to find this factor significant. This could be attributed to the fact that the unsure circumstances were presented after the sure circumstances in the test procedure. On the other hand, it could indicate that the length of time that the ball was viewed when the circumstances were unsure was sufficient to elicit the same procedure as was followed when sure circumstances were employed. Surety of ball flight trajectory may still be a factor influencing ball-catching success, but only when shorter viewing time or higher ball velocities are applied.

Although success in catching ability increased with advance in age, the size of the increment between the three age groups is unequal. There appears to be a larger difference between the percentage success of 6- and 8-year-olds than between 4- and 6-year-olds. This is contrary to the findings reported by Gutteridge (1939), who indicated a larger spurt in the development of catching ability between the 4- and 6-year-olds than between 6- and 8-year-olds. It must be noted, however, that Gutteridge measured the percentage of subjects who were proficient in the catching skills within each age group. A subject was considered proficient when he or she could catch at least 50% of the projected balls. It appears, therefore, that although subjects became more "proficient" in the skill between ages 4 and 6 than between ages 6 and 8, the percentage of balls they were able to catch showed a higher increment between ages 6 and 8 than between ages 4 and 6. The increment between ages 6 and 8 is even larger when the small ball is involved compared with large ball involvement. When the results of both ball sizes are combined, the percentage success rate seems to double with each age advancement of 2 years and thereby accentuates the spurt of the percentage successful catches between the ages of 6 and 8.

When the detailed effect of ball size is considered, it seems that although the small ball results in constantly lower success rates, the detrimental effect of this ball size on catching ability decreases as age increases. If the success rate results of catching the small ball were expressed as an approximate percentage of that of catching the large ball, the following comparison could be made: the 4-year-olds are 50% as proficient at catching the small ball, the 6-year-olds 70% as proficient, and the 8-year-olds 90% as proficient.

Table 3 indicates that the large ball during the high trajectory and the small ball during the low trajectory are significantly ($p < .05$) more difficult to catch when compared with other trajectories.

Table 3
Mean Success Rate (%) in Catching Balls of Different Sizes Projected at Different Trajectories

Trajectory	Ball Size	
	Large	Small
Low	[57.50]	37.98
Medium	[56.02]	[44.31]
High	50.14	[44.00]

Note. All means differ significantly at $p < .05$ except those encased in brackets.

In the case of the large ball and high trajectory, the time of flight of the ball and the balance problems encountered—particularly by the 4-year-olds in following the ball flight to its peak and consequently losing sight of the ground—could probably account for the difficulties experienced with this combination of independent factors. The change in response strategy from a scoop to a momentum absorption response by the 4- and 6-year-olds (Du Randt, 1981), and the increased horizontal velocity which affects the 8-year-olds as well, may account for the problems experienced in the case of the small ball and low trajectory.

CONCLUSION

It is evident that the ball-catching proficiency of girls aged 4, 6, and 8 is significantly influenced by factors such as age, ball size, and ball flight trajectory. The three age groups also seem to be influenced significantly in different ways by ball size and by ball flight trajectory. These facts should be considered when teaching the ball-catching skill to young children. The first teaching implication is that if any ball size is considered, the average percentages of balls expected to be caught by 4-, 6-, and 8-year-olds are more or less 20, 40, and 80 respectively. The second implication is that a small ball (e.g., the size of a tennis ball) stimulated the occurrence of a more mature catching response in 8- and 6-year-olds, but not in 4-year-olds. It is therefore recommended that 8- and 6-year-olds be encouraged to play with a small ball as often as possible, whereas 4-year-olds need not be confronted formally with a small ball until they are relatively proficient with a larger ball. The third implication concerns which ball flight trajectory should be concentrated on first: low trajectory for 4-year-olds and medium trajectory for 6- and 8-year-olds. For the latter two age groups, an advance to the other two ball flight trajectories should follow sooner than for 4-year-olds.

REFERENCES

Bruce, R.D. (1966). *The effects of variations in ball trajectory upon the catching performance of elementary school children.* Unpublished doctoral dissertation, University of Wisconsin.

Du Randt, R. (1981). *A spatial and temporal analysis of the gross motor response of an open skill with specific reference to 4, 6, and 8-year old girls.* Unpublished doctoral dissertation, University of Stellenbosch, Stellenbosch, South Africa.

Espenschade, A.S., & Eckert, H.M. (1980). *Motor development* (2nd ed.). Columbus, OH: Merrill.

Gentile, A.M. (1972). A working model of skill acquisition with application to teaching. *Quest, 17,* 3–23.

Gutteridge, M. (1939). A study of motor achievements of young children. *Archives of Psychology, 34* (Whole No. 244).

Halverson, L.E. (1966). Development of motor patterns in young children. *Quest, 4,* 44–53.

Katzenellenbogen, E.H. (1976). *Specific components of the perceptual motor ability of girls 7 to 11 years of age with specific reference to movements in the physical education programme.* Unpublished doctoral dissertation, University of Stellenbosch, Stellenbosch, South Africa.

Keele, S.W. (1968). Movement control in skilled motor performance. *Psychological Bulletin, 70,* 387–403.

Lawther, J.D. (1977). *The learning and performance of physical skills.* Englewood Cliffs, NJ: Prentice-Hall.

Meyer, M. (1956). Unpublished data from Randall School, Madison, WI.

Pederson, E.J. (1973). *A study of ball catching abilities of first, third and fifth-grade children on twelve selected ball catching tasks.* Unpublished doctoral dissertation, Indiana University.

Seils, L. (1951). The relation between measures of physical growth and gross motor performance of primary grade school children. *Research Quarterly, 22,* 244.

Smith, H.M. (1970). Implications for movement education experiences drawn from perceptual-motor research. *Journal of Health, Physical Education and Recreation, 41,* 30–33.

Snedecor, G. W., & Cochran, W. G. (1980). *Statistical methods* (7th ed.). Ames, IA: Iowa State University Press.

Sweeney, J. M. (1965). *The effects of instruction and practice only on the motor learning of elementary school children.* Unpublished doctoral dissertation, Ohio State University.

Victors, E. (1961). *A cinematographic analysis of catching behavior of a selected group of 7 and 9 year old boys.* Unpublished doctoral dissertation, University of Wisconsin.

Warner, A.P. (1952). *The motor ability of third, fourth and fifth grade boys in the elementary school.* Unpublished doctoral dissertation, University of Michigan.

Wellman, B. L. (1937). Motor achievement of preschool children. *Child Education, 8,* 311-316.

Winer, B. J. (1971). *Statistical principles in experimental design* (2nd ed.). New York: McGraw-Hill.

4

Fitts' Law and Motor Control in Children

ROBERT KERR
University of Ottawa

Fitts' law has been shown to be applicable to children (Kerr, 1975; Sugden, 1980; Wallace, Newell, & Wade, 1978), but there is disagreement as to the nature of the changes in children's ability to process information; that is, their motor capacity (Hay, 1981; Salmoni & McIlwain, 1979). The present study used a reciprocal tapping task to investigate the motor performance of subjects 4, 5, 6, and 7 years of age. Although overall performances improved with age, there were no significant changes in motor capacity. Results are discussed in terms of the potential contribution of changes in motor capacity to improvements in motor performance.

One of the common characteristics of children's motor development is the increase in their ability to make movements quickly and accurately. The improvement in movement efficiency is due partly to increases in strength which allow the children to stop and start movements more quickly, which in turn allows their physical response to movement-generated feedback to be faster and more precise. The improvement in motor performance, however, is also thought to reflect an improved ability to process information; that is, an increased motor capacity.

The term "motor capacity" is an intuitively relevant concept which eludes definition. To use a computer analogy, one can enhance the performance of a computer by changing either the hardware or the software. One can increase the computer's memory storage—the capacity of the system—or one can write more programs which can function within the existing capacity of the system. Thus, improvement in the motor performance of a child could reflect changes in motor capacity—for example, the ability to store or process larger amounts of motor information—or it could reflect the adoption of new strategies which would allow the child to process

An earlier draft of this paper was presented at the joint conference of the Canadian Society for Psychomotor Learning and Sports Psychology and the North American Society for the Psychology of Sport and Physical Activity, Michigan State University, May 1983.

information at a faster rate or would require the processing of less information due to an improved selection or sampling process.

To investigate the question of motor capacity, researchers have turned to the reciprocal tapping task as described by Fitts (1954), or the discrete version of Fitts and Peterson (1964). By changing the movement amplitude *(A)* between pairs of targets or the actual target width *(W)*, Fitts (1954) was able to vary the difficulty of the task. The index of difficulty *(ID)* was expressed as $ID = \log_2 (2A/W)$. What has since become known as Fitts' law makes movement time constant for any given ratio between movement amplitude and target width, with proportional changes in either parameter producing equivalent changes in movement time: $MT = a+b \log_2 (2A/W)$.

The determination of motor capacity from Fitts' law, however, has given rise to two quite different concepts. In the Fitts and Peterson (1964) paper "capacity" was considered to be analogous to a person's capacity for executing a given class of movements: in this case, at one particular level of the *ID*. It was expressed as $C = ID/MT$. In this sense "capacity" *(C)* is not some global measure of processing capacity, a sort of motor IQ, but is simply a measure of performance on one particular task. With practice at that particular task both movement time *(MT)* and *C* may improve (Kay, 1962). *C* will also vary from task as the *ID* level changes.

An alternative view of motor capacity may be determined by plotting the regression line between *MT* and *ID*. The reciprocal of the slope coefficient ($1/b$), the response to changes in task difficulty, may be regarded as a measure of the channel capacity of the motor system (measured in bits per second). Using this formulation Fitts and Peterson (1964) found that although extended practice led to decreases in *MT*, these improvements were consistent across conditions and there was, therefore, no change in the slope of the regression coefficient. Clearly, an assessment of motor capacity (i.e., $1/b$) that is not susceptible to practice effects and is not tied to specific variations of a task is very attractive.

Fitts' law has proved quite robust and has been shown to be applicable to children (Kerr, 1975; Sugden, 1980; Wallace, Newell, & Wade, 1978). Even so, there has been disagreement as to the nature of the changes in children's ability to process information (Salmoni & McIlwain, 1979). My study (1975) with children 5-9 years of age and Sugden's (1980) study, using a serial task with children 6-12 years of age, found a decrease in *MT* with age but no significant change in the slope coefficient, that is, the response to changes in task difficulty. Salmoni and McIlwain, however, indicated significant changes in the slope coefficients between children in Grade 1 and children in Grades 5 and 9, and Hay (1981) also showed a decrease in the slope coefficient from 5 to 9 years of age. Using a discrete task Sugden did observe differences in slope coefficients across ages, but these were not tested statistically.

A somewhat different interpretation of Fitts' law was provided by Welford, Norris, and Shock (1969), who felt that two separate processes ought to be distinguished: a faster one concerned with distance covering and a slower one for "homing onto" the target. Using this distinction Hay (1981) argued that differences in performance over age could be accounted for by changes in the contribution of these two factors. Hay suggested that whereas 5-year-olds were more influenced by the required precision, 7- to 11-year-olds were more affected by the distance to be moved. I observed differences in the mean value of the slope coefficients where either *A* or *W* was held constant (6.13 bits and 8.20 bits, respectively, for the 5-year-old group), but found no significant differences in the contribution of these same two factors in children aged 5, 7, or 9 (Kerr, 1975). Hay's conclusions requiring this aspect of Fitts' law were drawn on descriptive data only.

In explaining some of the discrepancies among these studies, Salmoni and McIlwain (1979) pointed to the limited range of *ID* used in my 1975 work and my failure to use target widths of less than 1 cm. Alternatively, Hay (1981) suggested that improvements in motor performance occur in a series of steps, thus whether significant improvements are noted may depend to some extent on the ages being compared.

Given that children aged 5 (Hay, 1981) and 6 (Salmoni & McIlwain, 1979) appeared to perform significantly differently from older children, I sought to reproduce or refute my 1975 data by focusing on these two age groups plus or minus 1 year. Wallace et al. (1978) showed Fitts' law to hold for preschool children. Thus, while accommodating the criticisms of Salmoni and McIlwain, I attempted to assess differences in the channel capacity ($1/b$) of children aged 4–7. I also attempted to assess separately the effect of changes in *A* and *W*.

METHOD

Subjects

The subjects were 64 children aged 4–7 from schools and day care centers in the Ottawa area. Children were tested within 3 months of their birthdays to create four age groups ($n = 16$): 4, 5, 6, and 7 years of age, respectively.

Apparatus

Pairs of targets were drawn on sheets of paper, five pairs per sheet. The first sheet had four pairs of targets not included in the experiment and was followed by a random sequence of 16 pairs of targets in which *A* was either 5, 9, 18, or 30 cm and *W* was either 3, 6, 15, or 35 mm. Thus the *ID* ranged from 1.50 to 7.64 bits. The tapping was performed with a sharp metal stylus.

Procedure

To familiarize the children with the task and the experimenter, the subjects at each test location were asked to complete a series of five practice trials (targets not included in the experiment) as a group demonstration. The next day subjects were tested individually, the first four pairs of targets being used to ensure that the children understood the task and performed it correctly. The four trials were not included in the data analysis. Each trial lasted 10 s. The experimenter, who gave the stop/start signal, also counted the total number of movements.

MT data were submitted to a 4 × 16 (Age Group × Task) analysis of variance (ANOVA), with repeated measures. Individual regression equations were calculated and the data used to compare group differences in the slope and intercept coefficients. Separate regression equations were also calculated to assess the effect of holding *A* and *W* constant.

RESULTS

The analysis of the *MT* data revealed significant main effects for group, $F(3, 60) = 96.13$, $p < .001$, and for task, $F(15, 900) = 31.55$, $p < .001$. The Scheffé test indicated that all age groups were significantly different from each other, $p < .05$, and the level of significance for task reflected the differences in the *ID*. Table 1 provides *MT*s.

Table 1
Mean Movement Times (ms) and Regression Equation Data

		All Targets		3-mm Targets Excluded	
Age	Mean MT	Intercept	Slope	Intercept	Slope
4	1255	567	145	554	145
5	1045	462	123	520	108
6	932	362	120	405	104
7	785	153	133	211	113

The overall error rate was 7.5%, ranging from 10% for the 4-year-olds to 4% for the 6-year-olds. With a paper-and-pencil test this is only an estimate, because one point (hole) may represent more than one hit. Percentage error may be misleading when the number of hits per target is not controlled; 1 error in 5 hits (20%) compared with 1 in 20 (5%). Slower (younger) movers may appear less accurate.

One-way ANOVAs applied to the group data, using the individual regression data, were calculated separately for the slopes and intercepts. Significant differences were found between age groups for intercept, $F(3, 60) = 8.21$, $p < .001$, but not for slope. Using the Scheffé test with the intercept data, the 7-year-olds were found to be significantly different from the 5- and 4-year-olds, $p < .05$, but not from the 6-year-olds. This finding agrees with that of Hay (1981).

In a further analysis of the data, separate regression equations were calculated where either A or W was held constant. For the case of $W = 3$ mm the slope was found to approach zero (for all ages), the implication being that the 3-mm target created sufficient difficulty that increasing A had little additional effect on MT. Because it was felt that these data might be biasing the overall interpretation of the MT/ID regression analysis, the major analysis was recalculated with the 3-mm data eliminated. Consequently, a significant difference was found for slope, $F(3, 60) = 2.78$, $p < .05$ (an F of 2.76 being required for significance). The Scheffé test revealed no significant differences.

To analyze the effects of accuracy and distance, I used the same approach as Hay (1981) in which separate slope coefficients were calculated for A and W. The overall impact of A or W is represented by taking the mean of these slopes (see Table 2). This mean value provides a description of the data but does not permit a test of statistical significance. In Table 2, the effect of A or W is shown as the mean of the coefficients for MT against ID where one of the variables

Table 2
Slope Coefficients (Expressed as $1/b$ in bits/s)

	All Data			3-mm Targets Excluded		
Age	Overall	Effect of Amplitude[a]	Effect of Width[b]	Overall	Effect of Amplitude[a]	Effect of Width[b]
4	6.90	8.62	6.37	6.90	6.67	6.76
5	8.13	20.83	7.94	9.26	11.10	8.20
6	8.33	15.38	7.25	9.62	10.99	8.85
7	7.52	12.50	6.67	8.84	10.20	7.87

[a] Mean of slopes with target width held constant.
[b] Mean of slopes with movement amplitude held constant.

(*A* or *W*) is held constant, expressed in bits per second. For all age groups, the effect of changes in *W* was greater than changes in *A*, producing a steeper slope coefficient (or fewer bits processed per second). However, when the 3-mm targets were eliminated the mean slopes for *A* or *W* were equivalent for the 4-year-old group: 6.67 and 6.76 bits.

DISCUSSION

In general, the present study appears to support my earlier (1975) findings and those of Sugden (1980) with a serial task. The children showed a significant improvement in their overall performance with increasing age but did not show any significant improvement in their channel capacity, as measured by the reciprocal of the slope coefficient ($1/b$). Thus, although practice and/or development may improve a child's overall ability to move faster and more precisely, constant increases in the difficulty of the task (as measured by changes in the informational load or *ID*) will still produce equivalent increases in *MT* across age levels.

The failure to find improvements in motor capacity ($1/b$) is not consistent with the work of Salmoni and McIlwain (1979) and Hay (1981). Salmoni and McIlwain found a significant improvement from 6 to 10 years of age and Hay from 5 to 9 years of age. Removing the smallest *W* from the present study and recalculating the slope coefficients did produce a significant *F* ratio, but not one that can be interpreted in any meaningful manner. Notwithstanding the discrepancies in these studies, three points emerge. First, the overall performance of children on a Fitts' law type of task improves markedly from year to year. Second, although there appears to be a clear increase in motor capacity (using $1/b$) from the young child (4–5) to the adult (Salmoni & McIlwain, 1979), the attempts to sample intervals within this range have produced inconsistent results. Third, children's motor performance is highly variable. Taken together these points would appear to lead to two further conclusions.

First, if there are gradual improvements in motor capacity from one age level to the next, these are largely masked by the impact of rapid changes in muscle strength and other physiological parameters. A more powerful musculature might both produce faster movement and permit the execution of faster movement corrections. Such improvements in movement efficiency could result in the movements approximating more precisely what the child intended, that is, fewer corrections leading to faster overall performance. *MT*s are faster at all levels of difficulty with increasing age, but the slope of the regression equation remains relatively unchanged.

Second, because the contribution an improvement in motor capacity might make to the overall improvement in motor performance is, at best, limited, the pattern of the "growth" of motor capacity over time might only be teased out by reducing the variability in the subject's movements. Extended practice may not improve performance in terms of motor capacity (Fitts, 1954), but it may reduce some of the variability in the children's performance. Only then may we assess the speculations of Hay (1981) regarding the sequence, if any, of increases and plateaus in sensorimotor development across ages. The Salmoni and McIlwain (1979) study of two children was insufficient to clarify the picture.

Hay (1981), using the model of Welford et al. (1969), also reviewed the separate effects of *A* and *W* on performance. Hay suggested that whereas 5-year-olds were affected by movement accuracy, 7-, 9- and 11-year-olds were influenced by *A*. This latter finding is not consistent with the original model of Welford et al., who refer to a "relatively faster" distance-covering component. I found no significant differences regarding the influence of these two factors in 5-, 7-, and 9-year-olds, although descriptively the 5-year-olds did show a similar bias toward movement accuracy (Kerr, 1975). In the present study, all age groups were affected differentially by *A* and *W*, with changes in *W* producing steeper slope coefficients; this is the reverse of what Hay (1981) found. It should be noted that Hay used a pointing task rather than a tapping task.

Kerr (1978) changed the environment by asking subjects to perform the Fitts task underwater. In this environment, Kerr also found a greater effect for *A*. The descriptive data from the present study regarding the separate impact on *MT* of *A* and *W* (see Table 2) provide almost a reverse image of Hay (1981). Given that changes in the environment or in the age range can produce contrary findings, one might suggest that these "differences" regarding the contributions of the two components *(A* and *W)* may be more anomalies of the task than characteristics of motor development.

Given the biasing effect of the 3-mm target, the a priori decisions (Kerr, 1975; Hay, 1981; Sugden, 1980) not to use targets less than 1 cm may have been justified. It appears that for all the age groups in the present study, subjects performed the 3-mm tasks more as a series of discrete movements than as a continuous task. The task of hitting the 3-mm targets was sufficiently difficult that *A* had little additional impact. It is possible, therefore, that the use of a single 2.5-mm target by Salmoni and McIlwain (1979) may have biased their results.

The potential change in strategy at high levels of *ID* is supported by Sugden (1980), who found that the "gain" in time, when comparing a serial and discrete task, disappeared at the higher *ID* levels. The implication is that at the higher *ID* levels subjects treated the serial task more like a discrete task. Small targets, close to the limits of the children's ability to move accurately, may produce similar changes in strategy.

That physical limits to Fitts' law exist has always been recognized. As *ID* is lowered a point is reached, before *ID* reaches zero, where the subjects cannot make any further increase in the speed of their movements. Similarly, there are physical limits as to how far and accurately we can move. By trying to identify and avoid these limitations, or control for them with arm length as Hay (1981) did, we may improve our ability to clarify the picture.

Finally, although there appear to be motor capacity differences between adults and 5-year-olds, there is no clear evidence for how this "improvement" may develop. An explanation suggested by Wade (1976) is that young children process more information to perform the same task as an adult. They do not have the strategies available to an adult and, therefore, are unable to capitalize on any redundancies present in the movement. What is a single movement to a target and back for an adult may be viewed as three separate movements by a child: moving forward, hitting the target, and moving back. Given the equivalency of the slope coefficients in the present study, it appears that the young children are spending more time "on target" and thereby treating the serial task as a series of discrete movements rather than a continuous task. If so, then comparing adults and children on the same task is a little like comparing apples and oranges. We may be seeking to demonstrate a change in motor capacity which does not exist.

REFERENCES

Fitts, P.M. (1954). The information capacity of the human motor system in controlling the amplitude of movement. *Journal of Experimental Psychology, 47,* 381-391.

Fitts, P.M., & Peterson, J.R. (1964). Information capacity of discrete motor responses. *Journal of Experimental Psychology, 65,* 103-112.

Hay, L. (1981). The effect of amplitude and accuracy requirements on movement times in children. *Journal of Motor Behavior, 13,* 177-186.

Kay, H. (1962). Channel capacity and skilled performance. In F.A. Geldard (Ed.), *Defense psychology* (pp. 161-169). New York: Macmillan.

Kerr, R. (1975). Movement control and motivation in elementary-grade children. *Perceptual and Motor Skills, 41,* 151-154.

Kerr, R. (1978). Diving, adaptation and Fitts' law. *Journal of Motor Behavior, 10,* 255-260.

Salmoni, A., & McIlwain, J.S. (1979). Fitts' reciprocal tapping task, a measure of motor capacity? *Perceptual and Motor Skills, 9,* 403-413.

Sugden, D.A. (1980). Movement speed in children. *Journal of Motor Behavior, 12,* 125-132.

Wade, M.G. (1976). Developmental motor learning. In J.F. Keogh & R.S. Hutton (Eds.), *Exercise and sport sciences reviews* (Vol. 4, pp. 375-394). Santa Barbara, CA: Journal Publishing Affiliates.

Wallace, S.A., Newell, K.M., & Wade M.G. (1978). Decision and response times as a function of movement difficulty in preschool children. *Child Development, 49,* 509-512.

Welford, A.T., Norris, A.M., & Shock, N.W. (1969). Speed and accuracy of movement and their changes with age. *Acta Psychologica, 30,* 3-15.

5

Interlimb Movement Control and Coordination in Children

DAN SOUTHARD
Texas Christian University

The purpose of this study was to investigate how children coordinate and control interlimb movements. Nine groups of children (five boys and five girls per group) ranging in age from 5 to 14 years performed single- and two-hand movements to targets of equal and disparate difficulty. Analysis of data showed similar changes for reaction times (RTs) and movement times (MTs) for all single- and two-hand movement conditions by age. MTs for the hand moving to the easy target in the two-hand (left easy-right difficult) condition were significantly elevated over the corresponding single-hand (left easy) condition. In addition, nonsignificant RTs and MTs between hands for two-hand conditions support the concept of a systematic linkage of muscles (coordinative structures) which constrain the actor to control and perceive two-hand movements as a unit. It was concluded that coordinative structures represent an invariant mode of interlimb control across changes in age.

Human movement frequently requires the control and coordination of more than one limb simultaneously. Indeed, a cursory view of the developing organism reveals the necessity of interlimb coordination for mature performances of the most fundamental of skills. Nonetheless, researchers in motor development have focused on data from single-limb paradigms to investigate the developmental aspects of motor control (Hay, 1981; Kerr, 1975; Salmoni & Pascoe, 1978; Sugden, 1980). Although such research contributes to knowledge concerning human development, single-limb designs may mask the processes controlling interlimb movement.

Recent interest in interlimb coordination was sparked by the Soviet physiologist Nicolai Bernstein (1967), when he posed a problem which not only focuses on interlimb control and coordination but is also a natural consequence of the developing organism: How can the many degrees of freedom of the body be regulated in the course of activity by a minimally intelligent executive intervening minimally? The problem increases in complexity when one considers adaptation to physical changes accompanying development. Or, as phrased by Kugler, Kelso, and Turvey (1982): What is the informational base for systematically constraining the body's degrees of freedom and how is that informational base coordinated with changes in the body's dimensions?

In attempts to solve Bernstein's problem it has been proposed that the brain does not control individual muscles; rather, control is delegated to lower centers which are capable of producing coordinated movement in an autonomous fashion (Gelfand, Gurfinkel, Tsetlin, & Shik, 1971; Turvey, 1977). A further reduction in the control problem is gained through the systematic linkage of individual muscles so that groups of muscle linkages act as a unit called a coordinative structure (Grillner, 1975; Shik & Orlovskii, 1976; Turvey, Shaw, & Mace, 1978). Kelso, Southard, and Goodman (1979) operationalized the coordinative structures concept by showing that when subjects were required to produce movements of the upper limbs to targets which varied in amplitude and precision requirements, they did so by releasing home keys, reaching peak velocity and acceleration, and arriving at respective targets virtually simultaneously.

Marteniuk and MacKenzie (1980) utilized an interlimb paradigm to examine interference effects between hands by manipulating amplitude and stylus weight held by subjects. Unlike the Kelso et al. (1979) study, they found significant differences in movement times (MTs) between hands when subjects were required to move different distances. In addition, they demonstrated systematic differences between hands for reaction times (RTs), MTs, and constant error. As a result of their findings, a model of two-hand coordination was proposed which was based on three basic control processes. The first two, intensity and equilibrium point specification, were seen as relatively independent and affected by mass and distance manipulations. The model predicted interference effects for both processes due to interaction of neural activity at subcortical and spinal levels as well as their modification by the third process—hand/hemisphere asymmetrical organization.

Whereas the importance of interlimb coordination is both intuitively and empirically well grounded, we know very little concerning the developmental aspects of processes underlying the control of human interlimb movements. Two primary questions concerning the development of interlimb control and coordination are addressed in this study: (1) How do children control bimanual movements? and (2) Does maturation affect the processes responsible for interlimb control?

METHOD

Subjects

Nine age groups—5, 6, 8, 9, 10, 11, 12, 13, and 14 years—were used in this study. There were 10 subjects (5 boys and 5 girls) in each group. The mean ages (in years and months) and standard deviations (in months) were $X = 5\text{-}4$, $SD = 4$; $X = 6\text{-}3$, $SD = 3$; $X = 8\text{-}7$, $SD = 3$; $X = 9\text{-}2$, $SD = 5$; $X = 10\text{-}4$, $SD = 4$; $X = 11\text{-}7$, $SD = 6$; $X = 12\text{-}6$, $SD = 5$; $X = 13\text{-}6$, $SD = 3$; $X = 14\text{-}4$, $SD = 4$. The subjects were randomly selected from public school classes in Fort Worth, Texas. Seven-year-olds were not available for testing.

Apparatus

The apparatus consisted of a plywood base 30 cm × 70 cm. Two home keys (normally closed keyboard switches) were mounted and centrally placed 5 cm apart. Two targets were positioned on the base laterally from the home keys and at distances between 8 and 32 cm. The targets were designated easy or difficult depending upon their width and distance from the home key (Index of Difficulty [ID] = $\log 2A/W$). Easy targets were wider (6 cm) and closer to the home key (10 cm) than difficult targets, which were 3 cm and 30 cm from the home key. The home keys and targets were connected to reaction/movement timers (Lafayette model 63017) which recorded RTs and MTs for each hand and also controlled the 1–5-s variable foreperiod, warning light, and auditory (Sonalert) stimulus to move.

Procedure and Design

The subjects were seated facing the apparatus. For two-hand movements they were instructed to depress the home keys with the index fingers. Then, following a Sonalert stimulus, subjects moved to the targets as fast and accurately as possible, touching them with only their index fingers. Instructions were similar to the single-hand movements, with the subjects depressing the right home key with the right index finger and the left home key with the left index finger. For single-hand movements only the appropriate target was placed on the board. All movements were lateral away from the home keys.

There were five experimental conditions (Figure 1), which varied according to the number of hands required and whether the target was easy ($ID = 1.74$) or difficult ($ID = 4.32$). The two-hand movement conditions were easy-difficult, difficult-difficult, and easy-easy. The single-hand movement conditions were left easy and right difficult.

Time constraints placed on data collection per subject necessitated an imbalanced design. That is, the two-hand easy-difficult condition was not balanced with a two-hand difficult-easy

Figure 1. Schematic representation of movement conditions.

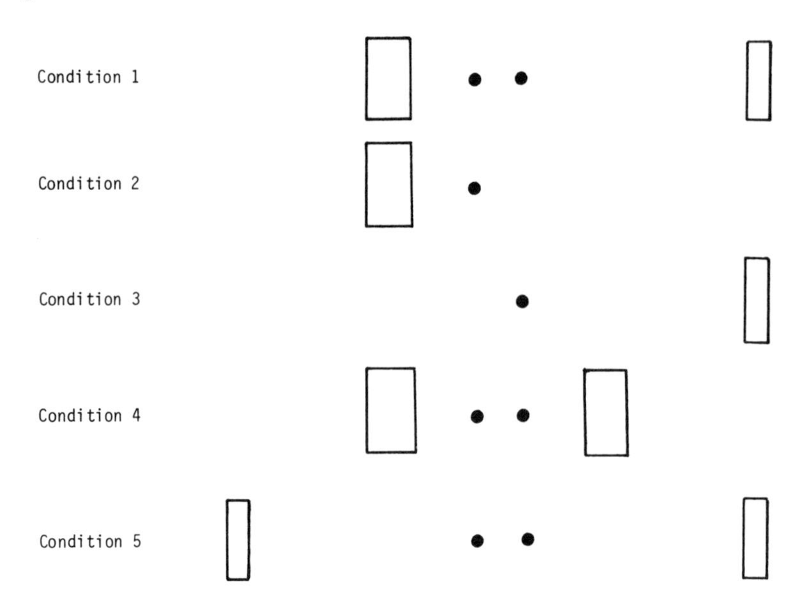

condition and subsequent single-hand (left difficult and right easy) conditions. This prohibited an examination of any systematic asymmetries between hands. However, an examination of the mutual influence between limbs was possible through the comparison of MTs for the hand moving to the easy target in the two-hand easy-difficult condition with MTs to the easy target in the single-hand condition. If there is mutual influence between limbs, MTs to the easy target in the two-hand condition should be significantly elevated over MTs to the easy target in the single-hand condition. Further support of mutual influence was investigated by examining differences between right and left RTs and MTs for two-hand conditions. No differences between hands for the temporal measures would indicate synchronous behavior of limbs.

Each subject performed all five conditions, which were presented in random order. There were 20 trials per condition with a 90-s rest period between each block of trials. Only the last 15 trials were used in data analysis, with the first 5 trials serving as familiarization. More time was taken explaining instructions to the younger children (ages 5, 6, and 8). The necessity to move as fast and accurately as possible was reinforced frequently during the practice trials.

Analysis

The overall error (missing one or both targets) rate for all conditions was 11%. The range was from 7%–9% for subjects over 10 years of age to 8%–13% for subjects 10 years and younger. Error rates for single-hand conditions were less (6%) across groups than for two-hand conditions (15%). Mean RTs and MTs were determined from the 15 test trials in each condition, for each hand (Table 1). The differences between RTs and MTs for right and left hands in two-hand conditions were also computed. RTs and MTs for each hand by condition and differences in temporal measures for two-hand conditions were plotted as a function of age. RTs and MTs, for the right and left hands, were analyzed by means of a 9 (Groups) × 4 (Conditions) analysis of variance (ANOVA) and trend analysis. Differences between hands for two-hand temporal measures were analyzed by means of a 9 (Groups) × 3 (Conditions) ANOVA and trend analysis. Scheffé's post hoc analysis was used to test differences between specific means.

RESULTS

ANOVA and trend analysis for left and right RTs showed a significant main effects for age (left hand, $F[8, 81] = 559.5$; right hand, $F[8, 81] = 380.5$, $p < .001$) and condition (left hand, $F[3, 243] = 860.8$; right hand, $F[3, 243] = 909.9$, $p < .001$) and an Age × Condition interaction (left hand, $F[24, 243] = 43.5$; right hand, $F[24, 243] = 30.0$, $p < .001$). MT analysis showed a significant main effects for age (left hand, $F[8, 81] = 159.0$; right hand, $F[8, 81] = 247.1$, $p < .001$) and condition (left hand, $F[3, 243] = 177.1$; right hand, $F[3, 243] = 352.6$, $p < .001$) and an age × condition interaction (left hand, $F[24, 243] = 3.6$; right hand, $F[24, 243] = 2.4$, $p < .001$).

An overall significant cubic trend (Figure 2) was found for both right- and left-hand RT and MT data ($p < .001$).

Reaction and Movement Times

Reaction Times. A comparison of single- and two-hand data for the left hand at ages 5–10 indicated that Condition 1 RT was not significantly different from the single-hand movement to the easy target (Condition 2, $p > .05$), but was greater than ($p < .05$) Condition 2 for ages 11–14. An examination of right-hand data indicated that RTs for the difficult component of Condition 1 (easy-difficult) were less than those for Condition 3 (right difficult) for ages 5–10 and age 12. Differences were significant ($p < .05$) for ages 5, 8, and 9.

There was a mutual influence between hands concerning the initiation of left and right components of Condition 1 (easy-difficult) when compared with single-hand counterparts. These effects were

Table 1
Mean Reaction Time (RTs) and Movement Times (MTs) in Single-Hand and Two-Hand Conditions (expressed in ms)

Condition		Age Group 5	6	8	9	10	11	12	13	14
1	Left RT	303.5	307.7	245.2	229.8	211.6	228.7	226.3	227.0	198.5
	Left MT	261.8	239.9	225.5	177.7	187.6	169.8	179.6	155.2	142.8
	Right RT	308.5	308.5	236.7	227.9	214.4	234.0	221.8	226.3	194.0
	Right MT	293.0	262.9	248.4	209.8	209.8	182.2	196.6	169.6	161.1
2	Left RT	312.9	299.6	250.4	226.2	200.7	200.4	210.5	203.0	180.2
	Left MT	206.5	184.4	173.0	146.1	163.8	144.8	148.3	130.6	110.7
3	Right RT	324.9	315.0	261.9	249.7	214.7	222.5	227.1	216.1	180.1
	Right MT	284.6	253.8	236.3	209.0	198.0	180.2	190.7	177.2	166.0
4	Left RT	263.6	250.1	236.9	227.8	201.2	195.8	203.0	203.1	168.4
	Left MT	206.8	200.8	188.2	163.0	161.5	149.5	152.0	138.2	108.7
	Right RT	264.5	271.5	232.7	225.0	205.5	200.0	203.4	203.6	160.9
	Right MT	210.3	198.0	202.2	177.1	173.6	151.2	158.8	141.0	117.5
5	Left RT	254.3	262.4	260.5	251.6	205.3	214.1	215.8	215.3	186.9
	Left MT	290.5	277.6	269.1	214.5	217.4	197.3	209.5	192.6	156.8
	Right RT	253.0	265.1	247.5	248.1	203.1	216.4	212.4	217.8	181.1
	Right MT	273.4	246.0	271.8	214.5	207.7	189.4	200.5	186.8	162.1

Note. $N = 90$, 10 subjects per group.

Figure 2. Left- and right-hand reaction and movement times according to age.

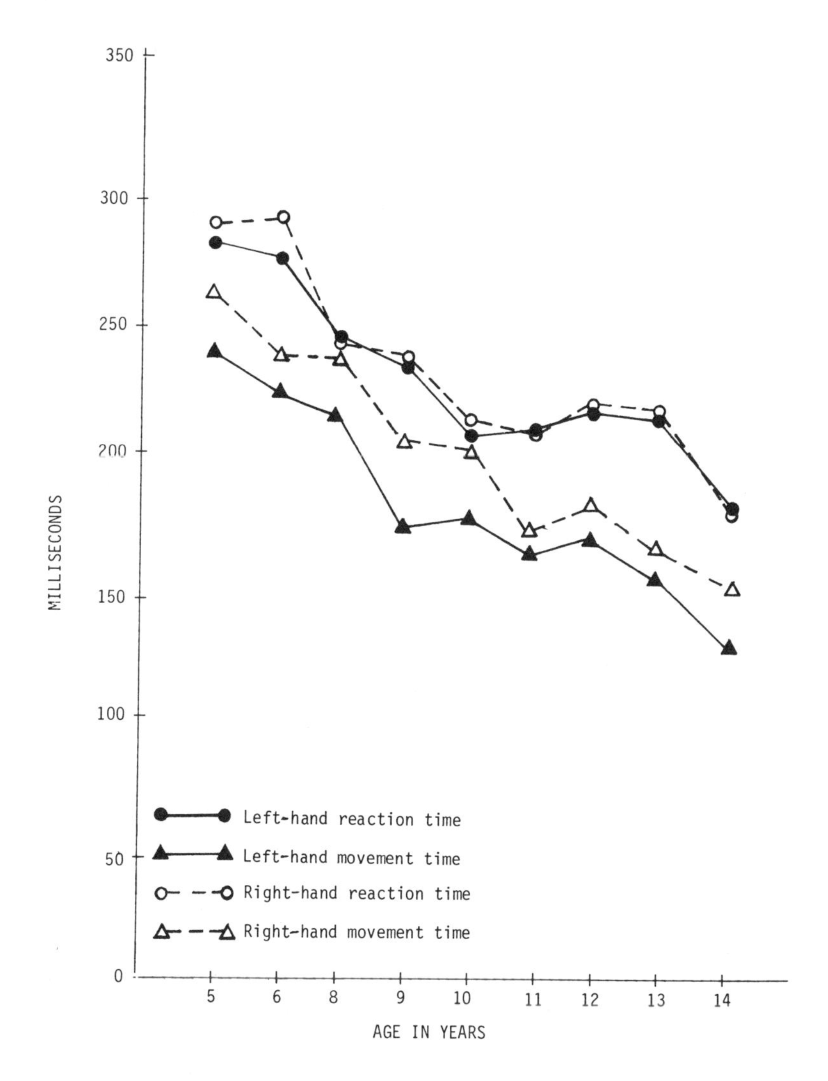

evident at the younger ages (5–10 years), where there seemed to be a facilitating effect of the left easy component on the right difficult component for Condition 1. In this respect the data do not support an interference effect predicted by Marteniuk and MacKenzie's (1980) model of two-hand control, because only the easy target in the easy-difficult condition revealed the deleterious effects of the opposite task. Furthermore, examination of two-hand same movements, in comparison with their single-hand counterparts, substantiates that

Figure 3. Differences in reaction times according to age, for two-hand movement conditions.

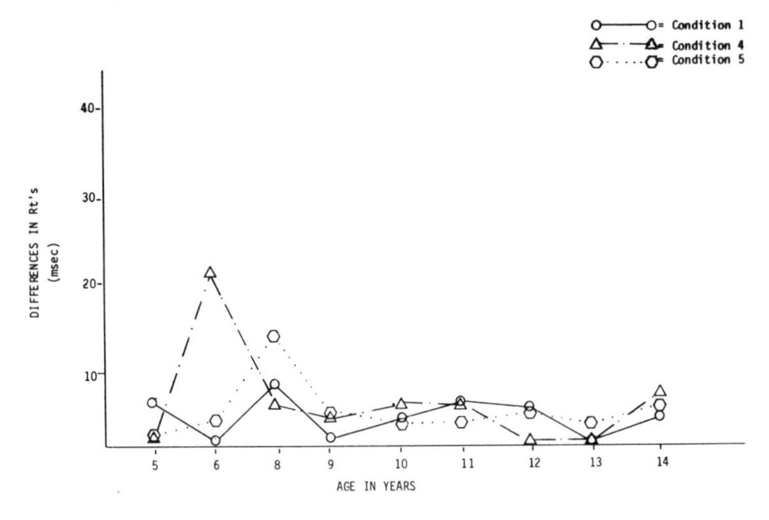

two-hand movements were not more complex in their initiation than single-hand movements across age. In fact, the two-hand same movements had consistently lower RTs for both right and left hands with significant differences occurring for ages 5, 6, and 8 ($p < .001$). It appears that for younger subjects (ages 5 and 6 particularly) the inclusion of a second task of the same difficulty facilitated RTs, relative to single-hand tasks.

Movement Times. Trend analysis for the left and right hands indicated a coherence of patterns across conditions. Post hoc analysis for the right hand showed no significant differences ($p > .001$) between Conditions 1, 3, and 5 across ages, except between Conditions 3 and 5 for age 8. In addition, Condition 4 was significantly less than Conditions 1, 3, and 5 for all ages, as would be predicted by Fitts' law. For the left hand, Condition 1 was significantly ($p < .001$) elevated over its single- and two-hand counterparts. The MTs to the difficult target were similar across conditions, whereas the easy component of Condition 1 was significantly elevated over its single- and two-hand counterparts. For Condition 1, the influence of the difficult component on the hand moving to the easy target indicates that the limbs are constrained to seek isochronous movement.

Concerning the comparison of two-hand same conditions (4 and 5) with their single-hand counterparts (Conditions 2 and 3); there were no significant differences excepting the right component of

Figure 4. Differences in movement times according to age, for two-hand movement conditions.

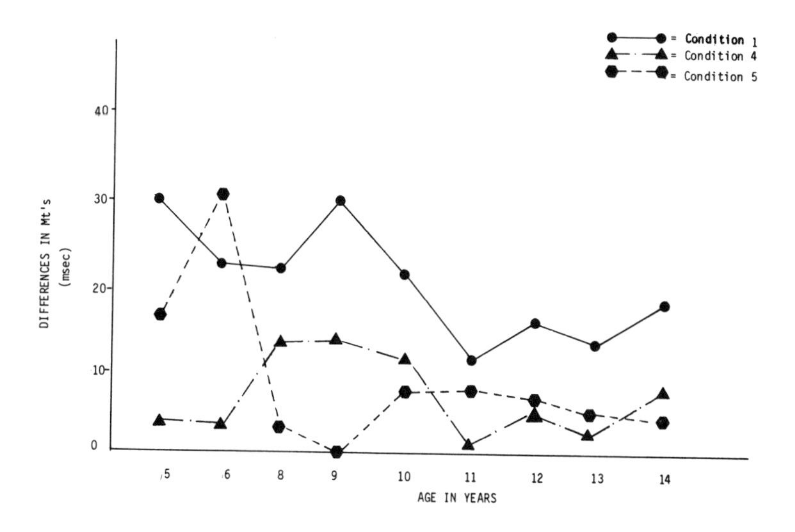

Conditions 5 and Condition 3 at age 8 ($p < .001$). Once again, the inclusion of an additional hand to a target of equal difficulty did not precipitate an interference effect between hands.

Temporal Differences Between Hands for Two-Hand Conditions

Whether there is mutual effect exerted by hands during bimanual movement is demonstrated by a comparison of respective RTs and MTs of disparate two-hand conditions with their respective single-hand counterparts. If there are differences between the left-hand and/or right-hand components of two-hand movements and their single-hand counterparts, then the temporal compatibility between hands may indicate the degree of mutual effect.

Reaction Times. A two-way ANOVA (Groups × Conditions) and trend analysis of differences between right- and left-hand RTs showed a significant main effects for groups—$F(8, 81) = 3.11$, $p < .001$—with no significant trends in data when differences are plotted by age. Differences in RTs as a function of age are represented in Figure 3. Post hoc analysis revealed significant differences for Condition 4 at age 6 (21.4 ms) and Condition 5 at age 8 (13.0 ms). Therefore, with the exception of the two significant differences, two-hand movements were initiated simultaneously across age.

Movement Times. ANOVA (Groups × Conditions) and trend analysis for differences between right- and left-hand MTs showed a significant main effects for groups—$F(8, 81) = 4.61$, $p < .001$—and conditions—$F(2, 243) = 74.89$, $p < .001$—with significant linear trends for Conditions 1 and 4 when differences were plotted by age. Differences plotted by age are represented in Figure 4. Post hoc analysis revealed significant differences ($p < .01$) for Condition 1 at ages 5, 6, 8, and 9, and Condition 5 for age 6. Whereas the two-hand same conditions (4 and 5) showed simultaneity of MTs across age, the left easy-right difficult condition was not simultaneous until age 10.

DISCUSSION

The independent inspection of each hand appears to confirm that developmental factors affect RTs and MTs of single- and two-hand movements similarly. Concerning the pattern of responses, the data indicate an overall increase in the temporal capacities of the motor system with an apparent plateau occurring from ages 10 through 12. When children mature, qualitative changes in temporal orderings accompany age, but these improvements may not be indicative of a change in underlying control processes for interlimb movements. Decreases in RTs and MTs, coupled with increases in age and fundamental skill proficiency, need not indicate an accommodating change in movement control and coordination. Changes in the temporal parameters of movement may not be by-products of action control changes. That is, as individuals mature they run faster, jump higher, and throw further, but the processes controlling and coordinating such interlimb movements may remain invariant.

In this study, the added degrees of freedom resulting from the necessity of controlling two-hands significantly increased MTs to the easy component (Condition 1) over single-hand counterparts. In addition, RTs were not significantly increased by the necessity of two-hand control. Actually, RTs for two-hand same conditions were often significantly less than their single-hand counterparts. These findings do not offer support for a separate prescription to each hand (motor program), nor are they conducive to an interference model between hands (Marteniuk & MacKenzie, 1980). Rather, the findings support the constraint of two-hand movements and their perception as a unit throughout the developmental period from 5 to 14 years. When children face the problem of controlling interlimb movement, they manage the added degrees of freedom by means of a coordinative structure. Similarly to adults, groups of muscles are linked to act cohesively in the performance of two-hand movement tasks.

When differences between hands for two-hand temporal measures were plotted as a function of age, there was a linear relationship of MTs for Conditions 1 and 5. This indicates a maturational effect on the constraint of two-hand movements.

However, the slope of each significant relationship was low (Condition 1 = − .125, Condition 5 = − .184), and Condition 1 was the only condition that showed an increase in the degree of limb constraint for a period greater than 2 consecutive years (3 years; 9-12). In addition, Condition 4, which consisted of two easy components, did not have a significant trend when differences were plotted by age. Previous studies using adult subjects and a similar paradigm (Kelso, Goodman, & Putnam, 1983; Kelso, Southard, & Goodman, 1979) determined that the more difficult component has the greater effect on the mutuality of limbs. It could be that the slopes of Conditions 1 and 5 are the result of a qualitative change in ability to deal with the difficult component and not a change in control processes. It is proposed that the mode of control (coordinative structures) for interlimb movements remains consistent despite structural changes resulting from physical maturation.

REFERENCES

Bernstein, N.A. (1967). *The coordination and regulation of movements.* London: Pergamon Press.

Gelfand, I.M., Gurfinkel, V.S., Tsetlin, M.L., & Shik, M.L. (1971). Some problems in the analysis of movements. In I. M. Gelfand, V. S. Gurfinkel, S.V. Fomin, & M.L. Tsetlin (Eds.), *Models of the structural-functional organization of certain biological systems* (pp. 160-171). Cambridge, MA: MIT Press.

Grillner, S. (1975). Locomotion in vertebrates: Central mechanisms and reflex interaction. *Physiological Reviews, 51,* 247-304.

Hay, L. (1981). The effect of amplitude and accuracy requirements on movement time in children. *Journal of Motor Behavior, 13,* 177-186.

Kelso, J.A.S., Goodman, D., & Putnam, C. (1983). On the space-time structure of human interlimb coordination. *Quarterly Journal of Experimental Psychology, 35A,* 347-375.

Kelso, J.A.S., Southard, D.L., & Goodman, D. (1979). On the nature of human interlimb coordination. *Science, 203,* 1029-1031.

Kerr, R. (1975). Movement control and maturation in elementary-grade children. *Perceptual and Motor Skills, 41,* 151-154.

Kugler, P.N., Kelso, J.A.S., & Turvey, M.T. (1982). On the control and coordination of naturally developing systems. In J.A.S. Kelso & J.E. Clark (Eds.), *The development of movement control and co-ordination* (pp. 5-78). New York: Wiley & Sons.

Marteniuk, R.G., & MacKenzie, C.L. (1980). A preliminary theory of two-hand coordinated control. In G.E. Stelmach & J. Requin (Eds.), *Tutorials in motor behavior* (pp. 185-197). Amsterdam: North Holland.

Salmoni, A.W., & Pascoe, C. (1978). Fitts' reciprocal tapping test: A developmental study. In C. G. Roberts & K. M. Newell (Eds.), *Psychology of motor behavior and sport 1978* (pp. 288-294). Champaign, IL: Human Kinetics.

Shik, M.L., & Orlovskii, G.N. (1976). Neurophysiology of locomotor automation. *Physiological Reviews, 56,* 465-501.

Sugden, D.A. (1980). Movement speed in children. *Journal of Motor Behavior, 12,* 125-132.

Turvey, M.T. (1977). Preliminaries to a theory of action with reference to vision. In R. Shaw & J. Bransford (Eds.), *Perceiving, acting and knowing: Towards an ecological psychology* (pp. 211-265). Hillsdale, NJ: Erlbaum.

Turvey, M.T. Shaw, R., & Mace, W. (1978). Issues in a theory of action: Degrees of freedom, coordinative structures and coalitions. In J. Requin (Ed.), *Attention and performance, VII* (pp. 557-595). Hillsdale, NJ: Erlbaum.

6

Developmental Direction of Action Programs: Repetitive Action to Correction Loops

CLARA ALLISON
Connecticut College

For the purpose of studying the developmental changes in action programs, 3- and 5-year-old children were observed using an easel paint brush in the natural setting of their school. As was hypothesized, the younger children's action programs were characterized by relatively simple repetitive actions, whereas the older children's programs included correction loops. The results are discussed in relation to Gibson's (1979) concept of affordances.

One of the major tasks for the young child is to develop skills to interact with and control the objects in the environment. To a large extent these interactions are accomplished through the manipulation of tools, a special class of objects that allows the child to control and influence the events in the world. Such skilled tool use, in turn, makes an important contribution to the child's social and intellectual development (Vygotsky, 1978), as well as to the more obvious area of motor skill development.

In developing skill in using a tool the child constructs an action program. Such action programs are made up of a serially ordered set of subunits, or subroutines. "A sub-routine is an act, the performance of which is a necessary but not sufficient condition for the execution of some more complex, hierarchically organized sequence of sub-routines of which it is a member" (Elliott & Connolly, 1974, p. 136). Each subroutine relates to a specific aspect of the more complex sequence, the action program. According to Connolly (1975), the constituent components, the subroutines, of an action program are organized into a sequence designed to solve a specific motor problem. Practice modifies and shapes the subroutines.

The study reported here is based on the concept that an action program evolves from the child's perception of the properties of the

---

I am indebted to June Patterson, Professor of Child Development and Director of the Children's School at Connecticut College, for facilitating the data collection and for sharing her insights and expertise. Special thanks are given to the advanced Child Development majors who assisted with the observations.

objects and materials with which he or she is interacting and the actions afforded by them. The child perceives these properties directly as the objects and materials are grasped, moved, and manipulated (Gibson, 1982). In other words, the action program results from the reciprocal relationship between the physical properties of the objects and the child's actions with the objects.

It follows, then, that an action program for a particular tool may change as a result of the child's interactions with the tool and the materials used in a specific task. Connolly's (1980) examination and description of the child's mastery of the use of a spoon during the first 2 years of life gives evidence that, indeed, there is a direction to changes in the action program as the child becomes more skillful. Using a modified flowchart, Connolly outlined the way in which the action program was elaborated as the child became more skilled in using a spoon. He found two initial subroutines: (1) repetitive dipping of the spoon in and out of the dish and (2) repetitive putting the spoon in and taking it out of the mouth. Finally, during the course of the skill's development, the sequence of repetitive action was elaborated by the appearance of correction loops, subroutines in which the main sequence could be interrupted and backtracking could take place if the program was not going according to expectation.

The purpose of the present study was to investigate developmental changes in action programs. The ages of the children and the tool they used were selected because they were different from the Connolly (1980) study and, thus, allowed a comparison with those findings. For this purpose, 3- and 5-year-old children were observed using an easel paint brush in the natural setting of their school. It was hypothesized that the older children's action programs would be more elaborate than those of the younger children. That is, it was expected that the younger children's action programs would be composed of relatively simple repetitive actions, whereas the older children's programs would include correction loops.

METHOD

Subjects

Two groups of children were selected for observation. The younger group consisted of the four youngest children in the youngest school group; they ranged in age from 2 years, 11 months, to 3 years, 6 months, with a mean age of 3 years, 2 months. The older group consisted of the five oldest children in the oldest school group; they ranged in age from 4 years, 6 months to 5 years, 8 months, with a mean age of 5 years, 2 months.

Apparatus

The children painted on large paper (18 in. × 24 in.) which was clipped to a standing easel (28 in. × 30 in.). The center of the easel was at approximately the child's shoulder height as he or she stood in front of it. The paint jars were in a tray attached to the easel; every day there were at least two jars of paint at each easel; and for each jar of paint there was a 1/2-in. brush with a 10-in. handle. There were two easels in each classroom.

Procedure

Each child was observed when he or she chose easel painting from the alternative learning opportunities offered in the normal plan for the school morning. No constraints were imposed on the activity by this investigation. Easel painting was a popular activity and the children chose it freely. As with the other activities planned, the teacher pointed out that painting was one of the alternatives, but no child was required to select it.

The observations were made during a 2-week period in the classroom of the school the children regularly attended. The observers sat at an oblique angle to the easel and approximately 10 ft away from it. Using the event sampling method, the observers recorded the painting actions used by each child. It is important to note that it was *actions* that were recorded rather than the individual movements and hand or arm postures that comprised the actions (Connolly, 1975).

Two independent observers observed each child during two separate occasions while the child was engaged in easel painting. The shortest occasion was 5 min and the longest was 20 min. The agreement between the observers was 94.2% and 92.6% for the younger and older children, respectively. An action program for each individual child was compiled from the two observers' records for both occasions, that is, from four records (two observers on two occasions). The summaries for each group were made from these individual descriptions of actions.

RESULTS

As predicted, the younger group's action programs were characterized by relatively simple repetitive actions whereas the older children demonstrated more elaborate action programs which included correction loops (Figure 1).

In general, the younger children used three sequences: (1) putting the brush in and out of the paint jar, (2) putting the brush in the paint jar and stirring, and (3) putting the brush in the paint jar, removing the brush from the jar, and "painting." All three of these

Figure 1. Action programs for use of an easel paint brush by 3- and 5-year-old children.

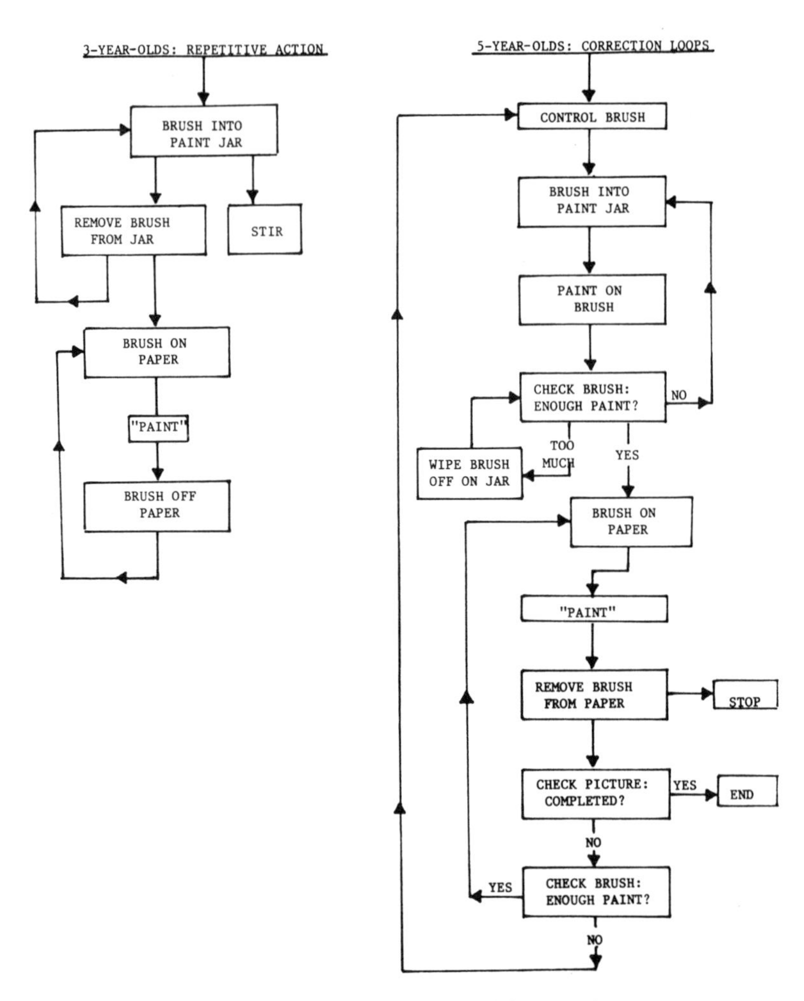

sequences were repetitive actions. For the older children, the sequence included the following checking routines:

1. After removing the brush from the paint jar, the brush was checked for enough paint. If there was not enough paint, the brush was returned to the jar. If there was too much paint, the excess was removed by wiping the brush off on the jar lip. If there was enough paint, the brush was put on the paper and painting was started.
2. After painting for awhile, the brush was removed from the paper and the picture was visually scanned. If the picture was complete,

> the task ended and the child either started a new picture or left the activity. If the picture was not complete, the brush was checked for enough paint. If there was enough paint, the brush was put back on the paper and painting continued; if there was not enough paint, the brush was put in the paint jar and the sequence started again.

These two routines were correction loops which allowed for backtracking in the sequence.

There was minimal overlap between the two groups' action programs. Regardless of the amount of time spent at easel painting, the action sequences were typical of the child's age group. That is, a younger child spending 15 min painting did not demonstrate an action program which was similar to the older child; nor did an older child spending 5 min use an action pattern typical of the younger children.

There were individual differences in both groups. Not all of the younger children used all of the repetitive actions. All of them did put the brush on the paper and painted, but none demonstrated any sequence which could be characterized as a correction loop. The older children rarely were observed using repetitive actions like those of the younger children. All of the older children demonstrated the correction sequence of checking for enough paint on the brush; however, only two children consistently scanned the picture to determine whether or not it was complete. The other children seemed simply to stop the action sequence.

DISCUSSION

The results of this study support the view that the acquisition of motor skills in using tools can be described as action programs. These action programs are made up of serially ordered subroutines and, as a child becomes more skillful in the use of a particular tool, the action program becomes more elaborate. The action programs described here for the use of the easel paint brush are consistent with Connolly's (1980) description of the action programs for mastery of spoon use; there is a correspondence between the progressive elaborations of the action programs for both tools. The beginning program for each skill is characterized by repetitive actions, the goals for which seem to be the action for its own sake, rather than the instrumental goal of painting or eating. The children's increase in skill is defined by action programs which increasingly include subroutines that allow the accomplishment of the instrumental goal in a direct yet more and more flexible fashion. For both skills, then, there is a progression from programs including subroutines of repetitive actions to programs including correction loops among the subroutines that define the skills.

These results lead to the question of how or why an action program becomes elaborated. According to Gibson's (1979) concept of affordances, the interaction with the specific tool and materials allows the child the opportunity to perceive what the tool and materials afford. The action program changes as a result of the child perceiving these affordances. For example, initially, the easel paint brush affords grasping and, together with the paint, relatively simple manipulations such as stirring. Later, the properties of the bristles of the brush and the paint afford making lines on the paper. The brush, paint, and paper afford the activity of painting because of their properties, and the affordances are there to be perceived directly by the child. "Perception is bound to action . . . and most affordances must be extracted in the course of action" (Gibson, 1982, p. 80).

The child's own actions are central to skill development, not because of "connections" between stimuli and responses, but because they allow the perception of affordances. Actions can be viewed as the interrelations between the child and the tool and are as much a property of the tool as a characteristic of the child (Reed, 1982). Skill development comes about because of the reciprocity between perceptions and actions.

REFERENCES

Connolly, K. (1975). Movement, action and skill. In K.S. Holt (Ed.), *Movement and child development* (pp. 102-110). Philadelphia: Lippincott.

Connolly, K. (1980). The development of competence in motor skills. In C.H. Nadeau, W.R. Halliwell, K.M. Newell, & G.C. Robert (Eds.), *Psychology of motor behavior and sport—1979* (pp. 229-252). Champaign, IL: Human Kinetics.

Elliott, J., & Connolly, K. (1974). Hierarchical structure in skill development. In K. Connolly & J. Bruner (Eds.), *The growth of competence* (pp. 135-168). New York: Academic Press.

Gibson, E.J. (1982). The concept of affordances in development: The renascence of functionalism. In W.A. Collins (Ed.), *Minnesota symposium on child psychology: Vol. 15. The concept of development* (pp. 55-81). Hillsdale, NJ: Erlbaum.

Gibson, J.J. (1979). *The ecological approach to visual perception.* Boston: Houghton-Mifflin.

Reed, E.S. (1982). An outline of a theory of action systems. *Journal of Motor Behavior, 14,* 98-134.

Vygotsky, L.S. (1978). Tool and symbol in child development. In M. Cole, V. John-Steiner, S. Scribner, & E. Souberman (Eds.), *Mind in society* (pp. 19-30). Cambridge, MA: Harvard University Press.

7

A Developmental Sequence of the Standing Long Jump

JANE E. CLARK AND SALLY J. PHILLIPS
University of Maryland

A developmental sequence for the arm and leg components of the standing long jump was hypothesized. Using a research strategy suggested by Roberton, Williams, and Langendorfer (1980), we tested a cross-sectional sample of children 3–7 years of age against a probabilistic model of the standing long jump's development. We filmed 110 children and digitized their film records to determine the spatial-temporal characteristics of the arm and leg actions of the jump. Three expert jumpers also were filmed and their performances analyzed. The results showed clear developmental ordering for the arm sequence. Developmental ordering of the leg sequence also conformed to the model with two exceptions.

Those who study motor development have long sought to understand the principles underlying the antecedent-consequent relationships among emerging forms of movement coordination. Before such principles can be derived, however, researchers must first identify the antecedent-consequent relationships for the movement pattern(s) of interest. In this paper we report our work on the validation of one such relationship, the developmental sequence for the propulsive phase of the standing long jump.

Although the standing long jump is considered one of the fundamental movement patterns of humans (Hellebrandt, Rarick, Glassow, & Carns, 1961; McClenaghan & Gallahue, 1978; Wickstrom, 1983), surprisingly little research has attempted to identify its developmental chronology. Indeed, except for the pioneering work of Hellebrandt and her colleagues, there are no empirically based

---

We wish to thank Ricardo Petersen and Hope Ellen Welker for their assistance in data collection and reduction, and the teachers and children of the Campus Center for Early Learning and St. Marks Elementary School for their willingness to give freely of their time and cooperation. Computer time for this research was supported in full through the facilities of the Computer Science Center of the University of Maryland.

Portions of this research were reported at the National Conference of the North American Society for the Psychology of Sport and Physical Activity, College Park, Maryland, May 1982.

studies in the literature that describe the development of the standing long jump. It was, therefore, our purpose to extend on the work of Hellebrandt et al. and delineate those antecedent-consequent relationships in the standing long jump that might prove to constitute a developmental sequence for this movement pattern.

It is well established that the most appropriate procedure for validating a developmental sequence is a longitudinal design in which cohort differences are controlled (Wohlwill, 1973). Although such designs are more desirable, they have well-known limitations which create substantial difficulties for developmental researchers. Roberton (1982; Roberton, Williams, & Langendorfer, 1980) elaborated on the work of Feldman and Toulmin (1976) and Wohlwill (1973) to provide a procedure for prelongitudinal screening of developmental sequences. The procedure described by Roberton et al. (1980) assumes that the developmental sequence revealed in a cross-sectional sample represents the sequence in the population from which it was drawn. At any given age, the frequency of behaviors in the sequence would vary such that with increasing age, the modal behavior would shift upward in the developmental sequence. Thus, less mature behavior would be expected or more probable in the younger groups and more mature or developmentally advanced behaviors would be expected in the older age groups.

To test a hypothesized developmental sequence with this procedure, one must first make an a priori determination of the sequence and a hypothetical longitudinal model depicting the occurrence of the sequence over the age range of interest. Roberton (1982) referred to this hypothetical model as the population or probabilistic model. Data are then collected on a cross-sectional sample and the investigator compares that sample to the hypothesized population or probabilistic model. Results of this comparison either support or refute all or parts of the hypothesized developmental sequence. Clearly, this procedure is superior to the traditional approach, which evaluated developmental sequences on the basis of an investigator's "best guess."

Accordingly, our purpose was to evaluate a developmental sequence for the standing long jump employing the prelongitudinal screening procedure described by Roberton et al. (1980). The sequence we sought was one which would capture the essential element(s) of the coordination pattern used by the child to provide the necessary force to project the body. We therefore focused only on the propulsive phase, namely the movements from the onset of preparation until the child leaves the ground.

METHOD

Subjects

The 110 subjects for this study were randomly selected from five age groups (3, 4, 5, 6, and 7 years) attending a preschool or a private elementary school in College Park, Maryland. Means and standard deviations for age, height, and weight for each age group are presented in Table 1.

Three highly skilled men from the University of Maryland track team served as subjects to confirm the mature skilled jumping pattern. Two of the adult subjects competed in the high jump event, and the third competed in the decathlon. Their mean age, height, and weight are reported in Table 1.

Table 1
Means and Standard Deviations for Age, Height, Weight, and Distance Jumped by Age Group

Age Group	Female *n*	Male *n*	Age (yr)	Height (cm)	Weight (kg)	Distance Jumped (cm)
3-year-olds	10	10				
M			3.5	100.4	15.8	44.7
SD			.31	3.8	2.0	18.5
4-year-olds	10	10				
M			4.5	107.6	17.6	69.0
SD			.28	4.1	2.8	23.0
5-year-olds	15	9				
M			5.4	115.3	21.1	89.9
SD			.26	3.7	3.4	12.2
6-year-olds	11	12				
M			6.4	117.5	23.8	109.0
SD			.24	3.6	2.7	14.7
7-year-olds	11	12				
M			7.4	123.8	27.8	110.3
SD			.24	4.8	4.5	16.9
Adults		3				
M			21.3	192.3	86.0	281.7
SD			1.5	8.0	1.2	10.6

Determination of the Hypothesized Sequences

Prior to data collection, developmental sequences were hypothesized for the arm and leg actions of the propulsive phase of the standing long jump. The arm and leg actions were studied separately so as not to mask or misrepresent the developing patterns of action. Others, in particular Roberton (1978), have argued rather persuasively that a developmental sequence based on a whole body configuration does not provide for the possibility that individual component action systems (such as arm or leg action) may develop at different rates.

The arm and leg sequences developed were based on (1) the previous research of others (Halverson, 1958; Hellebrandt et al., 1961; Roy, 1971; Zimmerman, 1956) and (2) an analysis of the data from a pilot study in which 80 children, ages 2-11, and four adult members of the University of Pittsburgh track team were filmed performing the standing long jump. Filming for the pilot study was done with a super 8mm camera at the University of Pittsburgh Laboratory School.

The hypothesized developmental sequence for the arm movement in the standing long jump included no arm action, shoulder flexion only, incomplete biphasic arm action, and complete biphasic arm action. Four actions were hypothesized for the developmental sequence of the leg movements in the standing long jump: stepping out, knee extension precedes heels up, knee extension and heels up simultaneously, and knee extension follows heels up. An example and description of each hypothesized arm and leg pattern are given in Figures 1-4. Congruent levels (i.e., arm action Level I with leg action Level I) are presented for illustrative purposes. As discussed later, congruence between levels is not required nor often demonstrated.

Figure 1. Level I. Arm action: No arm action; arms remain immobile throughout propulsive phase; may exhibit shoulder girdle retraction ("winging") close to take-off. Leg action: Stepping out; a one-footed take-off.

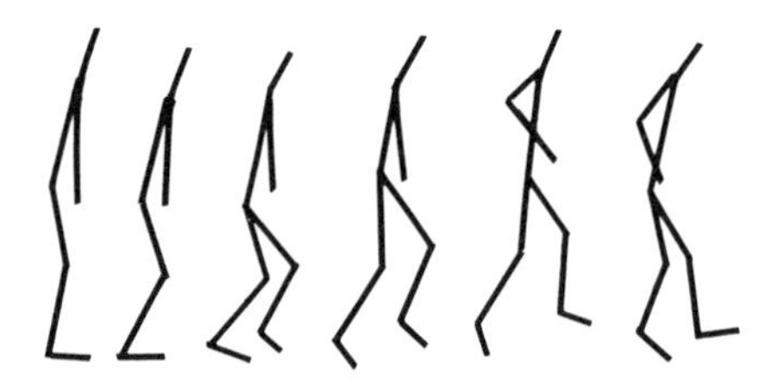

Design

To validate the developmental sequence, we first selected a cross-sectional sample which encompassed the age groups where the movement patterns of the hypothesized sequence were most likely to occur. Based on our pilot work, it was determined that a sample

Figure 2. Level II. Arm action: Shoulder flexion only; arms remain immobile during lower extremity flexion. Shoulder flexion occurs with lower extremity extension; some shoulder abduction may be seen. Leg action: Knee extension precedes heels up.

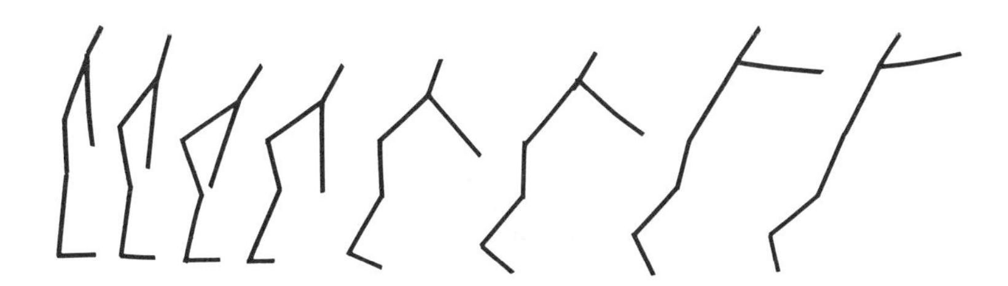

Figure 3. Level III. Arm action: Incomplete biphasic arm action; shoulder hyperextension occurs during lower extremity flexion; shoulder flexion occurs with lower extremity extension; shoulder flexion incomplete (less than 160°) at take-off. Leg action: Knee extension and heels up simultaneously.

Figure 4. Level IV. Arm action: Complete biphasic arm action; same as Level III except that shoulder flexion is complete (greater than 160°) at take-off. Leg action: Knee extension follows heels up.

including children from 3 to 7 years of age would represent the age range needed. Expert adult jumpers were included to confirm the mature arm and leg patterns.

After data reduction, the observed frequencies of each pattern's occurrence were compared to a probabilistic model (see insets of Figures 5 and 6). This model represents a hypothetical set of curves which describe the frequency of occurrence of the action pattern

Figure 5. Observed frequency of occurrence for the four levels of arm action. The inset illustrates the placement of the observed data on the hypothesized sequence's curves.

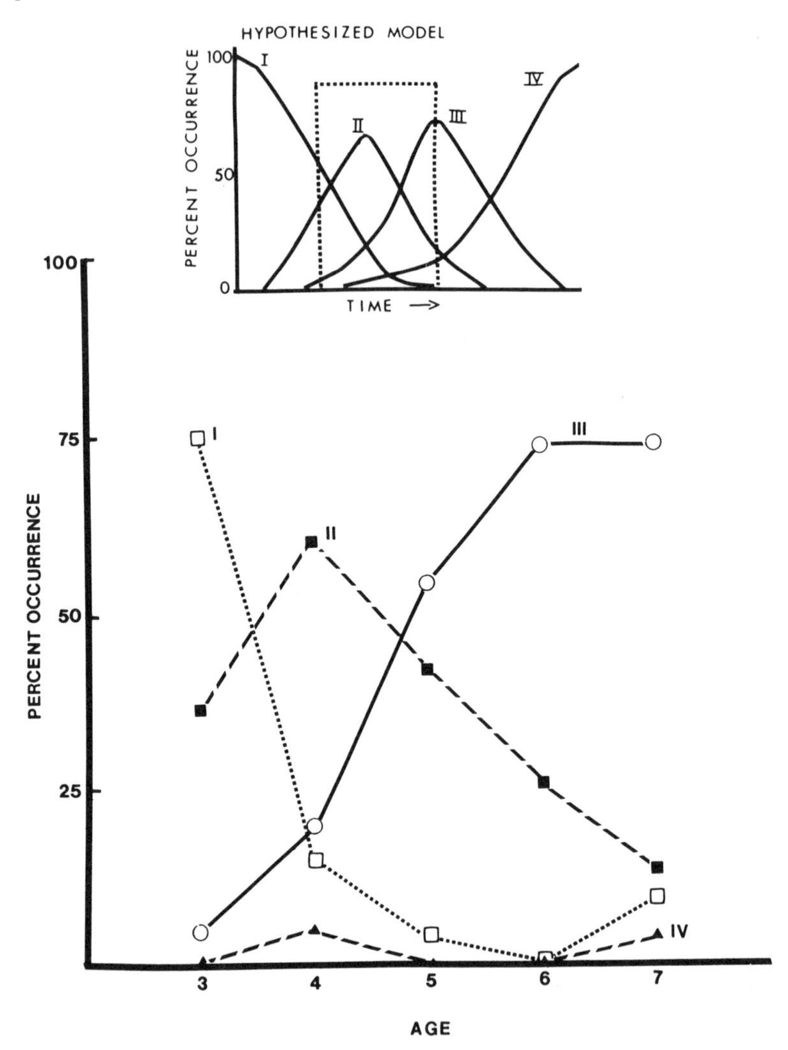

longitudinally. Criteria for testing the "goodness" of the developmental sequence are as follows:

1. *Proper sequence order* (Roberton et al., 1980)—Were the least mature patterns observed in the youngest performers and the most mature patterns observed in the oldest children?
2. *Sign of the function* (Roberton et al., 1980)—Did the curves rise and fall in accordance with the predictions of the probabilistic model?

Figure 6. Observed frequency of occurrence for the four levels of leg action. The inset illustrates the placement of the observed data on the hypothesized sequence's curves.

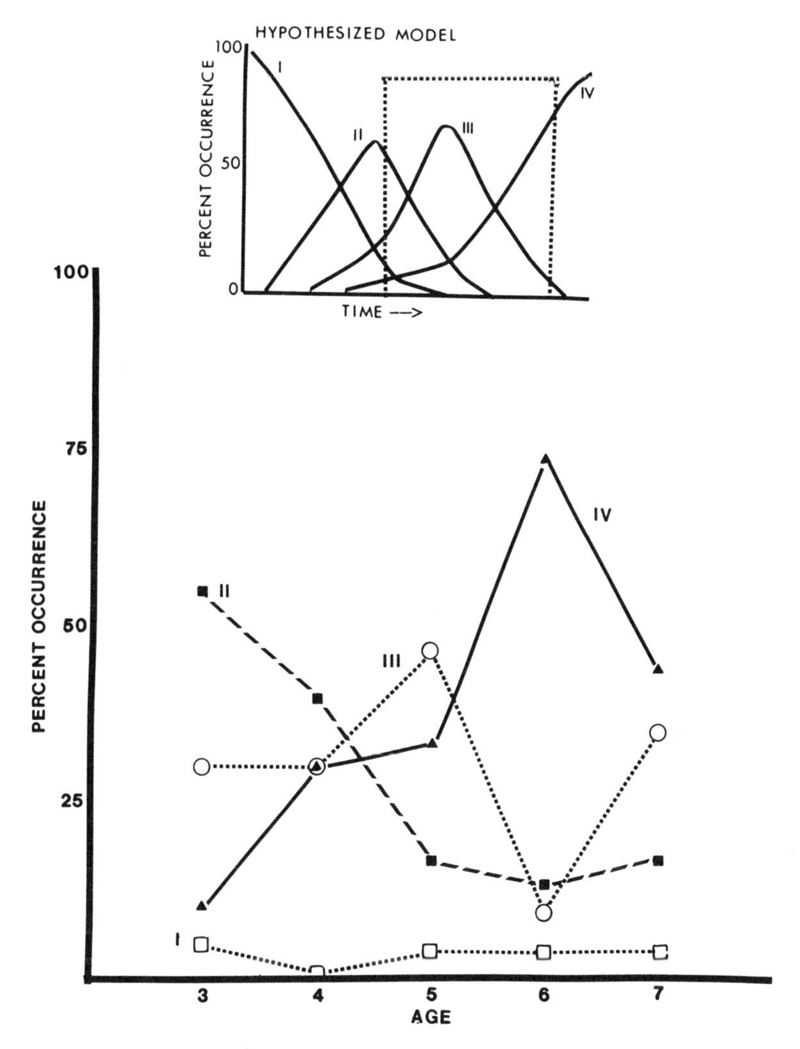

3. *Comprehensiveness and inclusiveness of the categories* (Williams, 1980)—Were the hypothesized categories observed in the sample? Were arm or leg patterns not hypothesized observed in the sample?

Data Collection, Reduction, and Analysis

Each child was filmed from a side view while performing three standing long jumps. Prior to the filmed trials, each child was given instructions on the task to be performed and was permitted two practice trials. Feedback was given if the child did not perform a two-footed standing long jump or did not understand the instructions. All children were given praise after each trial as well as encouragement to jump as far as possible. Height, weight, and age were determined at the time of data collection or shortly thereafter. Filming was done with a 16mm Photosonics camera fitted with a 25mm lens with a constant framing rate of 32 fps and an exposure time of 1/125 s. The lens-to-subject distance was 9.35 and 9.5 m for the elementary school and preschool filming sites, respectively.

The first step of data reduction was the calculation of the distance jumped on each trial from the digitized linear coordinates of the toe at takeoff and the heel at landing. A rear projection system magnified the film image 75×, and coordinates were determined using a Numonics 1224 digitizer. The reliability for the distance-jumped measures was calculated by randomly redigitizing 150 trials. This test-retest procedure resulted in a Pearson product-moment correlation coefficient of .99.

Using the distance measures, a child's farthest jump was determined. Subsequent analyses were conducted on the trial eliciting the farthest jump of each child. This seemed a reasonable criterion for determining the trial for analysis. However, it should be noted that all three trials were visually inspected to determine if the trial selected was representative of the child's performance across all three trials. Only in a few instances was another trial selected. In all cases the trial analyzed represented the child's "best" jump with the modal pattern of action.

Estimated joint centers of the knee, hip, shoulder, and elbow as well as the subject's toe and heel were then digitized throughout the propulsive phase. Segmental and intersegmental angles were calculated and smoothed at 6 Hz using a digital filtering technique. A subject's angular kinematic parameters were then used to determine which of the four categories of arm or leg action was exhibited. The subject's data were tabulated across all ages and categories and compared to the expected probabilistic model for that sequence.

RESULTS AND DISCUSSION

The results (children's data only) for the arm and leg developmental sequences are presented in Figures 5 and 6, respectively. Analysis of the data from the three skilled adults revealed, as expected, that they exhibited arm and leg patterns hypothesized as the developmentally most mature (i.e., Level IV).

As illustrated in Figure 5, the degree to which the observed data for the arm sequence conformed to the probabilistic model of sequential development can be seen by comparing the observed curves with the probabilistic model's curves (see inset). All levels demonstrated not only the proper ordering but also the appropriate sign of the function. Although Level IV did not appear to any extent within the children tested, it should be noted that the three skilled jumpers exhibited this pattern of arm action on all trials. The category system for the arm action was not only comprehensive, with every category represented, but also inclusive, with no instance of a failure to classify a child's arm pattern.

The hypothesized developmental sequence for the leg action also appeared to conform to our hypothesized model, with two exceptions. The first exception was the lack of occurrence of Level I. Based on the work of others, particularly Hellebrandt et al. (1961), the absence of Level I in our study may be due to our failure to include a younger sample (i.e., 2-year-olds). Our own observations would bear this out, but, of course, would require a more formal confirmation. We find no evidence now to suggest that stepping out is not the most primitive and earliest level of leg coordination used by the child in horizontal projection, thus we maintain that it is an appropriate first level in our leg sequence.

The second exception to our hypothesized model of leg action was the function of the curve for Levels III and IV where the curve reversed slope between the 5- and 7-year-old groups. This finding may be a function of our sampling. Roy, Youm, and Roberts (1973) argued, and we tend to agree, that the basic patterns of coordination for the standing long jump are established by about age 7. Indeed, at age 6, 75% of the children we tested had attained the most advanced level of leg coordination. In our 7-year-old group nearly 50% had achieved this level. Why were there fewer 7-year-olds at a higher level of leg action than 6-year-olds? Perhaps our 7-year-olds were less skilled than the 6-year-olds. This suggestion receives support from an analysis of the distance-jumped measures (see Table 1). Each year there were almost linear increases in the average distance jumped by the age groups, except between ages 6 and 7. This type of plateau in product scores between 6 and 7 years has not been reported in the literature; in fact, most studies report linearlike increases until at least puberty (Clark & Al-Shatti, 1980; Espenschade, 1960; Keogh, 1965). Such findings suggest that this particular sample of 7-year-olds may have been less skilled than the 6-year-old sample. Notwithstanding this exception, it should be emphasized that the three skilled jumpers exhibited Level IV leg action on all of their jumps.

The results of our study support the hypothesized developmental sequences of arm and leg action which focus on the essential patterns of coordination necessary for horizontal body projection. We intentionally did not focus on the flight or landing phases of the jump which, of course, influence the actual distance a child may travel. Rather, we sought to describe a sequence that captured the neuromuscular system's "action plan" for creating the necessary force to project the body horizontally. We sought essential actions, not those that seemed a consequent of the action plan. For example, Hellebrandt et al. (1961) characterized the most primitive arm action as a "winging" action. In our pilot study many of the youngest subjects who exhibited no arm action during the early and middle portions of the propulsive phase exhibited winging (i.e., scapular retraction) during the latter portions of the propulsive phase. However, some subjects who had other arm actions (e.g., incomplete biphasic action) began winging very near takeoff—a consequence of their off-balance position. If we had defined "winging" as a category, children who had initiated a more advanced pattern of arm action would have been categorized at a lower developmental level merely because they "reacted" to the forces their bodies were generating. Winging is a *consequence* of threatened balance, not a centrally organized pattern of coordination intended to produce a maximum horizontal body projection. We sought to identify movement sequences that would capture the essential, invariant patterns of coordination.

No doubt there are other developmental sequences which may capture the changes occurring in the standing long jump. In fact, Haubenstricker, Seefeldt, and Branta (1983) presented quite another sequence for the standing long jump. They included actions from all phases of the jump (i.e., propulsive, flight, and landing) and did not use the component approach (i.e., separating arm and leg actions). Analysis of our data suggests several problems which may lead to differences between the studies. Table 2 summarizes our findings on the percentage of agreement for arm and leg categories. Looking at the congruence between developmental levels of the leg and arm action, it is clear that a child may well be developmentally advanced in arm action and delayed in leg action, or vice versa.

Although it is theoretically unimportant if the actual levels (numerically) are equal, it is important that there be consistency as to which component (arms or legs) is developmentally in advance of the other. Examining Table 2, one can see that there are no clear patterns evident in the data. These results raise a number of questions regarding a category system in which both actions are to be included. As an example, at what level is a child categorized if the arm action does not fit the level indicated by the leg action? Investigating such differences between various hypothesized sequences and their significance, however, is the task of future research efforts.

Table 2
Percentage Agreement Between Arm and Leg Levels

		Legs in Advance		Arms in Advance	
Age Group	Agreement	One Level	Two Levels	One Level	Two Levels
3-year-olds $n = 20$	20	45	35	0	0
4-year-olds $n = 20$	25	45	20	10	0
5-year-olds $n = 24$	29	37.5	16.7	16.7	0
6-year-olds $n = 23$	4.3	65.2	13	17.4	0
7-year-olds $n = 23$	26.1	39.1	13	17.4	4.3

In sum, the data support the hypothesized developmental sequence for the arm action of the standing long jump. The data were less clear-cut as to the leg action, perhaps requiring further cross-sectional sampling. Both arm and leg sequences, of course, require future longitudinal validation. For now, however, the sequences appear to capture the developmental order for arm and leg action in the standing long jump.

REFERENCES

Clark, J.E., & Al-Shatti, S. (1980). *Evaluation of the motor development of elementary school children.* Unpublished manuscript.

Espenschade, A. (1960) Motor development. In W.R. Johnson (Ed.), *Science and medicine of exercise and sports* (pp. 419–439). New York: Harper & Row.

Feldman, D.F., & Toulmin, S. (1976). Logic and the theory of mind. In W.J. Arnold (Ed.), *Nebraska Symposium on Motivation—1975* (pp. 409–476). Lincoln: University of Nebraska Press.

Halverson, L.E. (1958). *A comparison of performance of kindergarten children in the take-off phase of the standing broad jump.* Unpublished dissertation, University of Wisconsin.

Haubenstricker, J.L., Seefeldt, V., & Branta, C. (1983, April). *Preliminary validation of a developmental sequence for the standing long jump.* Paper presented at the meeting of the American Alliance for Health, Physical Education, Recreation and Dance, Minneapolis.

Hellebrandt, F.A., Rarick, G.L., Glassow, R., & Carns, M. (1961). Physiological analysis of basic motor skills. I. Growth and development of jumping. *American Journal of Physical Medicine, 40,* 14–25.

Keogh, J.F. (1965). *Motor performance of elementary school children.* Los Angeles: University of California, Department of Physical Education.

McClenaghan, B.A., & Gallahue, D.L. (1978). *Fundamental movement: A developmental and remedial approach.* Philadelphia: W.B. Saunders.

Roberton, M.A. (1978). Stages in motor development. In M.V. Ridenour (Ed.), *Motor development: Issues and applications* (pp. 63–81). Princeton, NJ: Princeton Book.

Roberton, M.A. (1982). Describing "stages" within and across motor tasks. In J.A.S. Kelso & J.E. Clark (Eds.), *The development of movement control and co-ordination* (pp. 293–307). New York: Wiley & Sons.

Roberton, M.A., Williams, K., & Langendorfer, S. (1980). Prelongitudinal screening of motor development sequences. *Research Quarterly for Exercise and Sport, 51,* 724–731.

Roy, B. (1971). *Kinematics and kinetics of the standing long jump in seven, ten, thirteen, and sixteen-year-olds boys.* Unpublished doctoral dissertation, University of Wisconsin.

Roy, B., Youm, Y., & Roberts, E.M. (1973). Kinematics and kinetics of the standing long jump in seven, ten, thirteen and sixteen-year-olds boys. In S. Cerquiglini, A. Venerando, & J. Wartenweiler (Eds.), *Medicine and Sport. Biomechanics III* (pp. 409–416). Basel, Switzerland: Karger.

Wickstrom, R.L. (1983). *Fundamental motor patterns* (3rd ed.). Philadelphia: Lea & Febiger.

Williams, K. (1980). Developmental characteristics of a forward roll. *Research Quarterly for Exercise and Sport, 51,* 703–713.

Wohlwill, J. (1973). *The study of behavioral development.* New York: Academic Press.

Zimmerman, H.M. (1956). Characteristic likenesses and differences between skilled and non-skilled performance of standing broad jump. *Research Quarterly, 27,* 352–362.

8

The Role of Balancing Ability in Performance of Fundamental Motor Skills in 3-, 4-, and 5-Year-Old Children

BEVERLY D. ULRICH
Michigan State University

DALE A. ULRICH
Southern Illinois University

We investigated (1) the relationship between balancing ability, age, and gender and (2) the role of balancing in performance of fundamental gross motor tasks when the effect of age is partialled out. A battery of 15 items was administered to 72 preschoolers aged 3, 4, and 5 years. Tasks included all eight items from the balance subtest of the Bruininks-Oseretsky Test of Motor Proficiency (Bruininks, 1978). Qualitative performance of six fundamental motor skills was assessed using stage descriptions developed by Seefeldt and Haubenstricker (Graham, 1980; Haubenstricker, Branta, & Seefeldt, 1983; Haubenstricker, Seefeldt, & Branta, 1983; Seefeldt & Haubenstricker, 1974–1976). Multiple regression analysis of the data suggested that age had a significant linear relationship to balancing ability, $F(1, 70) = 68.32$, $p < .001$. *A gender difference was not found. Multivariate analysis of covariance with age as the covariate suggested that balancing ability was significantly related to level of performance of fundamental gross motor tasks,* $F(7, 63) = 3.87$, $p < .0015$.

Balance activities are commonly included in programs designed to facilitate the acquisition of gross motor tasks in young children. The rationale for this may be the claims frequently made by experts in the field (e.g., DeOreo & Keogh, 1980; Espenschade & Eckert, 1980) that balance is important to the development of the fundamental motor skills. Such a relationship is inherently appealing, but empirical evidence is lacking. In fact, only a few researchers have investigated balancing ability alone for 3-, 4-, and 5-year-olds. DeOreo (1971) examined the performance of this age group on four dynamic and two static balance tasks and found a significant linear increase in skill level by age across tasks. Girls performed more proficiently than boys on the static balance items only. Morris, Williams, Atwater, and Wilmore (1982) included one static balance item in the battery of performance tasks presented to children 3–6 years of age. Mean balance scores demonstrated an increase with age, but the year-to-year differences were not significant except between ages 5 and 6. A gender difference was not found until that age also, when the performance of 6-year-old girls differed from all other age by gender groups.

The importance of this relationship for preschoolers is underscored by the fact that fundamental motor skills such as throwing, kicking, and jumping emerge during these years. As proficiency increases, such skills form the foundation for more complex skill acquisition. If practitioners are to be expected to base instructional content on empirical evidence, then this relationship must be investigated.

The purpose of our study was to examine the relationship between balancing ability and the ability to perform fundamental motor skills in preschool-age children. The following specific research questions were asked:

1. Is there a linear relationship between age and the ability to balance in preschoolers?
2. Is there a gender difference in balancing ability at this age?
3. Are age and gender significant factors in the ability to perform each of six fundamental motor skills?
4. When age is controlled, what is the relationship between the ability to balance and the ability to perform fundamental motor skills?

METHOD

A battery of 15 items measuring balancing ability and developmental level of gross motor skills was administered individually to 33 girls and 39 boys aged 3–5. Mean age, in months, and standard deviations (in parentheses) for the 3-, 4-, and 5-year age groups were 43.08 (2.95), 52.54 (3.73), and 64.88 (3.59), respectively. Sample size for each age group was 24.

Balance tasks within the test battery included all eight items from the balance subtest of the Bruininks-Oseretsky Test of Motor Proficiency (Bruininks, 1978). The only modification of instructions to subjects from those in the test manual was that children were not required to maintain hands placed on hips. Examples of items included are standing on preferred foot on floor, standing on preferred foot on balance beam with eyes closed, walking forward heel-to-toe on balance beam. Raw scores on the balance items were transformed according to procedures specified in the test manual, to obtain a total point score for all items. This total point score was used for subsequent analyses.

The additional seven items in the test battery assessed qualitative performance of specific fundamental gross motor skills. Specific skills assessed included throwing, kicking, striking, jumping, hopping on preferred and nonpreferred foot, and skipping. Subjects were given five trials on each task. All trials were visually judged by one experimenter as the subject performed each skill. The subject's modal score (which corresponded to developmental level) for each skill was used in subsequent analyses. For example, a child demonstrating a throwing pattern best described by Stage 1 criteria received a score of 1 for that skill.

Stage descriptions used were those developed by Seefeldt and Haubenstricker (Graham, 1980; Seefeldt & Haubenstricker, 1974–1976; Seefeldt, Reuschlein, & Vogel, 1972); they are summarized in Table 1. Stage descriptions were derived from inspection of films of approximately 150 children performing fundamental motor tasks. The primary criterion for determination of stages was the commonality of segmental relationships among performers. An additional concern was that they be readily discernible by visual inspection and not so time consuming as to lack practical utility (Seefeldt et al., 1972).

Table 1
Stages of Development for Six Fundamental Motor Skills

Skill	Stage	Description
Throw	1	Arm motion posterior-anterior in direction, feet stationary, force comes from hip flexion, shoulder protraction and elbow extention.
	2	Arm motion is in transverse plane, body rotates as a unit about the vertical axis.
	3	Arm begins throw with ball placed above shoulder followed by diagonal throw, ipsilateral step is taken, little or no spine and hip rotation.
	4	Arm preparatory movement is vertical and posterior, contralateral step is taken, little trunk rotation.
	5	Throwing hand winds up by moving in downward and backward arc, contralateral step is taken, sequential rotation and derotation of shoulder, spine, and hip.
Kick	1	Body stationary, force applied more of a "push" from hip and knee flexion extension anterior to the midfrontal plane.
	2	Body stationary, leg winds up behind coronal plane, opposition of upper and lower extremities.
	3	Deliberate approach utilized, trunk vertical at impact.

	4	Rapid approach with leaping step just prior to contact followed by a hop after on support leg, trunk inclined backward at contact.
Strike	1	Feet stationary, chopping action of arms in the posterior to anterior direction.
	2	Feet remain stationary or one foot may step as body moves toward the approaching ball, body rotates as a unit with bat moving transversely.
	3	Ipsilateral step is taken, bat movement in oblique-vertical plane.
	4	Contralateral step is taken, rotation and derotation of shoulder, spine, and hip, elbow extension and supination-pronation of hands occur as lever is extended fully to meet the ball.
Horizontal Jump	1	Arms move backward during flight, jump mostly vertical.
	2	Preparatory arm movement is anterior to posterior with motion during flight being sideward in "winging" fashion, center of gravity over feet at landing.
	3	Arms move backward then forward in preparatory phase with knees and hips flexing fully, at takeoff arms extend forward but not above head, center of gravity close to feet at landing.
	4	At takeoff arms extend vigorously forward and above head with hips and knees fully extended, body is at a 45° angle or less, prior to landing feet are thrust forward and arms down, at contact knees flex and arms thrust forward.
Hop	1	Thigh of nonsupport leg held anterior to body and parallel to surface, hands held near shoulder height, little distance achieved.
	2	Thigh of nonsupport leg held lower in front in a diagonal position with foot near buttocks, trunk inclines forward, bilateral arm force.
	3	Thigh of nonsupport leg is vertical with knee flexion of 90° or less, trunk inclined well forward, arms aid in force production moving up and down bilaterally.
	4	Nonsupport leg swings pendularly to aid in force production, arms carried close to body.
Skip	1	Deliberate step-hop pattern, action appears segmented.
	2	Rhythmical movement, exaggerated vertical component.
	3	Smooth rhythmical pattern with foot of nonsupport leg remaining near surface, arms swing easily at sides.

Note. From *Developmental Sequences of Fundamental Motor Skills* by V. Seefeldt and J. Haubenstricker, 1974-1976. Unpublished manuscripts.

Preliminary examination of several of the developmental sequences (Haubenstricker, Branta, & Seefeldt, 1983; Haubenstricker, Seefeldt, & Branta, 1983) suggests adherence to the prelongitudinal paradigm for validation of developmental levels as proposed by Roberton, Williams, and Langendorfer (1980). Test-retest analysis of the data for 10 subjects generated an average Pearson product-moment correlation of .77 across all motor items.

ANALYSES AND RESULTS

The general linear model for multiple regression procedures was used to examine the relationships between balancing ability and age and balancing ability and gender. Results suggested a significant linear relationship between age and ability to balance $F(1, 70) = 68.32$, $p < .05$. No gender difference was found for balancing ability.

A two-way multivariate analysis of variance design was used to test the significance of age (at 3, 4, and 5 years) and gender to the qualitative performance of the six fundamental motor skills. Wilk's criterion yielded an approximate F ratio of 4.10 (14, 120), $p < .05$ for the main effect age and 10.43 (7, 60), $p < .05$ for gender. The interaction effect was not significant. Subsequent univariate analysis indicated that age had a significant relationship to level of performance for each of the fundamental motor skills tested, $p < .05$.

Post hoc comparison of the age effect using the Student Newman-Keuls test revealed significant differences among all three ages for throwing, kicking, striking, and hopping on the preferred foot (Table 2). For skipping and hopping on the nonpreferred foot, 3-year-olds differed from the 4- and 5-year-olds, who did not differ from each other. Subjects aged 3 and 4 did not differ from each other on jumping ability but were significantly less advanced than 5-year-olds.

Table 2
Post Hoc Analyses of Age Differences by Skill Using Student Newman-Keuls Test

Motor Skill		Subset	
Throw	3	4	5
Kick	3	4	5
Hop (preferred foot)	3	4	5
Hop (nonpreferred foot)	3	4, 5	
Skip	3	4, 5	
Jump	3, 4		5
Strike	3	4	5

Table 3
Means and Standard Deviations of Fundamental Motor Skill Stages and Balance Score by Age and by Gender

	Age (yr)						Gender			
	3		4		5		Girls		Boys	
Motor Skill	*X*	*SD*	*X*	*SD*	*X*	*SD*	*X*	*SD*	*X*	*SD*
Throw	2.46	.98	3.00	.93	3.71	.75	2.48	.80	3.54	.94
Kick	2.08	.77	2.58	.78	3.08	.58	2.24	.79	2.87	.73
Hop (preferred foot)	1.13	.80	1.71	.55	2.17	.70	1.76	.66	1.59	.91
Hop (nonpreferred foot)	.88	.68	1.58	.58	1.79	.59	1.52	.62	1.33	.81
Skip	.67	.76	1.25	.85	1.63	.65	1.42	.66	.97	.93
Strike	1.92	.83	2.54	.78	3.08	.83	2.12	.70	2.85	.99
Jump	1.54	.59	1.88	.61	2.29	.69	1.82	.64	1.97	.74
Balance	12.54	4.29	17.04	4.50	21.88	5.04	16.91	4.40	17.36	7.07

A significant gender difference was found for four of the movement skills, $p < .05$ (Table 3). Mean values indicated that boys were more advanced than girls in throwing, kicking, and striking, whereas girls were more proficient in skipping than boys. Boys and girls did not differ significantly on stage for hopping and jumping.

Multivariate analysis of covariance (MANCOVA) was used to examine the main effect of balance on fundamental motor skills, using age as the covariate. General linear model for multiple regression procedures (Helwig & Council, 1979) were used in the MANCOVA to allow for the use of age and balance as continuous independent variables. Results indicated that when age was partialled out, balance was significantly related to the level of performance of fundamental motor skills (Table 4). Wilk's criterion yielded an approximate F ratio of 3.87 (7, 63), $p < .05$. The interaction effect for age by balance was not significant. Univariate analysis of the fundamental motor skills indicated that the stages of hopping on the preferred and nonpreferred foot, jumping, and striking were significantly related to balancing ability ($p < .05$). The relationships between balance and the skipping, throwing, and kicking stages were not significant. The final two columns of Table 4 report the coefficients of determination for each of the full models, and the amount of variance accounted for by balance after age was partialled out. For skills in which age and balance together accounted for a

Table 4
Relationship of Balance to Motor Skills With Age as the Covariate

Motor Skill		Univariate F^a	p	R^2	r^2
Hop (preferred foot)	Age	31.21	.0001	.3526	.2929
	Balance	6.37	.0139		.0597
Hop (nonpreferred foot)	Age	38.31	.0001	.4652	.2969
	Balance	21.72	.0001		.1683
Jump	Age	22.76	.0001	.3017	.2303
	Balance	7.06	.0098		.0714
Strike	Age	30.48	.0001	.3419	.2901
	Balance	5.37	.0235		.0512
Skip	Age	15.20	.0002	.2015	.1758
	Balance	2.22	.1407		.0251
Throw	Age	23.73	.0001	.2710	.2507
	Balance	1.92	.1703		.0203
Kick	Age	27.02	.0001	.2903	.2779
	Balance	1.21	.2758		.0124

[a]df = 1, 69 throughout
Note. Wilk's lambda (balance) = .699; approximate $F = 3.87$ (7, 63 df), $p < .001$

significant amount of variance, the coefficients of determination ranged from .302 (jumping) to .465 (hopping on the nonpreferred foot). When the variance accounted for by balance alone was computed, only .051 to .168 of the total variance was accounted for.

Several researchers have suggested that balancing ability consists of both static and dynamic components (Drowatsky & Zuccato, 1967; Peterson, Reuschlein, & Seefeldt, 1974). Krus, Bruininks, and Robertson (1981) provide evidence for the representativeness of a composite score for balance, but separate subtotal point scores for static and dynamic items were also calculated for each subject. The general linear model procedures were again used to analyze the relationship between each fundamental motor skill and separate static and dynamic balance scores. As was demonstrated with the analysis using the total balance score, developmental level for skipping, throwing, and kicking was not significantly related to either static or dynamic balance scores. Of those skills found significantly related to the total balance score, this analysis further identified them as related more to static, dynamic, or both balance components. Static balance scores were significantly related ($p < .05$) to hopping stage (on the preferred foot) $F(1, 69) = 7.11$ and striking $F(1, 69) = 7.42$. Dynamic balance scores were significant ($p < .05$) for jumping, $F(1, 69) = 9.73$. Both static and dynamic balance scores accounted for a significant ($p < .05$) amount of the variance for hopping on the nonpreferred foot, with $F(1, 69) = 13.90$ for static and $F(1, 69) = 15.30$ for dynamic balance.

DISCUSSION

The results of our study suggest that for preschoolers balance plays a statistically significant role in the performance of several fundamental motor skills (i.e., hopping, jumping, and striking). Inspection of the proportion of total variance accounted for indicates that its practical significance may be low. Other variables such as strength-power or experience may account for a larger proportion of the variance in skill level. In a qualitative assessment such as this, strength may be a requirement for minimal performance, but because *how* a child moves is of greater concern than *how far*, experience or exposure may well be more relevant. Of those skills not significantly related to balance, each displayed a gender difference. At this age only minimal physical differences are evident, so cultural or experiential differences may be the important determinants.

Balance has frequently been noted for its importance to performance of basic motor skills (Espenschade & Eckert, 1980; Wickstrom, 1977). In view of the fact that the results of this study showed a statistically significant but low relationship between balance and the fundamental motor skills tested, two approaches to understanding the nature of balancing ability may be suggested. One approach is that balancing ability is task specific and must be measured differently for different tasks or sports. Conversely, our current tests may be too specific, measuring components of balance such as static and dynamic, which in true motor performance situations cannot be separated.

One might argue that the Bruininks' Sub-test for Balance was able to assess at least a portion of the body control or balancing ability necessary for skillful performance of hopping, jumping, and striking, although it was unable to measure the type of control necessary for skipping, throwing, and kicking. These skills may well be performed more efficiently by young children who can "balance" well as many suggest (DeOreo & Keogh, 1980; Williams, 1983), but the movement control required for these skills differs too widely from the test items to be represented by them. Skipping and kicking may be classified as dynamic skills, but the relationship of developmental level of performance to a composite score of only the dynamic balance items still was nonsignificant. The balancing ability necessary to perform well may change from task to task and therefore must be measured according to specific task requirements, with task-specific items.

The second approach to understanding the nature of balancing ability suggests that the Bruininks' Sub-test for Balance, like many others, is too specific. Balance tests are commonly categorized as measuring two separate components of balance, static and dynamic (Baumgartner & Jackson, 1975; Johnson & Nelson, 1979; Kirkendall, Gruber, & Johnson, 1980). However, research comparing several tests purported to measure these components may suggest their failure to actually reflect two distinct elements. Drowatsky and Zuccato (1967) examined the intercorrelations among six commonly used static and dynamic balance test items, finding only one significant (and very low) correlation. Hempel and Fleishman (1955) included six static and dynamic balance items in a large factor analysis study. Several loaded on nonbalance factors or cross-loaded on two distinct factors. Additionally, some nonbalance items loaded on the factors designated as static and dynamic balance. It may be that a score obtained by a subject on a static or dynamic test item reflects only the ability to perform that discrete task, not the ability to control gross body movement or balance in a more sport-related situation. Seldom in sport can dynamic (or moving) and static (nonmoving) elements be separated. To relate the ability to balance to level of performance of gross motor skills, we may need an assessment instrument that *combines* such elements and thus resembles more closely the control of movement required for skilled motor performance.

In sum, the present data suggest a linear relationship between age and ability to balance. No significant difference was found between boys and girls in balancing ability. Qualitative performance of six fundamental motor skills improved significantly between the ages of 3, 4, and 5, with boys performing more proficiently than girls in throwing, kicking, and striking and girls demonstrating a more advanced level of skipping ability than boys. We did not demonstrate a significant relationship between gender and hopping or jumping performance.

The data further suggest statistical significance for the role of balance in performance of fundamental motor skills when the variance due to age is partialled out. Specifically, level of ability for jumping, striking, and hopping on the preferred and nonpreferred foot were skills significantly related to balancing ability. No such relationship was demonstrated for skipping, throwing, and kicking. For those skills in which balance was found to have a statistically significant relationship, the small proportion of variance accounted for may raise doubts about its practical significance.

REFERENCES

Baumgartner, T., & Jackson, A. (1975). *Measurement for evaluation in physical education.* Boston: Houghton-Mifflin.

Bruininks, R. (1978). *Bruininks-Oseretsky Test of Motor Proficiency.* Circle Pines, MN: American Guidance Service.

DeOreo, K. (1971). Dynamic and static balance in children. *Dissertation Abstracts International, 32,* 769A. (University Microfilms No. 71-72, 106).

DeOreo, K., & Keogh, J. (1980). Performance of fundamental motor tasks. In C. Corbin (Ed.), *A textbook of motor development* (2nd ed., pp. 76–91). Dubuque, IA: Brown.

Drowatsky, J., & Zuccato, F. (1967). Inter-relationships between selected measures of static and dynamic balance. *Research Quarterly, 38,* 509–510.

Espenschade, A.S., & Eckert, H.M. (1980). *Motor development* (2nd ed.). Columbus, OH: Merrill.

Graham, G. (1980). *Children moving: A reflective approach to teaching physical education.* Palo Alto, CA: Mayfield.

Haubenstricker, J., Branta, C., & Seefeldt, V. (1983, May). *Preliminary validation of developmental sequences for throwing and catching.* Paper presented at the annual meeting of the North American Society for the Psychology of Sport and Physical Activity, East Lansing, MI.

Haubenstricker, J., Seefeldt, V., & Branta, C. (1983, April). *Preliminary validation of a developmental sequence for the standing long jump.*

Paper presented at the annual meeting of the American Alliance for Health, Physical Education, Recreation and Dance, Minneapolis.

Helwig, J., & Council, K. (Eds.). (1979). *SAS user's guide.* Cary, NC: SAS Institute.

Hempel, W.E., Jr., & Fleishman, E.A. (1955). A factor analysis of physical proficiency and manipulative skill. *Journal of Applied Psychology, 39,* 12-16.

Johnson, B., & Nelson, J. (1979). *Practical measurements for evaluation in physical education* (3rd ed.). Minneapolis: Burgess.

Krus, P., Bruininks, R., & Robertson, G. (1981). Structure of motor abilities in children. *Perceptual and Motor Skills, 52,* 119-129.

Kirkendall, D., Gruber, J., & Johnson, R. (1980). *Measurement and evaluation for physical educators.* Dubuque, IA: Brown.

Morris, A., Williams, J., Atwater, A., & Wilmore, J. (1982). Age and sex differences in motor performance of 3 through 6 year old children. *Research Quarterly for Exercise and Sport, 53,* 214-221.

Peterson, K., Reuschlein, P., & Seefeldt, V. (1974). *Factor analyses of motor performance for kindergarten, first and second grade children. A tentative solution.* Paper presented at the annual meeting of the American Alliance for Health, Physical Education, Recreation and Dance, Anaheim, CA.

Roberton, M.A., Williams, K., & Langendorfer, S. (1980). Pre-longitudinal screening of motor development sequences. *Research Quarterly for Exercise and Sport, 51,* 724-731.

Seefeldt, V., & Haubenstricker, J. (1974-1976). *Developmental sequences of fundamental motor skills.* Unpublished manuscripts, Michigan State University, Department of Health and Physical Education, East Lansing.

Seefeldt, V., Reuschlein, P., & Vogel, P. (1972, March). *Sequencing motor skills within the physical education curriculum.* Paper presented at the annual meeting of the American Association for Health, Physical Education and Recreation, Houston.

Wickstrom, R. (1977). *Fundamental motor patterns.* Philadelphia: Lea & Febiger.

Williams, H. (1983). *Perceptual and motor development.* Englewood Cliffs, NJ: Prentice-Hall.

9

Play Patterns of Primary School Children

JULIE F. CRUM
Los Angeles Unified School District, Los Angeles, California

HELEN M. ECKERT
University of California, Berkeley

In two primary grade schools, seventy-two 6- and 8-year-old boys and girls were videotaped during recess and noon-hour free play periods for two 5-min sessions. The tapes were analyzed at 15-s intervals for activity organization, activity orientation, size and sex of play group, and motor skill competency. The only sex difference that occurred at 6 years was in activity orientation. At 8 years there were significant sex differences in activity organization, activity orientation, and size of play group, with boys having the higher mean values in all instances. There were no significant sex differences in motor skill competency at either age level. Significant age differences occurred for boys in all measures in a developmental manner, whereas increases in size of play group were the only significant age effects for girls. At both ages, same sex children were the preferred playmates.

In an extensive review of sex differences by Maccoby and Jacklin (1974), the cited research dealing with play patterns of children indicated that play groups are largely sex segregated; sex preference exists for various activities; male-preferred activities tend to become more complex than female-preferred activities; and the size of play groups increases more with increasing age for boys than it does for girls. Preschool and third- to sixth-grade children were the subjects for the majority of the studies investigating gross motor play patterns. Research on the primary school-aged child's play patterns and use of gross motor activities is minimal, so the progressive nature of these trends is not fully established. For example, Laosa and Brophy's (1972) observations of the size of play groups for kindergarten children indicate that boys play more frequently in groups containing more than two and girls play in pairs. At the fifth-grade level, boys play in groups larger than four whereas girls play in groups smaller than four (Lever, 1976, 1978).

Investigators of children's play patterns have used a variety of data collection and measurement techniques and explored different aspects, so cross-study interpretations present difficulties. Sutton-Smith and Rosenberg (1960) and Walker (1964) used game checklists to determine the sex-preferred game choices for boys and girls in the third to sixth grades. Games and pastimes were considered to be either masculine or feminine if they significantly discriminated between the two sexes' choices. Boys' choices tended to narrow to a small number of organized sports with increasing grade level, whereas girls' choices changed from feminine to more masculine play activities with increased grade level. Lever (1976, 1978), who associated the size of play group and the complexity of activity with the socialization process for the sexes, used a variety of methods to collect her data: direct observations of children during recess and physical education classes, interviewing children about their play activity, written questionnaires, and studying the children's diaries in which they recorded each day's play. In her analysis of play activities, Lever (1978) did not include playing alone, for which there was no sex difference and which accounted for about 20% of all play. She concluded that boys' play more frequently involved specialization of roles, interdependence of players, explicit group goals, larger group membership, and numerous rules. On the other hand, girls' play usually occurred in smaller groups, had fewer rules, involved turn-taking activities where competition was indirect, and favored individual achievement over group goals. More defined and standardized methods of measurement may provide more precise information on the role of size of play group and complexity of activity with respect to the socialization process. Observations of children's play activities at an age level when many children initially encounter a school environment may also prove of value.

The developmental sequences for the acquisition of gross motor skills, required for effective participation in gross motor activities, are well documented. With the exception of the overhand throw for distance, there are no sex differences in either the pattern or rate of acquisition of gross motor skills (Espenschade & Eckert, 1980; Wickstrom, 1977). In general, the acquisition of patterning of gross motor skills is accomplished during the first 6 years, and the basic skills are refined and modified thereafter to accommodate to various activity and game requirements. Mean performance scores for basic motor skills indicate that boys tend to perform better in tests involving distance which use application of strength, such as throwing, kicking, jumping, and running, whereas girls are faster and more precise in jumping and hopping (Espenschade & Eckert, 1980; Keogh, 1965). Lever (1976) suggests a higher ceiling of skill for boys' games and a lower motor skill level for girls to account for the shorter duration of girls' games in comparison with those of boys at the fifth-grade level.

Lockhart (1973) believes that children gain motor control, or skill, when they are sufficiently motivated to practice until control of a specific skill is gained. Although many primary school children are taught basic motor skills in physical education classes, the fact remains that to gain sufficient expertise they must practice these skills in activities and games played in free play sessions such as recess, the noon hour, or after school. If children view certain play activities as exclusively "masculine" or "feminine" because only one sex plays them, then their skillful performance may be limited to certain types of activities which they perceive as sex appropriate, or from which they gain same-sex peer reinforcement. An examination of this aspect of skill development may be appropriate at an age level in which there is a transition not only in developmental aspects of skill acquisition but also in the social environment in which skill is acquired.

It was the purpose of our study to examine the free-choice play patterns of primary school children to determine if there are age and sex differences in the selection of activities, the size of play group, the organizational complexity of selected activities, and the gross motor skill competency of the children. In keeping with the previously reported research, specific hypotheses predicted age differences in each of the variables. Sex differences were predicted for all variables except gross motor skill competency of the children.

METHOD

Subjects

To minimize confounding variables, two elementary schools in the suburban Los Angeles area were chosen on the basis of racial, socioeconomic, equipment, and free play period similarities as the locus for this study, and data interpretations are limited accordingly. The white, middle-class schools had morning recesses of 13 and 15 min and noon-hour play periods, excluding lunch time, of 25 min. Although one school had approximately twice the population size of the other (224 vs. 105 6- and 8-year-olds), the size of the playgrounds and the number of pieces of equipment were roughly proportional on a per student basis. Both schools had separate, supervised playgrounds for each of the two age groups in this study. In any natural environment there are always some limitations to free play choice based upon the availability of fixed apparatus (e.g., jungle gyms) or small pieces of equipment (e.g., balls, bats, ropes) and no attempt was made to change playground procedures at either school.

The subjects were seventy-two 6- and 8-year-old children. The 36 children from each school comprised equal numbers of boys and girls at each of the two age levels ($n = 18$ in each age by sex cell) who were randomly selected from a parental consenting pool. At the time of the first videotaping session in November and December, the mean age of the 6-year-olds at both schools was 6 years, 6 months; the mean age of the 8-year-olds at one school was 8 years, 7 months and 8 years, 5 months, at the other. The second videotaping session took place in the following January and February, and because of the mild weather there were no constraints on playground activity choices.

Procedure

A pilot study of 16 children from the larger school was conducted to determine the number and duration of videotaping sessions and the length of recording intervals. In addition, the pilot study was used to determine the reliability of the motor competency rating scale developed by the principal investigator. A professor of physical education at San Francisco State University and the principal investigator, who had 8 years of experience in teaching physical education, viewed the tapes independently and rated each child on developmental motor competency for those gross motor skills undertaken by the child. Using Van De Warder's normal scores (Marascuilo & McSweeney, 1977), the two sets of ratings were found to correlate at .96, giving satisfactory evidence that the rating technique was reliable and the principal investigator was competent in the analysis of this aspect of the study. The children who participated in the pilot study were excluded from the main study selection pool.

The pilot study indicated that two 5-min continuous recording sessions with 15-s recording intervals would provide a representative taping of play behavior and adequately reflect the changes in activity. All subjects at both schools were taped for one 5-min session before the second taping was made. The taping sessions were adjusted so that each subject was recorded during a morning recess and during a noon-hour free play period.

An experienced operator videotaped all observations using a 1/4-in. Akaii Porta-Pac videotape camera with zoom lens. The taping began when the subject arrived on the playground and became engaged in some sort of activity. The audio track was used to record the name of the subject, identify the child, and periodically record the number and sex of children playing with the subject. Most of the observations were made from a minimum of 10–20 ft.

Several arrangements were made to ensure that the presence of the camera, operator, and principal investigator would not interfere with the children's normal play. Teachers in all classrooms explained to the children that the tapes would be looked at only by the investigator to determine how children played. Most importantly, it was stressed that the tapes were not going to be used for a television show. In addition, prior to the actual recording sessions, several taping sessions were undertaken at each school with each age group to accustom the children to the data collection procedures. Any time a child asked a question about the camera, the response was that the investigator was writing a paper for the university about children's play. Many subjects, especially those involved in games, were never aware that they were being observed. However, subjects who were sitting and talking with friends, or just walking around, sometimes became aware that the camera was focused on them. If they continued with their activity, the session was recorded. On only two occasions, 6-year-olds began either to hide from or to "show off" for the camera. These two observations were discarded because they did not reflect representative play behavior, and both subjects were videotaped at a later date when they were unaware of the camera.

Following each taping session all observations were transferred from the 1/4-in. tape to 3/4-in. videotape cassettes, which provided a check that the subject had been properly recorded and allowed for viewing of the projection on a large monitor. The videotape recordings were analyzed on the basis of activity organization, activity orientation, size of play group, and motor skill competency. The sex of the subject's play group was also recorded.

Measures

Activity Organization. Activity organization categories were devised taking into account the complexity of motor skills used in games and activities. The two criteria defining the organization categories were (1) the environment in which the skill was performed, that is, "open" or "closed," and (2) the number of motor skills required for a game or activity. Gentile (1972) defines a closed skill as one that takes place in a stable, unchanging environment in which performance can be carried out successfully with minimum reference to the environment; in an open skill the constantly changing environment requires that the motor activity be regulated and appropriately modified to conform to the external situation. The second criterion emphasizes the fact that some activities, such as jumping rope, require one skill (jumping), whereas other activities, such as playing kickball, use various motor skills (kicking, catching, throwing, and running).

Developmental considerations were also given to the following organizational categories:

Nonmotor Activities (2 points)—In any free play period there are always some children who are not involved in gross motor activity. The nonmotor category includes such activities as playing imaginative games, talking with friends, watching others play, or digging in the sand.

Low-Organization Activities (4 points)—Activities that require one or two motor skills and are performed in a closed environment are placed in this category. They include swinging, climbing on the jungle gym, running, hopscotch stunts on the bars, unstructured chase games, and jump rope.

Medium-Organization Activities (6 points)—Included in this category are activities that require more than two skills in a closed environment or that use one or two skills in an open environment. The rationale for combining these types of activities in the same category is based upon the theory that closed skills develop into open skills along a continuum, and this classification appears to be an intermediate phase. Examples of activities using more than two skills in a closed environment are performing many stunts on the bars, jump rope games that involve a variety of jumping skills or tempos, and shooting baskets. Activities such as tag, dodgeball, tetherball, foursquare, handball, and kick and catch are play examples using one or two motor skills in an open environment.

High-Organization Activities (8 points)—Defined as using more than two motor skills in an open environment, this category includes such activities as volleyball, kickball, basketball, baseball, and soccer.

To obtain a score, the subject's activity choice was assigned the value of the activity category and multiplied by the number of 15-s intervals the child spent in that category. When a subject changed activities during a 15-s interval, the activity in which the child spent the major portion of the 15 s was considered the choice for that interval. The mean score was obtained by dividing these summed scores by the total number of 15-s intervals (20) for each session. In addition, a combined mean was obtained for both sessions.

Activity Orientation. Three activity orientation categories were used to determine the designated sex typing of the activities engaged in by 6- and 8-year-olds. Based upon previous research of sex preference in activity selection (Lever, 1978; Sutton-Smith & Rosenberg, 1960; Sutton-Smith, Rosenberg, & Morgan, 1963; Walker, 1964) and prior observations by the principal investigator, play choices of the children were classified as being masculine, feminine, or neutral preferred. In instances where previous research had indicated a sex preference for a specific activity, that classification was accepted for the rating of activity orientation. Activities such as rings, bars, and handball, which had not been previously listed, were categorized by the principal investigator on the basis of their similarity to previously categorized activities and on the basis of personal experience.

Maccoby and Jacklin (1974) raise the question of degree of sex typing in that "sex constancy" was found not to be well developed in children aged 4–6, and the children undergo age-related changes associated with sex typing. To indicate changes in degree, it is necessary to assign graduations in numerical values. Our assignment of numerical values to sex-preferred activities is based upon statistical considerations and not upon any bias as to the relative value of masculine- or feminine-preferred activities. Lever (1978) indicated that masculine-preferred activities include a larger-sized play group and are more complex in organization than are feminine-preferred activities. Therefore, to avoid negative value comparisons, we assigned feminine-preferred activities lower numerical values than masculine-preferred activities to indicate the degree of activity orientation. The categories are as follows:

Feminine Activities (2 points)—These activities include talking to friends, swings, chase games or tag, apparatus play on bars or rings, and turn-taking games such as jump rope, hopscotch, Follow the Leader, and Mother May I?

Neutral Activities (4 points)—Both sexes generally participate in activities such as standing or sitting, using the slide, foursquare, running or walking, tetherball, and bouncing or dribbling a ball.

Masculine Activities (6 points)—Included in this category are such activities as sand play, jungle gym, catch, handball, running races, and team sports such as football, kickball, basketball, and soccer.

The scoring for this measure was similar to that for activity organization in that the activity orientation value was multiplied by the number of 15-s intervals of participation in that activity and then divided by the total number of intervals per session to obtain the mean score for each subject.

Motor Skill Competency. As they participated in the various chosen activities, the children in the study performed 26 different gross motor skills. Categories based upon immature, minimal, and mature skill form were developed for each of these motor skills, using Wickstrom's intratask phases for development (1977) and other sources for skills such as ball bouncing, climbing, hopping, and stunts on bars (Espenschade & Eckert, 1980; Halverson & Roberton,

1977; Schmid & Drury, 1973). For example, in Wickstrom's classification model, the mature pattern of the overarm throw is defined as initiating the action with the trunk, transferring weight to the opposite leg from the throwing arm, and leading with the elbow as the release movement begins to follow through with an extended throwing arm. The child with immature form lacks some of these skill components, and the child with minimal form displays the mature pattern but lacks timing, accuracy, or smoothness in the performance. The mature categorization is achieved when the child displays the mature form in conjunction with all spatial and temporal aspects of the skill so that the child exhibits a high degree of motor control in the performance.

The rating scale used to assess the relative maturity of each subject's motor skill pattern was as follows:

Low Ability (2 points)—The child exhibits a developmentally immature motor pattern which lacks one or more of the essential features of the mature pattern.

Average Ability (4 points)—The child's performance has all the essential features of the mature skill pattern but lacks the timing, accuracy, or smoothness that is displayed in the mature form of the skill.

High Ability (6 points)—The child has mastered control of the skill to combine the mature pattern with optimal timing, accuracy, and smoothness appropriate to the skill.

In the course of this study, each subject did not undertake all of the motor skills which were used as the basis for rating motor skill competency. In addition, the complexity of the motor skill pattern was not the determinant for rating motor ability; rather, each gross motor skill was rated independently for maturity level. For example, a child who exhibited mature control of jungle gym climbing was accorded the same motor skill rating as a child who had skillfully mastered the more complex overarm throw. Each child was rated only on the gross motor skills undertaken during their free play period, and an average motor ability score was derived by summing the rating for each motor skill undertaken and dividing the sum by the number of skills undertaken.

Size and Sex of Play Group. The size of play group score was obtained by recording the number of children in the subject's play group every 15 s. Any additions to or subtractions from the play group during an interval were made only when more than half of the 15 s had elapsed following change. A mean score for size of play group was obtained by multiplying the number of children in a subject's play group by the number of 15-s intervals and then dividing by the total number of intervals (20) per session.

The sex of play group categorizations included playing alone, only with boys, only with girls, or in a mixed group. Subjects had to spend at least 50% of their time in one category during a session to be considered in one of these categories.

To derive additional data on whether boys or girls at 6 and 8 years of age participated in activities that required different types of motor skills, activities were grouped as follows: whole-body skills (involving hopping, jumping, skipping, galloping, running); apparatus skills (involving sliding, climbing, pumping, swinging from bar to bar, stunts on a bar); and skills with balls (involving throwing, kicking, catching, striking, dribbling, bouncing). Data were gathered on the amount of time subjects spent in each type of activity for both sessions.

Data Analysis

The data were analyzed by two-way analysis of variance (ANOVA) with nested-design using planned comparisons with age and sex as the independent variables and each of the following as the dependent variable: activity organization, activity orientation, size of play group, and motor skill competency. The planned comparisons tested the specific hypotheses relevant to age and to sex differences for each of the four dependent variables using Dunn's multiple comparison procedure with an alpha of .05 (Kirk, 1968). The nested, planned comparison design did not yield age comparisons within each sex, so these analyses were made using *t* tests at the .05 level of significance. In addition, correlation matrices for age, sex, and each age by sex group were used to determine the significant relationships between the four dependent variables. Data were analyzed for the first, second, and combined sessions, but the results for the separate sessions were similar to those for the combined sessions so only the results for the combined sessions are reported here.

RESULTS

The a priori nature of planned comparisons precludes statistical constraints concerning significant differences of main effects. However, significant main effects differences were found for the ANOVAs for each of the dependent variables; namely, for sex, $F(1, 68) = 24.45$, $p < .01$, and for age, $F(1, 68) = 21.79$, $p < .01$, in the activity organization variable; for sex, $F(1, 68) = 107.47$, $p < .01$, and for age, $F(1, 68) = 4.34$, $p < .05$, in the activity organization variable; in group size, $F(3, 68) = 16.11$, $p < .01$; and for age, $F(1, 68) = 8.05$, $p < .01$, but not for sex in motor competency.

Analysis of data using planned contrasts yielded the significant age and sex differences indicated in Table 1. There is little sex difference in the degree of physical activity organization at age 6, but at age 8 boys chose activities which were significantly more complex than those chosen by girls of the same age.

Table 1
Means and Standard Deviations for Various Measures

	6 Years		8 Years	
Variable	*M*	*SD*	*M*	*SD*
Activity organization				
Boys	3.64	1.11	6.28[a,b]	1.85
Girls	3.57	0.53	3.56	0.89
Activity orientation				
Boys	4.41[a]	1.09	5.53[a,b]	0.88
Girls	2.89	0.82	2.65	0.77
Size of play group				
Boys	2.91	1.34	7.81[a,b]	4.69
Girls	2.44	1.26	3.35[b]	1.47
Skill competency				
Boys	4.26	1.40	5.47[b]	0.60
Girls	4.52	1.47	5.03	1.04

[a] Significant difference between the sexes for one age grouping.
[b] Significant difference between age grouping for one sex.

The shift to more complex organizational structure in the activities selected by boys from 6 to 8 years was marked by a pronounced increase in the amount of time spent by 8-year-old boys in open environment team games which require more than two motor skills. On the basis of the categorizations listed in Table 2, there was a marked increase in the amount of participation time, from 19% at age 6 to 85% at age 8, for boys in team-type activities using balls. This increased participation time in team games for boys with increased age resulted in a decreased participation time in all of the other activity categories.

The significant increase in mean organizational scores for boys from ages 6 to 8 reflects a developmental trend in activity organization that did not occur for girls from age 6 to 8, where there was no change in level of activity complexity (see Table 1). Although the organizational level of activities selected by girls remained consistent with age, there was a shift in percentage of participation time in various activities, with older girls spending less time on playground apparatus (61% reduced to 21%) and more time (0% increased to 17%) on games with balls (see Table 2).

Table 2
Percentage of Time Spent in Sex-Typed Activities Categorized by Type of Motor Skill Required, by Age and Sex

Type of Motor Skills Required and Sex-Typed Activities	6 Years		8 Years	
	Boys	Girls	Boys	Girls
Playground apparatus skills: rings (fem.),[a] bars (fem.),[a] swings (fem.), jungle gym (masc.)	18	61	0	21
Whole-body skills: chase and tag games (fem.), Follow the Leader (fem.), jump rope (fem.), hopscotch (fem.)	26	22	4	24
Skills with balls: kickball (masc.), basketball (masc.), Kick and Catch (masc.), handball (neut.),[a] foursquare (neut.)	19	0	85	17
Activities requiring no motor skills: talking to friends (fem.), digging in the sand (masc.)	30	17	11	34
Other	7	0	0	4

[a]Predicted by principal investigator prior to data collection.

Team sports have generally been classified as masculine in terms of gender preference, so it is not surprising that the activity orientation scores also reflect a significantly higher value for 8-year-old boys than for 6-year-olds (see Table 1). Moreover, the significant sex difference in activity orientation at age 8 is undoubtedly also attributable to the much higher percentage of time spent by boys in team games at that age. The significant sex difference in activity orientation at age 6 may be accounted for by a greater percentage of participation by girls in feminine-categorized apparatus activities and lack of participation in team-type activities. The percentage distribution in activity participation categories for the 8-year-old girls closely approximates that of 6-year-old boys, but the activities selected within these broad categories were sex typed as feminine, whereas the higher activity orientation scores for the 6-year-old boys indicate a higher selection of masculine and neutral activities. The lack of trend toward masculine-preferred activities from 6 to 8 years for girls does not support the findings of Sutton-Smith et al. (1963), who reported more masculine choices for older girls.

The increased choice of team games by 8-year-old boys is also reflected in the significantly increased mean size of the play group in comparison with boys at age 6 and girls at both age levels (see Table 1). The much higher standard deviation for the boys at 8 years of age reflects a range in average individual group size from 1.3 to 13.1, with 11 of those boys playing in group sizes larger than 8. The average individual group sizes for the remaining subjects were very similar, with that of 6-year-old boys being 1.1-6.6 and those for girls being 1.1-6.2 and 1-6.2 at 6 and 8 years, respectively. Although there was no significant difference in the size of play groups between the sexes at 6 years of age, girls also improved significantly in play group size from 6 to 8 years of age. The much smaller increase with age for girls may be attributed to the 21% participation time in more solitary apparatus activities and the increased participation time in medium organization games and in nonmotor activities such as talking with friends (see Table 2).

An examination of the descriptive data of the sex of the subjects' play groups indicated that more than 75% of the 6-year-old boys and girls and the 8-year-old girls played exclusively with playmates of the same sex as themselves. Fifty percent of 8-year-old boys played only with other boys; the other 50% spent at least one session in a mixed group. Most of the mixed group play was in kickball games with 17-20 players; each of these groups was made up mostly of boys with one or two girls. None of the girls who were subjects in this study participated in the observed kickball games, and, although the boys participating in these games were classified as playing in a mixed group, the players were predominantly boys.

In view of the higher level of activity organization and the greater percentage of participation in team activities for boys, it might be anticipated that the motor skill competency of boys would be greater than that of girls. However, such is not the case for the mean scores of motor skill competency as measured in this study. The fact that mean motor skill competency scores increased with increasing age for both sexes indicates that the measures did account for developmental improvements in motor skill with increasing age, even if these were only significant for the boys (see Table 1). In assessing these results, it should be kept in mind that the selection of activities was different for the sexes, yet both boys and girls chose activities in which they had a similar degree of competency of performance.

An overall rating of motor performance with respect to type of activity (i.e., activity organization level multiplied by motor skill competency level) would result in a much higher level of complexity competence in motor activities for 8-year-old boys and fairly similar levels for 6-year-old boys and 8-year-old girls. Girls did exhibit a change in the percentage of participation in various activities from ages 6 to 8 and they were able to achieve a level of motor skill competency in the selected activities similar to that of boys, so the difference in an overall rating of motor performance for the sexes at age 8 appears to be a factor more of the selection of the type of activity rather than basic motor competency differences between the sexes.

The interrelationships between activity organization, size of play group, and activity orientation for boys tend to support the relationships suggested between these variables by the data in Tables 1 and 2. The common variance of 62% between activity organization and size of play group (r = .79), which shows the very strong relationship that exists between the complexity of an activity and the size of the play group for combined age boys' data, is exemplified by participation in team games. A high value in the activity orientation variable reflects masculine-preferred activities, so it is not surprising that the relationship between this measure and activity organization is .58 (r^2 = .32) for all the boys in this study. In short, as the complexity of an activity increased for boys, it involved a larger-sized play group and there was a likelihood that the activity would be masculine preferred.

The interrelationships for the combined age girls' data are low in comparison with those of boys and range from −.36 (r^2 = .13) between activity orientation and size of play group to .34 (r^2 = .12) between motor competency and size of play group. The low positive relationship between motor competency and size of play group indicates a very slight trend for the more highly skilled girls to participate in larger-sized groups. However, the low negative relationships between activity orientation and size of play group and between the latter variable and activity organization (r = − .33; r^2 = .11) reflect tendencies toward a decrease in complexity of activities with increased group size and the likelihood that participation in feminine-preferred activities would increase with greater group size. (Lower values in the activity orientation measure indicate the feminine end of the scale.) The low and somewhat ambiguous interrelationships for girls may in part be explained by the fact that the most complex activities selected were handball, foursquare, the rings, and performing more than two stunts on a single iron bar—all of which required small groups or individual performance. However, girls did play in large groups in nonmotor and low-organization activities that were feminine preferred, such as talking with friends, Follow the Leader, and chase games.

DISCUSSION

In general, the 6- and 8-year-olds in this study were similar in their preference for same-sex playmates as are younger and older children described in previous studies (Lever, 1978; Serbin, Tonick & Sternglanz, 1977). However, previously reported differences in play group size for kindergarten boys and girls (Laosa & Brophy, 1972) were not found in our study for 6-year-olds where there was no significant difference in the size of play group. On the other hand, the significant sex difference in play group size for 8-year-olds supports previously reported larger size of play groups for boys in the fifth grade (Lever, 1976, 1978), although the numbers reported differ somewhat.

The use of rating scales for activity organization, activity orientation, and motor skill competency measures allows for a different statistical treatment and analysis of these variables in comparison with previously reported analyses. The significant sex difference at both age levels for the activity orientation measure indicates that this rating scale adequately distinguishes between masculine- and feminine-preferred activities. This aspect of the measure and the significantly greater masculinization of the mean score with increasing age for boys support the previous results with respect to sex preference in game choices reported by Sutton-Smith and Rosenberg (1960) and Lever (1978). However, the lack of significant age difference in activity orientation for girls in this study does not support the observation of Sutton-Smith and Rosenberg that girls' choices changed from feminine to more masculine play activities. Rather, the slightly lower mean, and hence more feminine rating, for the older girls seems to support Lever's analysis of the characteristics of girls' play. These results indicate that the masculine-feminine socialization process generates significant differences in sex-preferred play choices before children enter primary school and that these choices become more firmly fixed during the early school years.

Activities can be rated not only on the degree of sex preference in choice situations but also on the degree of quantity of basic skill usage and the complexity of skill organization. The significant age difference in activity orientation means for boys reflects the change in degree of organization complexity, from the relatively broad choice of activities at varying levels of organization at age 6 to the concentration on the much more highly organized team games at age 8. These results support the observations of Sutton-Smith and Rosenberg (1960) and Walker (1964) that boys' choices tended to narrow to a small number of organized sports. Again, as with the activity orientation rating, the activity organization means do not support the trend toward more complexity (hence masculinity) for the girls. Rather, the results of our study support Lever's (1978) observations that girls' play had fewer rules and involved turn-taking activities when competition was indirect.

In view of the significant sex difference in sex-preferred activities (activity orientation means) at age 6, the lack of sex difference in activity organization means is of decided interest in terms of physical performance development. It appears that the socialization factors that cause differences in masculine and feminine choices cannot override the inherent developmental sequences that apply to the acquisition of basic skills for both girls and boys. However, once the basic skills have been acquired, around 6 years of age, the subsequent refinement of these skills is undertaken in an environment of significantly greater complexity by boys at 8 years of age than it is for girls of the same age. Whether this is a factor of the change from a preoperational representation mode to a concrete operations mode (Piaget, 1962), or is a factor only of the socialization process, is a matter of some interest. The highly consistent activity organization means for girls at both ages in the face of changing percentage of participation patterns suggests that the girls' play patterns are not developmentally static but are highly influenced by the socialization process.

To some extent the lack of sex differences in motor skill competency reinforces the paramount role of socialization in the selection of free play activities. In those activities selected by the girls, they exhibited motor skill competency which was equal to that of the boys. For both sexes there was an increase in motor skill competency with increased age as may be expected on a developmental basis, although only the increase for the boys was significant. It may be argued that the motor skill competency of the 8-year-old girls was equal to that of the 8-year-old boys because they chose activities that were not so demanding in terms of activity organization, or conversely, that these girls would not have displayed the same motor skill competency with similar experience at the higher levels of activity organization as that of 8-year-old boys. Certainly this developmental question cannot be resolved until the sociological parameters are equalized for the sexes.

REFERENCES

Espenschade, A.S., & Eckert, H.M. (1980). *Motor development* (2nd ed.). Columbus, OH: Merrill.

Gentile, A.M. (1972). A working model of skill acquisition with application to teaching. *Quest, 17,* 3-23.

Halverson, L.E., & Roberton, M.A. (1977). *Physical edcuation for children: A focus on the teaching process.* Philadelphia: Lea & Febiger.

Keogh, J. (1965). *Motor performance of elementary school children.* University of California, Los Angeles, Department of Physical Education.

Kirk, R.E. (1968). *Experimental design: Procedures for the behavioral sciences.* Belmont, CA: Brooks/Cole.

Laosa, L. M., & Brophy, J. E. (1972). Effects of sex and birth order on sex role development and intelligence among kindergarten children. *Developmental Psychology, 6,* 409-415.

Lever, J. (1976). Sex differences in the games children play. *Social Problems, 23,* 478-487.

Lever, J. (1978). Sex differences in the complexity of children's play and games. *American Sociological Review, 43,* 471-483.

Lockhart, A. (1973). The motor learning of children. In C. B. Corbin (Ed.), *A textbook of motor development* (pp. 151-162). Dubuque, IA: Brown.

Maccoby, E. E., & Jacklin, C. N. (1974). *The psychology of sex differences.* Stanford, CA: Stanford University Press.

Marascuilo, L. A., & McSweeney, M. (1977). *Nonparametric and distribution-free methods for the social sciences.* Monterey, CA: Brooks/Cole.

Piaget, J. (1962). *Play, dreams, and imitation in childhood.* New York: W.W. Norton.

Schmid, A.B., & Drury, B.J. (1973). *Introduction to women's gymnastics.* Palo Alto, CA: Nation Press.

Serbin, L.A., Tonick, I.J., & Sternglanz, S.H. (1977). Shaping cooperative cross-sex play. *Child Development, 48,* 924-929.

Sutton-Smith, B., & Rosenberg, B.G. (1960). A revised conception of masculine-feminine differences in play activities. *Journal of Genetic Psychology, 96,* 165-170.

Sutton-Smith, B., Rosenberg, B. G., & Morgan, E. R. (1963). Development of sex differences in play choices during preadolescence. *Child Development, 34,* 119-126.

Walker, R.N. (1964). Measuring masculinity and femininity by children's game choices. *Child Development, 35,* 961-971.

Wickstrom, R. (1977). *Fundamental motor patterns.* Philadelphia: Lea & Febiger.

10

The Effects of Selected Sociocultural Factors Upon the Overhand-Throwing Performance of Prepubescent Children

WHITFIELD B. EAST AND LARRY D. HENSLEY
University of Northern Iowa

The purpose of this study was to determine if selected sociocultural factors could explain a significant degree of the variability of the overhand throw for distance among prepubescent boys and girls Grades K–3. Performance on the overhand throw of 280 children was measured as the average of four maximum throws. Sociocultural information was obtained from the parents by way of a questionnaire. Approximately 58% of the parents responded to the questionnaire, establishing a final sample of 162 children for the regression analyses. Stepwise multiple regression was used to analyze the relative contribution of each sociocultural variable to overhand-throwing performance. Separate regression equations for gender and grade were developed. The multiple Rs *exhibited a decreasing trend with chronological age: boys .87–.62 and girls .90–.66. This suggests that as a child becomes older, factors other than sociocultural determinants become relatively more important in the explanation of overhand-throwing performance. The sociocultural variables that consistently loaded high in the regression analyses were those pertaining to the influence of the mother and the father, hours of television watched, and extracurricular play experiences.*

The acquisition of motor skills may be described as a developmental sequence progressing from simple fundamental movement pattern to complex specific skills. Although not every fundamental movement pattern may be generalized to a specific skill, there are certain patterns which intuitively lead to the acquisition of specific skills. One such pattern is the overhand throw. This fundamental movement pattern establishes a movement sequence which affects the development of later specific skills such as the throw in football, full-court pass in basketball, spike in volleyball, serve in tennis, and overhead strokes in badminton and racquetball. Although the movements for each of these skills are not identical,

---

This study was supported by a Graduate College Faculty Research Award.

they are similar enough to make the development of a mature overhand-throwing pattern an integral step in the acquisition of many specific sports skills.

Although individuals develop differently, Gallahue (1982) suggested that there are four basic factors that regulate fundamental movement pattern development: maturation, physical development, hereditary factors, and environmental experiences. There have been numerous studies concerning the first three factors. Several of the more notable studies of the development of the overhand-throwing pattern were conducted by Wild (1938), Keogh (1973), Halverson, Roberton, Safrit, and Roberts (1977), and Roberton, Halverson, Langendorfer, and Williams (1979). From these studies, age and sex appear often as the primary delimiters of fundamental movement pattern development. Keogh (1973) concluded "that regardless of the testing procedure used, boys performed markedly better than girls on throwing for distance and accuracy at even the earliest ages" (p. 61).

An intuitive analysis of the overhand throw was provided by Eckert (1973). She made three significant observations. First, sex differences in the overhand throw for distance appear to be a reflection of sex differences in the throwing pattern. Second, "although boys do, on the average, have larger length and girth in the forearm . . . which gives them a mechanical and strength advantage in the propulsion of projectiles, the morphological and strength differences between the sexes are not great enough to account for the extremely large sex differences in this skill" (p. 168). Third,

> It is logical to attribute the noted sex differences in phylogenetic physical skills to sex differences in body size, anatomical structure, and physiological functioning. However, it is also possible that social and cultural factors may influence mean performance in running, jumping, and throwing in such a way that the sex differences in performance are magnified. (p. 173)

Eckert's observations are analogous to Singer's (1973) statements concerning intelligence. He concluded that since intelligence develops most rapidly before the age of 4, the child's environment is a major consideration for future development. Perhaps the environmental experiences provided by parents, teachers, and peers are the critical factors in the development of fundamental movement patterns such as the overhand throw.

Malina (1973) outlined two levels of sociocultural factors that influence motor development during infancy and early childhood. The first level is intrinsic factors, including familial characteristics such as family size, number of siblings, birth order, and socioeconomic background. The second level is extrinsic factors, which center around nurture experiences—opportunity for practice, infant stimulation, availability of toys and equipment, and so forth. Malina discussed the influence of the sociocultural factors, although no empirical evidence was given to support the relative contribution of individual sociocultural factors to the development of fundamental movement patterns.

In recent years more attention has been focused upon the influence of specific sociocultural factors upon motor development. Schnabel-Dickey (1977) analyzed the effects of the child-rearing attitudes upon the jumping and throwing performance of preschool children. She concluded that a permissive, indulgent home environment was associated with superior throwing skills. A direct relationship also has been reported between birth order and participation in dangerous sports (Alberts & Landers, 1977; Casher, 1977). Casher found that the third-born child was significantly more likely to participate in dangerous leisure-time activities than older siblings. Greendorfer and Lewko (1978) studied the socializing influence of parents and peers upon male and female siblings. Their results indicated that the parents, specifically the father, were the most significant influencing agent upon the sport socialization of young children. In a subsequent discussion of the greater differences in physical activity, Greendorfer (1980) concluded that toy and play behavior were learned. Girls were socialized away from competitive, aggressive activities and boys were socialized for competition.

The overhand-throwing pattern is a complex fundamental movement pattern which develops primarily during the prepubescent period. For boys this process occurs at a younger chronological age than for girls. Since there is no apparent physiological or maturational basis for these developmental differences (Keogh, 1973), perhaps the sociocultural status of the individual may account for the significant variability found in the performance of the overhand-throwing pattern.

The purpose of this study was to determine the effects of selected sociocultural factors upon the performance of the overhand-throwing pattern of young children. If the factors that significantly contribute to the overhand-throwing pattern can be identified, perhaps developmental experiences and nurture relationships can be restructured to equalize the opportunity for fundamental movement pattern development. With the orderly development of fundamental movement patterns, children may enter specific skill-learning situations with an enhanced movement repertoire that will increase the probability of successful achievement.

METHOD

Subjects and Procedure

For this study 280 children, Grades K-3, were selected from elementary schools in Cedar Falls, Iowa. The overhand throw for distance was selected as the criterion measure of overhand-throwing performance. Throwing for distance was measured as the absolute distance thrown (to the nearest tenth of a foot). To standardize the measure of throwing performance, subjects threw from a stationary stance; no run-up was allowed. Subjects were encouraged to warm up individually. No practice throws were allowed. Four successive trials were administered.

A questionnaire was developed to assess the sociocultural milieu of the child. The questionnaire was modeled after several similar questionnaires designed to assay sociocultural status, therefore this questionnaire was assumed to be valid and reliable based on face concurrent validity. The child's parents were asked to complete this questionnaire, which is presented in Figure 1. Questions on the instructions were selected to represent three general areas of sociocultural influence: (a) sibling influence—birth order, number of siblings, and so forth; (b) parental influence—education and work of the mother and father; and (c) sport activity influence—leisure-time rating, sport participation, and so forth. The questionnaire was introduced and explained by the child's teacher at a quarterly parent/teacher conference. Along with general instructions, several key points were covered and questions answered by the teacher. Questionnaires were returned by mail. Approximately 58% of the parents responded to the questionnaire, so the final sample for the regression analyses was 162.

Data Analysis

The data analysis was designed to determine the relative contribution of each sociocultural factor measured to overhand-throwing performance. Missing data were handled through a casewise deletion of cases. A stepwise multiple regression analysis was computed using the overhand throw for distance as the dependent variable. The sociocultural predictor variables used to describe overhand-throwing performance are presented in Table 1. The SPSS regression subprogram was used to compute the regression statistics. Because overhand-throwing performance is confounded by grade and gender, separate regression equations were computed for each male and female sample by grade. The sample size for the subsamples broken down by grade and gender was K_m— 20, K_f— 19, 1_m— 19, 1_f— 20, 2_m— 22, 2_f— 20, 3_m— 19, 3_f— 23.

Figure 1. The Parent Questionnaire.

PARENT QUESTIONNAIRE

Student I.D. ______ School ______
Student Birthdate ______ (month day year)
Student Height ____ feet ____ inches Student Weight ____ lbs.

Family Profile

1. Number of children in family. 1 2 3 4 5 6 7 8 9 10
2. Birth order of student. 1 2 3 4 5 6 7 8 9 10
3. Number of older brothers. 1 2 3 4 5 6 7 8 9 10
4. Number of older sisters. 1 2 3 4 5 6 7 8 9 10
5. Education of parents. (Indicate last grade or year completed.)
   Mother: 6 7 8 9 10 11 12 College 1 2 3 4 5 6 7 8 9
   Other ______
   Father: 6 7 8 9 10 11 12 College 1 2 3 4 5 6 7 8 9
   Other ______
6. List the sports you have played on a regular basis in the past. Place an (*) beside those in which you still participate.
   Mother ______
   Father ______
7. Child lives with: Both Mother and Father ____
   Father ____ Mother ____ Gaurdian ____
8. Work Status of Parent(s):
   Mother: No ____ Part time ____ Full time ____
   Father: No ____ Part time ____ Full time ____

DEVELOPMENTAL HISTORY OF CHILD

1. Was the pregnancy of full term? Yes ____ No ____
   Days Early ____ Days Late ____
2. Weight of child at birth: ____ lbs. ____ oz.
3. At what age (months) did the child sit alone? ____
   Walk ____ Talk ____
4. Did the child have any pre-school experiences?
   Yes ____ No ____

	Yes	No	Yrs.
Private Group Day Care (Parents pay fee)	____	____	____
Public Day Care (Public supported)	____	____	____
Individual Day Care (Less than 5 children)	____	____	____

5. Please describe your past play experiences with your child. Place a mark on the bar graph to indicate the play activities with your child.
   Example: If you played occasionally with your child at age 2:
   Seldom (One day a week or less) Frequently (Every day during the week)
   I——+——————I

Age		Mother (Seldom Frequently)		Father (Seldom Frequently)
2	Active Play	I————I	Active Play	I————I
	Quiet Play	I————I	Quiet Play	I————I
3	Active Play	I————I	Active Play	I————I
	Quiet Play	I————I	Quiet Play	I————I
4	Active Play	I————I	Active Play	I————I
	Quiet Play	I————I	Quiet Play	I————I
5	Active Play	I————I	Active Play	I————I
	Quiet Play	I————I	Quiet Play	I————I
6	Active Play	I————I	Active Play	I————I
	Quiet Play	I————I	Quiet Play	I————I
7	Active Play	I————I	Active Play	I————I
	Quiet Play	I————I	Quiet Play	I————I

6. Child illnesses or accidents:
   Ever hospitalized? Yes ____ No ____
   Last illness/accident and age? ____
   Allergies? Yes ____ No ____
   What allergies (age first noticed)? ____
7. Are there any physical or health problems that interfere with your child's play activities?
   Yes ____ No ____
   If so, what are they? ______
8. Leisure activities: Please mark those activities in which your child participates frequently (f); occasionally (o); and seldom (s).

____ Music(specify instrument)	____ Creative Play
____ Football	____ Gymnastics
____ Chior	____ Reading
____ Kickball	____ Swimming
____ Jump Rope	____ Baseball
____ T.V. (hours/day)	____ Wrestling
____ Running	____ Soccer
____ Dance	____ Cycling
____ Basketball	____ Art
____ Other	____ Other

9. Organized play experiences: Please include ate of experience.
   Church school: ______
   YMCA/YWCA: ______
   Day camp: ______
   Camp: ______
   Sports camp (sport): ______
   ______
   Sports lessons (sport): ______
   ______

The analysis had two objectives: (1) to determine if selected sociocultural variables could explain a significant degree of the variability of the overhand throw for distance and (2) to identify the sociocultural variables that accounted for a significant degree of the variability of overhand-throwing performance. After a variable was entered into the equation, the change in the R^2 value was analyzed to determine if the new variable contributed significantly to the variability of the overhand throw. The criterion for inclusion into the stepwise multiple regression equation was a significant change in the R^2 value for $df = N - 1$. These values were obtained from a bivariate r

Table 1
Sociocultural Predictors Grouped by Area of Influence

Area of Influence	Predictor Variable
Sibling influence	Birth order Number of older brothers Number of older sisters
Parental influence	Education of the mother Education of the father Active play of the mother Active play of the father Quiet play of the mother Quiet play of the father Sports of the mother Sports of the father
Sports activity influence	Preschool experiences Severe illnesses Leisure activities rating Organized play experiences

significance table (Ferguson, 1976, p. 494). Using a stepwise approach, once a variable was rejected (i.e., computed change in R^2 was less than table R^2) no more variables were entered into the equation.

RESULTS AND DISCUSSION

Analysis of Variance for Overhand Throw

Although the relationships between selected movement patterns (e.g., kicking, throwing, catching) and grade and gender are fairly well documented, it was of interest to determine if these data conformed to past findings. A two-factor analysis of variance model was used to examine the effects of grade and gender upon overhand-throwing performance. A significant Grade × Sex interaction ($p < .001$) was obtained, $F(3, 254) = 5.428$. Examination of the means and standard deviations presented in Table 2 reveals that the interaction results from a convergence of mean performance by gender for the kindergarten sample. This same interaction pattern was obtained by Halverson et al. (1977) when overhand-throwing velocity was analyzed by grade and gender. This finding should be of significant interest to developmental theorists, because it indicates that at some younger chronological age mean performance for boys and girls may not be significantly different. If this is the case, then subsequent gender differences in overhand-throwing performance can be directly related to differential environmental influences.

Table 2
Means and Standard Deviations by Grade and Gender on Overhand-Throwing Performance

	Grade			
Gender	K	1	2	3
Boys				
n	30	37	38	30
X	38.49	51.82	62.76	76.51
SD	10.98	15.11	16.32	12.36
Girls				
n	21	35	36	44
X	22.25	26.49	33.10	41.59
SD	4.49	7.92	8.20	14.24

Simple main effects were computed for boys and girls at each grade level. This analysis revealed a singularly interesting finding. The *F* ratios, representing the ratio of true score variance to error score variance, by gender were *K*— 18.93*, 1— 76.35*, 2— 102.59*, 3— 144.18* (*$p < .01$). The increasing magnitude to the *F* ratios supports what is witnessed performance-wise with regard to gender differences and overhand-throwing performance. For every two-group comparison by grade, successive grades performed significantly better ($p < .01$). The only exception was kindergarten and first-grade girls. The results obtained from the simple main effects analysis provides a rationale for computing separate regression equations by grade for each gender.

Regression Analysis for Sociocultural Factors

Multiple *R* coefficients were computed for each subsample by grade and gender. The dependent variable was the overhand throw for distance, and the predictor variables were the sociocultural variables taken from the parental questionnaire (see Table 1). For boys, the multiple *R*s were $R_k = .87$, $R_1 = .75$, $R_2 = .79$, $R_3 = .62$. For girls, the multiple *R*s were $R_k = .90$, $R_1 = .72$, $R_2 = .73$, $R_3 = .66$. Each coefficient was significantly greater than zero ($p < .01$). It is interesting to note the general trend of the multiple *R* coefficients from the kindergarten to the third-grade sample for both boys and girls. The decreasing magnitude of *R* may indicate a general lessening of the influence of the selected sociocultural variables as overhand-throwing ability matures. If data were collected for Grades 4-6, one might expect to see the contribution of the sociocultural factors accounting for even less of the variability of the overhand throw for distance.

Regression Model for Boys

Considering the relatively high magnitude of the multiple *R* coefficients, it was surprising that only a few variables accounted for such a high degree of the variability. Table 3 presents the results of the multiple regression analysis for each male subsample, Grades K-3. For the male kindergarten sample, there were four significant factors: quiet influence—mother, active influence—father, hours of television, and number of siblings. The only factor that loaded positively for the kindergarten boys was the "quiet influence of the mother," a measure of the mother/child interaction for quiet activities (e.g., reading, quiet games, music). The other three factors were negatively correlated with overhand-throwing performance.

Table 3
Results of Stepwise Multiple Regression Analysis for the Overhand Throw for Distance (Boys)

Grade Level	Variable	Multiple *R*	R^2	Simple *R*
Kindergarten	Quiet influence of mother	.483	.233	.483
	Active influence of father	.646	.417	-.416
	Hours of TV	.797	.635	-.420
	No. of siblings	.871	.759	-.195
First grade	Hours of TV	.545	.297	-.545
	Leisure rating	.664	.440	.493
	Quiet influence of mother	.745	.556	-.371
Second grade	Sports of father	.503	.253	.503
	Education of father	.790	.624	-.462
Third grade	Play experience rating	.616	.379	.616

For first-grade boys, the significant variables were hours of television, leisure rating, and quiet influence—mother. For both kindergarten and first-grade boys, hours of television loaded negatively, suggesting that children who spent extended periods of time watching television did not throw as far as those who used that time in some other manner. The quiet influence of the mother shifted to a negative loading among first-grade boys. Leisure rating was the only variable showing a positive relationship with overhand-throwing performance. The leisure rating (− 1 to 1) was indicative of how the individuals spent their leisure time (passive to active). Individuals who elected to spend their free time pursuing gross motor activities (e.g., football, wrestling, ballet) exhibited a more mature throwing performance than those with more sedentary extracurricular lifestyles. This supports a rationale for specific developmental experiences designed to enhance fundamental movement performance.

By the second grade, the factors had shifted completely to sports of father and education of father. The father had apparently now become the primary influencing agent, and the subject whose father was currently more active in sports tended to perform better on the overhand throw for distance. The educational level of the father was negatively correlated with performance.

For the third-grade sample, the play experience rating was the only significantly contributing factor. This rating was a measure of extracurricular physical activities in which the child participated. These activities had to be organized experiences such as swimming lessons, gymnastic lessons, and sports camps. The correlation between the play rating and overhand-throwing performance was .616. Thus, the organized nurture experiences provided for the child accounted for over one third of the total variability of overhand-throwing performance.

Regression Model for Girls

The female sample exhibited sociocultural trends similar to those of the boys (Table 4). This was somewhat surprising considering the significant performance differences that exist between the genders for the overhand throw. For the kindergarten sample, three factors contributed significantly to the variability of the overhand throw: education of the mother, hours of television, and active influence—mother. The mother appeared to be the primary influencing agent for the kindergarten girl, with the hours of television again exhibiting a negative influence.

For first-grade girls, the significant factors were quiet influence— mother, work status—mother, and education—mother. The mother was again the primary source of influence. The only change at this level was in the effect of the education of the mother. Although the simple correlation was nearly spurious, this factor now exhibited a negative relationship with throwing performance.

There were four significant factors for the second-grade female sample. This marks a slight change in the trend of decreasing numbers of significantly contributing factors. This change may be explained in part by the fact that the development of overhand-throwing performance is generally delayed for the young girl. For

Table 4
Results of Stepwise Multiple Regression Analysis for the Overhand Throw for Distance (Girls)

Grade Level	Variable	Multiple R	R^2	Simple R
Kindergarten	Education of mother	.456	.208	.456
	Hours of TV	.738	.545	-.051
	Active influence of mother	.895	.802	.308
First grade	Quiet influence of mother	.432	.186	.432
	Work of mother	.620	.384	.335
	Education of mother	.722	.522	-.219
Second grade	Sports of father	.395	.156	-.395
	Active influence of father	.535	.287	.357
	Education of mother	.644	.415	-.165
	Work of mother	.734	.538	.203
Third grade	Play experience rating	.562	.317	-.563
	Sports of father	.659	.434	-.543

example, the average second-grade girl performed at the same level or below the level of the kindergarten male (see Table 2). Therefore, similar sociocultural patterns for significantly contributing factors might not be expected across gender. The significant factors for the second-grade girls were sports—father, active influence—father, education—mother, and work status—mother. The two critical factors emphasize the relative importance of the parents as socializing agents. The active influence of the father and work status of the mother were positive influences. The sports of the father, which was a major positive influence for the boys, was a negative influence for the girls. The education of the mother remained a negative factor at this level.

For the third-grade female sample, the trend toward a decreasing overall sociocultural influence and decreasing number of significantly contributing factors reappears. The multiple R was .659 with two significant factors: play experience rating and sports of the father. The negative simple correlation for these two factors is somewhat difficult to understand. It should be remembered that play experience rating was the single significant factor for the third-grade male sample ($r = .616$). One possible explanation could be that the organized play experiences in which girls participate are different than those for boys (e.g., dance vs. basketball camp, gymnastics vs. junior league baseball). The play experiences of the females in this sample did not enhance overhand-throwing performance. The negative loading of sports of the father may be a predictable cultural phenomenon. The athletic father may perceive the movement needs of the daughter from a stereotypically male perspective. The daughters may be encouraged to dance or participate in gymnastics, but may not be allowed to play little league baseball.

CONCLUSIONS

From a macroscopic perspective, similar trends are seen in the influence of the sociocultural factors for the male and female samples. First, the statistical influence of the selected sociocultural factors decreased with chronological age. Multiple *R*s decreased from .87 for the kindergarten boys to .62 for the third-grade boys. For the female samples multiple *R*s ranged from .90 to .66, respectively. Although these statistics appear relatively consonant, one must consider the limitation of the relatively small sample size per subsample. However, these results seem to indicate that, as the individual becomes more proficient in overhand-throwing performance (i.e., has learned the skill), the influence of the socializing factors diminishes. One might speculate that as the skill is "learned" more performance-oriented factors (e.g., angle of release, strength, lag time) supplant the sociocultural factors as the primary contributors to overall performance. This may be evidenced by the further widening of the performance gap for overhand throw for distance demonstrated by postpubescent boys and girls.

Second, with an increase in chronological age there was a decrease in the number of significantly contributing sociocultural factors. For boys the number of significant factors decreased linearly from four to one for the respective subsamples. This trend was not yet as clear for the female sample, perhaps because the overhand throw exhibited by the girls was generally less mature than that of the boys. Kindergarten boys threw farther (38.49 ft) than every female sample except the third-grade girls (41.59 ft). The female subsamples did, however, exhibit a decreasing trend in the number of significantly contributing sociocultural variables.

A third trend pertained to the sociocultural factors themselves. Although there was some expected variability across gender, the intrinsic sociocultural factors (e.g., sports of the father, work status of the mother) appear to be the primary influencing factors for the kindergarten and first-grade subsamples in this study. This was especially true for the female subsamples. By the second and third grades the extrinsic factors began to emerge (e.g., leisure time rating and play experience rating). For boys both variables loaded positively. Active sports-minded fathers had active sons who performed well on the overhand throw for distance. For girls both variables loaded negatively. Over 25% of the total variance for overhand-throwing performance was attributable to the stereotyped father-figure who socialized the daughter away from sports and physically competitive situations. These conclusions directly parallel those of Greendorfer and Lewko (1978). It was interesting to note that in every instance hours of television loaded negatively. Other factors were of interest because they did not contribute significantly to overhand-throwing performance. With a changing economy we have heard many accusations concerning the effects of the working mother on child development. With regard to preschool experiences, there appears to be no significant difference in the overhand-throwing performance of boys and girls who remain at home with a parent, attend private day care, or attend public day care.

In conclusion, nurture experiences play a varied role in the socialization and development of motor behaviors. Movement patterns develop rapidly during the preschool years and are primarily affected by the attitudes, predilections, and encouragement of the parents. It is now becoming apparent that when fundamental movement patterns are not developed during this active developmental period (2-6 years), subsequent performance of fundamental and general movements is limited. It is a common experience to witness high school and even college girls exhibiting an immature overhand-throwing performance. With an inadequate fundamental movement pattern foundation, these individuals are often frustrated when they attempt to learn specific sport skills. The frustration of repeated failures causes many to abandon sports, losing the lifetime benefits these activities provide. Therefore, the orderly development of fundamental movement patterns is essential and is predicated to a large extent upon appropriate nurture experiences provided within the sociocultural milieu of the child.

REFERENCES

Alberts, C.L., & Landers, D.M. (1977). Birth order, motor performance and maternal influence. *Research Quarterly, 48,* 661-670.

Casher, B.B. (1977). Relationship between birth order and participation in dangerous sport. *Research Quarterly, 48,* 33-40.

Corbin, C.B. (1973). *A textbook of motor development.* Dubuque, IA: Brown.

Eckert, H.H. (1973). Age changes in motor skills. In G.L. Rarick (Ed.), *Physical activity: Human growth and development* (pp. 154-175). New York: Academic Press.

Ferguson, G. A. (1976). *Statistical analysis in psychology and education* (4th ed.). New York: McGraw-Hill.

Gallahue, D. L. (1982). *Motor development and movement experiences for young children.* New York: Wiley & Sons.

Greendorfer, S. L. (1980). Gender differences in physical activity. *Motor Skills: Theory into Practice, 4,* 83-90.

Greendorfer, S. L., & Lewko, J. H. (1978). Role of family members in sport socialization of children. *Research Quarterly, 49,* 146-152.

Halverson, L. E., Roberton, M. A., Safrit, J., & Roberts, T. W. (1977). Effects of guided practice on overhand-throw ball velocities of kindergarten children. *Research Quarterly, 48,* 311-318.

Keogh, J. (1973). Development in fundamental motor tasks. In C. B. Corbin (Ed.), *A textbook of motor development* (pp. 57-74). Dubuque, IA: Brown.

Malina, R. M. (1973). Factors influencing motor development during infancy and childhood. In C. B. Corbin (Ed.), *A textbook of motor development* (pp. 31-53). Dubuque, IA: Brown.

Roberton, M. A., Halverson, L. E., Langendorfer, S., & Williams, K. (1979). Longitudinal changes in children's overarm throw ball velocities. *Research Quarterly, 50,* 256-264.

Schnabel-Dickey, E. A. (1977). Relationships between parent's child-rearing attitudes and the jumping and throwing performance of their preschool children. *Research Quarterly, 48,* 382-390.

Singer, R. N. (1973). Motor learning as a function of age and sex. In G. L. Rarick (Ed.), *Physical activity: Human growth and development* (pp. 176-200). New York: Academic Press.

Wild, M. R. (1938). The behavior pattern of throwing and some observations concerning its course of development in children. *Research Quarterly, 9,* 20-25.

11

Developmental Differences in Motor Schema Formation

GAIL M. DUMMER
Indiana University

This study was designed to determine whether motor schema acquisition by mentally retarded children could be enhanced by providing training conditions that facilitate information processing, and whether mentally retarded children would demonstrate motor-learning behaviors similar to those exhibited by nonretarded children of equal mental age. Subjects were 72 trainable mentally retarded (TMR) children aged 9-16 years. The procedures involved a replication of the Kelso and Norman (1978) study in which subjects learned a linear positioning task under variable practice, constant practice, or no practice conditions. Following practice, all subjects participated in a transfer task consisting of two novel target positions. Nonparametric data analyses revealed little evidence of motor schema formation by TMRs. Inspection of mean absolute and variable error scores revealed similar performance levels on practice and transfer trials by TMRs and like-mental-age nonretarded preschool children from the Kelso and Norman sample.

Research evidence indicates that mentally retarded individuals generally acquire motor skills at a slower rate and to a lesser degree of proficiency than do nonretarded children of the same chronological age (Bruininks, 1974; Francis & Rarick, 1959; Malpass, 1963; Mann, Burger, & Proger, 1974; Rarick, 1973). Although the motor performance deficits of mentally retarded persons have been documented by numerous investigators, little is known about the motor educability or motor-learning potential of these children (Dummer, in press). The retardate's apparent inability to transfer skills from familiar to unfamiliar situations (Belmont & Butterfield, 1977; Borkowski & Cavanaugh, 1979; Brown, 1974) and the trait of high intra-individual variability of performance among retardates (Baumeister & Kellas, 1968; Dummer, 1978; Dunn, 1978; McGown, Dobbins, & Rarick, 1973; Rarick & Dobbins, 1972; Rarick &

This manuscript was based upon a doctoral dissertation completed at the University of California at Berkeley under the direction of Professor G. Lawrence Rarick.

McQuillan, 1977) suggest that they do not learn motor tasks readily.

Although several factors probably contribute to the retardate's difficulties in motor skill acquisition, perhaps the most limiting factor is deficient information-processing skills. Information processing refers to the use of information acquisition and retrieval strategies or memory skills to facilitate performance. Some scholars (e.g., Marteniuk, 1976) define motor learning as changes in the information-processing component of motor skill performance. Learning occurs and motor skill levels improve when appropriate information-processing strategies are used.

Research in verbal learning has revealed numerous developmental differences in information-processing abilities. Young children process information less efficiently than older children or adults (Clark, 1978; Wade, 1977), and mentally retarded individuals process information less efficiently than nonretarded persons (Belmont, 1978; Belmont & Butterfield, 1977; Brown, 1974, 1975; Brown & Campione, 1978; Mercer & Snell, 1977). In comparison with adults, young children and mentally retarded individuals have a smaller repertoire of information acquisition strategies such as rehearsal, organization, elaboration, mediation, or deliberate nonprocessing of irrelevant information (Belmont & Butterfield, 1971; Brown, 1974; Ellis, 1970; Flavell & Wellman, 1977; Spitz, 1966). Children and retardates also seem unaware of the usefulness of their learning strategies (Brown, 1974; Flavell, 1970), and they may lack the ability or experience necessary to select and coordinate appropriate information-processing strategies to meet particular task demands (Belmont & Butterfield, 1977). The results of verbal-learning research further indicate that information-processing skill may be a function of mental age (MA). Young children and retardates of equal MA tend to perform similarly on tasks that require the use of information acquisition or retrieval skills (Belmont, 1978; Brown, 1975).

Since information-processing skills are an integral aspect of motor learning as well as verbal learning, the developmental differences in information-processing abilities which have been noted by verbal-learning researchers should also be manifested in motor-learning situations. Furthermore, the similarities in information-processing abilities between retardates and their equal-MA peers on verbal-learning tasks suggest potential similarities in the motor-learning and performance characteristics of the two populations (Dummer, 1978; Poretta, 1982; Sugden, 1978).

Schmidt's (1975b) theory of motor learning has perhaps the greatest potential for predicting and explaining developmental differences in motor learning. According to Schmidt's theory, the performer solves motor problems by responding to a motor schema, which is an abstraction of four sources of information: the desired outcome of the movement; the initial conditions, or physiological and postural readiness for the movement; knowledge of past actual outcomes of similar movements; and knowledge of past actual sensory consequences of similar movements. The motor schema is developed as the performer discovers the relationship among these sources of information. The motor schema can be characterized as a set of rules which generate instructions for producing movement.

Schmidt's (1975b) description of the motor schema suggests that several information-processing skills are involved in successful motor performance. To succeed at a motor task, the performer must (a) recognize the current task to be either like or unlike previously learned skills; (b) retrieve from memory examples of past similar movements and sensory consequences; (c) decide upon a motor plan for the current task by interpolating new response specifications from past response specifications and movement outcomes; (d) execute the motor plan; (e) correct the movement in progress by updating the motor plan (if the movement is of more than one reaction time in duration); (f) evaluate the completed movement in terms of both actual outcome and sensory consequences; and (g) update and revise the motor schema.

The best conditions for schema formation involve numerous trials on a wide variety of task requirements (Schmidt, 1975a). Schmidt suggests that during skill acquisition the learner gradually develops a schema which can be compared to a graph with response specifications on the abscissa and movement outcomes on the ordinate. Over the course of a very large number of responses to an entire range of task requirements, the learner acquires a good idea of which specifications produce which outcomes. Alternately, the child who responds to a single task requirement will have less information about the relationship between specifications and outcomes. He or she will be able to develop only a truncated version of the correlation schema, and will therefore be less prepared to respond to later variations of the same task.

There is evidence to suggest that Schmidt's schema theory is valid for young children and mentally retarded individuals. The first finding of interest is that children apparently do learn generative rules for the direction and construction of movement (Bruner, 1973; Eckert & Eichorn, 1974; Hogan & Hogan, 1975). Additional support for the hypothesis that children learn schemata for motor tasks was provided by Kelso and Norman (1978).

In a direct test of schema theory, Kelso and Norman (1978) demonstrated that 3-year-old intellectually normal children were able to learn a strategy or set of rules for force production in a linear positioning task. These researchers reasoned that children given variability of practice would develop stronger schemata than children not provided with variability of practice. To test these ideas, Kelso and Norman studied 36 3-year-olds as they performed a ballistic force production task under one of three experimental conditions. A variable practice group practiced propelling a toy car to four different locations on a 2.6-m long track. A constant practice group practiced propelling the car to only one location on the track, and a control group received no practice sessions. As predicted by Schmidt's theory, the variable practice group exhibited superior performance on a transfer task consisting of trials practice group practiced kicking a Nerf soccer ball over four terrains of different slope to a target 5 m distant. Subjects in a constant group practiced kicking the ball over only one of the four terrains, and those in a control group participated in a catching and throwing task. As predicted by Schmidt's theory, the variable practice group exhibited superior performance on a transfer task consisting of trials at two novel target positions.

Poretta (1982) found evidence of schema formation in a sample of 24 10-year-old educatable mentally retarded (EMR) boys and among control groups of equal MA and chronological age (CA). Subjects assigned to a variable practice group practiced kicking a Nerf soccer ball over four terrains of different slope to a target 5 m distant. Subjects in a constant group practiced kicking the ball over only one of the four terrains, and those in a control group participated in a catching and throwing task. As predicted by Schmidt's theory, the variable practice group performed better on a transfer task consisting of trials over a novel terrain. Consistent with verbal-learning research, EMR boys and their equal-MA peers performed similarly during both practice and transfer trials; whereas the equal-CA control group outperformed both the EMRs and the equal-MA controls.

Any enthusiasm over these tentative results supporting schema formation by young children and retardates should be tempered by a recognition of factors that may make schema formation a relatively difficult or slow process for them. One factor that may adversely affect schema formation and schema operation is the frequent failure of developmentally young individuals to use efficient response strategies (Schmidt & Johnson, 1972; Sugden, 1978; Todor, 1974; Wade, 1977; Wade & Craig, 1970). Wade surmised that the use of inefficient strategies was at least in part due to an inability to determine task requirements. The performer who cannot determine task requirements cannot generate response specifications for the current task by comparing it to previously learned skills. Therefore, motor performance is likely to be impaired.

The relatively limited motor experience of young children and retardates is another factor to consider with respect to schema formation and operation. Todor (1974) suggested that response strategies for a particular task are selected on the basis of an individual's knowledge and experience with various kinds of strategies. The older or skilled performer probably has more motor experiences, and hence a greater knowledge of strategies that can be used to solve various motor tasks. In Schmidt's terms, the older or skilled performer may have stronger and more numerous schemata to use in solving new motor problems.

Wade's (1977) and Todor's (1974) suggestions about developmental differences in motor learning are similar to hypotheses proferred by Flavell (1970) and Brown (1975) concerning verbal learning. In both cases, children and retardates are seen to be deficient compared with adults in their ability to acquire, select, and use efficient information acquisition and response strategies. These developmental differences in information-processing skills may in turn contribute to difficulties in schema development by young children and mentally retarded individuals.

The present study was designed to determine whether motor skill acquisition by mentally retarded children could be enhanced by providing training conditions that facilitate information processing, and whether mentally retarded children demonstrate motor-learning behaviors characteristic of the behaviors exhibited by nonretarded children of similar MA. I replicated the procedures of the Kelso and Norman (1978) study of motor schema formation. Trainable mentally retarded (TMR) children were used as subjects to determine the nature of motor schema learning by TMRs and to permit comparisons of motor schema learning by the present sample with the similar-MA Kelso and Norman sample. The specific hypotheses of this study were as follows: (a) subjects in a variable practice group were expected to perform better on two transfer tasks than subjects assigned to any of four constant practice groups, who were in turn expected to perform better than control group subjects; (b) subjects were expected to show evidence of learning the car-pushing task during the practice trials; and (c) the mentally retarded children who participated in this study were expected to perform similarly to the Kelso and Norman nonrelated preschool subjects on both practice trials and transfer tasks.

METHOD

Subjects

The subjects for this experiment were 72 TMR children aged 9–16 from three northern California public schools. The mean CA of these children was 13.99 years (*SD* = 2.02 years). These TMRs may be characterized as poor motor skill performers based upon motor test scores. Most of these children had been previously tested on a battery of over 50 motor ability tests (Rarick & McQuillan, 1977). In general, they scored more than 2 *SDs* below the average performance of same-age nonretarded children on the same test items. Their mean Stanford-Binet or WISC IQ score was 40.36 (*SD* = 10.49), and their average MA was 4.29 years (*SD* = 1.33 years). The TMRs in this sample were therefore about 1 year older in MA than the 3.33-year-old subjects in the Kelso and Norman (1978) study.

Apparatus

The apparatus used in this experiment was that specified by Kelso and Norman (1978). It consisted of a toy car which traveled along a 2.6-m horizontal linear trackway. The trackway was a stainless steel rod mounted on wooden brackets. The toy car was mounted upon a Thompson ball bushing which traveled on the steel rod with near-frictionless movement.

Subjects were directed to use a ballistic movement to propel the ball bushing/car to designated stop positions along the trackway. Stop positions were designated by a toy stop sign which was inserted into holes drilled at 30, 55, 75, 95, 120, and 140 cm from the starting position. To permit evaluation of subject errors, a meter rule graduated in centimeters was positioned next to the trackway. Subject errors were assessed by measuring the distance in centimeters from the front bumper of the car to the position of the stop sign. An overshot was scored as a positive deviation from the target; an undershot was scored as a negative deviation.

Design

As in the Kelso and Norman (1978) study, a transfer design was used to assess the effectiveness of different practice conditions upon the performance of a two-part criterion task. The 72 TMRs were randomly assigned and equally distributed to six groups: a variable practice group, one of four constant practice groups, and a control group.

The variable practice group received 80 practice trials, consisting of 20 trials at each of four target locations placed at 30, 55, 95, and 120 cm from the starting point. Within each block of 20 trials, a different random order of targets was presented to each subject. Subjects in the four constant practice groups also received 80 practice trials. Each constant practice group practiced at only one of the target locations, 30, 55, 95, or 120 cm. The control group did not receive practice trials.

Following the practice trials, children in each of the five experimental groups and the control group participated in a two-part criterion transfer task consisting of 20 consecutive trials at a 75-cm target (within the range of earlier experience for the variable practice group) and 20 consecutive trials at a 140-cm target (outside the range of earlier experience for the variable practice group). The order of presentation of the two transfer targets was counterbalanced among all 72 subjects. Children with a well-developed motor schema for this task, presumably those in the variable practice group, were expected to respond accurately to both novel target positions. In contrast, subjects in the constant practice groups were expected to be less prepared to respond to the transfer tasks and to perform best at the transfer distance that most closely approximated their training task.

Procedure

All children were tested individually in a school-room on the school grounds. Once in the testing room, the child was seated in a chair facing the starting end of the linear trackway apparatus, which was set upon a table of standard height. The task was then described and demonstrated for the subject. This involved grasping the toy car in a pincer grip and applying sufficient ballistic force to propel the car to the designated stop position. Each subject was permitted several orientation trials to become familiar with the task. If after several orientation trials the subject could not master the ballistic movement required or could not identify the toy car or the stop sign, that subject was dropped from the study. Eight children were so excluded from the study.

Subjects completed 60 of the 80 practice trials immediately following the orientation trials. To ensure attention to the task and to avoid fatigue, the child was then returned to the classroom for a rest period of 1-1 1/2 h. Following this rest period, the subject returned to the testing room to complete the additional 20 practice trials and the 40 transfer trials.

Reliability

Separate Spearman-Brown reliability estimates were computed on an odd-even trial basis for each block of 20 trials for each experimental group. For the practice trial blocks, the average reliability estimate was .43 for subjects in the variable practice group and .86 for subjects in the combined constant practice groups. The random target sequence presented to the variable practice group mitigated against high reliability for the practice trials. For the transfer trial blocks, the average reliability estimate was .82 for the variable practice group, .91 for the combined constant practice groups, and .90 for the control group.

Data Analysis

Assuming validity of Schmidt's (1975a, 1975b) theory and of the experimental hypotheses, the variable practice group could be expected to demonstrate superior learning in comparison with the constant practice and control groups. Because one index of learning is reduced variability of performance, the parametric assumption of equal variance for these data appeared to be suspect. Therefore an a priori decision was made to employ nonparametric data analysis procedures.

A Kruskall-Wallis test model with planned Mann-Whitney U pairwise comparisons was used to test the hypothesis concerning differences between groups on the two transfer tasks. Separate sets of data analyses were performed to evaluate differences in mean constant, absolute, and variable error scores. For each set of comparisons, the family error rate was set at .05 using the Dunn method of distributing alpha over specific comparisons. All three types of error were expected to be lowest in the variable practice group and highest in the control group on each of the transfer tasks. No difference in error scores was expected among the four constant practice groups.

The hypothesis regarding evidence of improved performance across the practice trials was evaluated using a Friedman model for repeated measures designs. Specifically, a series of Page tests (Marascuilo & McSweeney, 1977) were used to test for monotonic trend in constant, absolute, and variable error scores over the four blocks of 20 practice trials for the variable and constant practice groups. A significant monotonic trend at $p \leq .05$ in the direction of reduced constant, absolute, or variable errors scores for any of the experimental groups was considered evidence that learning had occurred.

The hypothesis of similar performance by TMR and nonretarded children of equal MA was tested by use of visual comparisons of the differences in mean variable and absolute error scores of the five experimental groups and the control group on the four practice trial blocks and the two transfer trial blocks. (Kelso and Norman (1978) did not report constant error scores.) Also included were inspections of the standard deviations about these mean error scores.

RESULTS

The first hypothesis concerned the ability of mentally retarded children to develop motor schemata for a novel car-pushing task, one in which the ballistic force requirements vary within a series of trials. It was predicted that mentally retarded children who are exposed to variable practice conditions should perform better on the transfer tasks than children who practice under constant conditions, who should in turn perform better that children who do not practice the task. Inspection of the mean constant, absolute, and variable error scores for the variable practice, combined constant practice, and control groups gives support for these hypotheses. On both transfer tasks, the variable practice group exhibited lower mean constant, variable, and absolute error scores than the combined constant practice group, which in turn had lower error scores than the control group (Tables 1, 2, and 3). In addition, the variable practice group demonstrated less variability of performance than the constant practice or control groups.

Table 1
Mean Constant Error Scores of Mentally Retarded Children

		Practice Trial				Transfer Trials[b]	
Experimental Group		B1[a]	B2	B3	B4	B1	B2
Variable practice	*M*	7.63	6.26	1.47	.88	6.02	-5.82
	SD	10.64	5.51	3.63	5.37	3.93	9.85
Constant practice							
30-cm group	*M*	16.38	12.73	10.43	14.66	13.23	-3.61
	SD	17.39	14.73	15.88	22.16	19.78	17.89
55-cm group	*M*	12.22	6.47	4.30	7.10	9.06	-5.64
	SD	14.91	9.49	6.81	10.16	11.37	9.81
95-cm group	*M*	9.90	4.12	1.87	8.58	11.74	-4.56
	SD	17.37	9.07	4.72	11.80	10.82	13.30
120-cm group	*M*	1.63	5.13	-1.73	.86	11.84	-6.91
	SD	16.69	15.92	12.35	16.71	14.51	13.07
Combined constant practice groups	*M*	10.03	7.11	3.72	7.80	11.47	-5.18
	SD	16.98	12.72	11.43	16.17	14.17	13.43
Control group	*M*					16.33	8.58
	SD					11.77	19.98

[a]Each block represents 20 trials.
[b]Transfer Block 1 trials were at the 75-cm target. Transfer Block 2 trials were at the 140-cm target.

Table 2
Mean Variable Error Scores of Mentally Retarded Children

Experimental Group		Practice Trial				Transfer Trials[b]	
		B1[a]	B2	B3	B4	B1	B2
Variable practice	*M*	18.51	14.60	17.69	15.53	12.63	18.81
	SD	7.26	4.50	5.72	4.69	4.01	5.30
Constant practice 30-cm group	*M*	14.87	14.14	11.25	15.77	16.91	24.42
	SD	13.04	13.84	10.04	16.08	11.07	13.34
55-cm group	*M*	20.14	13.28	14.21	12.22	13.57	21.48
	SD	15.20	5.56	7.35	4.61	7.39	7.85
95-cm group	*M*	19.57	16.96	13.56	17.40	14.05	18.23
	SD	9.90	9.30	5.71	8.71	6.64	7.21
120-cm group	*M*	25.63	23.52	18.73	22.47	19.33	20.79
	SD	12.02	13.09	8.25	12.36	15.93	10.25
Combined constant practice groups	*M*	20.05	16.97	14,51	16.96	15.97	21.23
	SD	12.87	11.35	8.20	11.52	10.80	9.89
Control group	*M*					19.75	24.47
	SD					12.36	6.98

[a]Each block represents 20 trials.
[b]Transfer Block 1 trials were at the 75-cm target. Transfer Block 2 trials were at the 140-cm target.

However, the results of a series of pairwise Mann-Whitney U test contrasts do not provide statistical support for this hypothesis. None of the pairwise comparisons of the five experimental groups and the control group for constant, absolute, or variable error for either of the two transfer tasks were statistically significant.

The second hypothesis suggested that retardates would demonstrate evidence of learning the car-pushing task during the practice trials. In general, this hypothesis was not supported by the results of a series of Page tests for monotonic trend in constant, variable, and absolute error scores for the five experimental groups that participated in practice trials. Only two of the 15 Page tests were statistically significant. Monotonic trends characterized the constant error scores of the variable practice group and the absolute error scores of the 55-cm constant practice group.

Although the results of the preplanned data analyses failed to support the learning hypotheses, post hoc tests suggested evidence to the contrary. A reduction in the mean constant, absolute, and variable error scores was apparent in most cases across the first three trial blocks, followed by a deterioration of performance during the fourth

Table 3
Mean Absolute Error Scores of Mentally Retarded Children

		Practice Trial				Transfer Trials[b]	
Experimental Group		B1[a]	B2	B3	B4	B1	B2
Variable practice	*M*	16.80	13.16	13.26	12.12	11.24	17.68
	SD	7.58	5.09	3.44	3.93	3.35	4.96
Constant practice							
30-cm group	*M*	18.73	16.25	14.18	18.36	21.12	24.28
	SD	15.73	13.69	13.26	19.97	13.02	10.58
55-cm group	*M*	18.63	12.89	11.59	12.32	13.95	19.73
	SD	12.25	6.01	5.48	7.92	9.23	5.79
95-cm group	*M*	19.10	14.95	11.53	16.62	16.09	18.58
	SD	16.34	7.77	4.47	9.24	8.43	5.78
120-cm group	*M*	21.93	22.98	17.14	21.49	17.96	20.98
	SD	10.20	11.76	6.80	10.37	11.74	7.82
Combined constant practice groups	*M*	19.60	16.77	13.61	17.20	17.28	20.89
	SD	13.48	10.65	8.31	12.82	10.75	7.80
Control group	*M*					20.12	25.25
	SD					10.75	13.17

[a] Each block represents 20 trials.
[b] Transfer Block 1 trials were at the 75-cm target. Transfer Block 2 trials were at the 140-cm target.

trial block. The deterioration of scores in Trial Block 4 may be related to the rest period administered between Trial Blocks 3 and 4. When post hoc Page tests were performed using data from only the first three trial blocks (60 trials), statistically significant monotonic trends were revealed in constant error for the variable practice group, in both constant and absolute error for the 55-cm constant practice group, and in variable and absolute error for the 95-cm constant practice group. These post hoc Page tests suggested that some learning did occur during the practice trials and that learning may have been significantly interrupted by the rest period.

A third hypothesis was that mentally retarded children and their nonretarded equal-MA counterparts should respond similarly to motor-learning tasks. Direct statistical comparisons of the car-pushing task performances of the mentally retarded children from this study and the nonretarded preschool children from the Kelso and Norman (1978) study could not be performed, because only limited summary data were available from the Kelso and Norman study, and because the experimental conditions varied slightly between the present study and that of Kelso and Norman. The subjects in the latter study received 160 practice trials, whereas the TMR children in my study received only 80 practice trials.

Nevertheless, marked similarities exist between the learning and transfer task performances of the TMR and the preschool children. Table 4 compares the mean variable error scores of the two subject groups over all trials, and Table 5 compares the mean absolute error scores. The mean error scores of the TMR and preschool groups are remarkably alike; however, the variability of error scores among the TMRs was greater than among the preschool children. In general, the standard deviations about the mean error scores of TMR subjects were approximately double the standard deviations about the mean error

Table 4
Comparison of Variable Error Scores of Mentally Retarded and Nonretarded Preschool Children of Similar Mental Age

		Kelso & Norman Subjects[a]		Mentally Retarded Subjects	
Trial Block Number		Combined Constant Practice	Variable Practice	Combined Constant Practice	Variable Practice
1	*M*	18.10	19.48	20.05	18.51
	SD	4.65	3.05	12.87	7.26
2	*M*	16.39	17.36	16.97	14.60
	SD	5.93	2.73	11.35	4.50
3	*M*	15.72	17.33	14.51	17.69
	SD	4.94	3.00	8.20	5.72
4	*M*	16.35	16.78	16.96	15.53
	SD	5.76	3.51	11.52	4.69
5	*M*	15.99	17.70		
	SD	4.07	2.33		
6	*M*	14.80	17.36		
	SD	4.93	3.17		
7	*M*	16.02	17.37		
	SD	3.63	3.43		
8	*M*	15.89	16.58		
	SD	5.30	2.98		
Transfer 75 cm	*M*	16.93	13.72	15.97	12.63
	SD	2.81	2.40	10.80	4.01
Transfer 140 cm	*M*	21.75	18.89	21.23	18.81
	SD	3.16	2.71	9.89	5.30

[a]Data reproduced from "Motor Schema Formation in Children" by J.A.S. Kelso and P.E. Norman, 1978 preliminary manuscript and *Developmental Psychology, 14,* pp. 153-156. Copyright 1978 by American Psychological Association. Permission by APA and J.A.S. Kelso.

scores of the preschool children. These results offer tentative support to the contention that children of equal MA perform similarly on fine motor tasks of this kind.

Table 5
Comparison of Absolute Error Scores of Mentally Retarded and Nonretarded Preschool Children of Similar Mental Age

		Kelso & Norman Subjects[a]		Mentally Retarded Subjects	
Trial Block Number		Combined Constant Practice	Variable Practice	Combined Constant Practice	Variable Practice
1	*M*	16.93	17.17	19.60	16.80
	SD	4.77	2.92	13.48	7.58
2	*M*	14.68	15.37	16.77	13.16
	SD	4.96	2.46	10.65	5.09
3	*M*	14.19	15.29	13.61	13.26
	SD	4.22	3.02	8.31	3.44
4	*M*	15.47	15.53	17.20	12.12
	SD	5.60	3.02	12.82	3.93
5	*M*	13.98	15.81		
	SD	3.64	2.53		
6	*M*	13.06	15.46		
	SD	4.49	3.31		
7	*M*	15.15	16.56		
	SD	4.02	2.50		
8	*M*	14.44	14.61		
	SD	4.89	2.12		
Transfer 75 cm	*M*	14.34	12.75	17.28	11.24
	SD	2.82	3.71	10.75	3.35
Transfer 140 cm	*M*	20.67	18.54	20.89	17.68
	SD	3.51	2.61	7.80	4.96

[a]Data reproduced from "Motor Schema Formation in Children" by J.A.S. Kelso and P.E. Norman, 1978 preliminary manuscript and *Developmental Psychology, 14,* pp. 153-156. Copyright 1978 by American Psychological Association. Permission by APA and J.A.S. Kelso.

DISCUSSION

The results of this experiment provide information about the validity of Schmidt's (1975a, 1975b) schema theory for TMR children. In addition, these results indicate that the motor-learning behaviors of mentally retarded and nonretarded children may be in part a function of MA.

With regard to Schmidt's theory, variability of practice should be the optimal condition for motor schema formation. If the TMRs in this study had developed motor schemata for the car-pushing task, there should have been clear evidence of learning during the practice trials by subjects in the variable and constant practice groups. If learning had occurred, members of the variable practice group should have developed schemata that permitted accurate response to both transfer tasks; whereas constant practice subjects could be expected to perform best at the transfer task distance that best approximated their training task. In addition, the variable practice group should have performed better than the other groups on the transfer tasks.

In fact, the data analyses revealed some evidence of learning. Several Page tests for monotonic trend in the direction of reduced error scores were found to be significant. Inspection of mean error scores revealed that the variable practice group did respond more accurately to the transfer tasks than the constant practice or control groups. As predicted, the 55-cm and 95-cm constant practice groups responded more accurately than the 30-cm and 120-cm groups to the 75-cm transfer target. Furthermore, the variable practice group did demonstrate lower error scores and less variability of performance than the constant practice of control groups. However, in most cases, these data were not sufficiently robust to yield statistically significant evidence of schema formation. The failure to obtain statistical significance may be due in part to the variability of performance exhibited by these TMR children. Indeed, with very similar mean error scores, Kelso and Norman (1978) obtained significant differences in favor of their variable practice group, and findings of no difference were obtained in the present study.

These results indicate that motor schema formation may be especially difficult for TMRs. Some factors that might account for this difficulty include inadequate memory or information-processing abilities, lack of motor competence, and lack of motivation. This experiment was designed to control somewhat for the last two alternatives. The car-pushing task was selected because it has minimal motor requirements, and TMR children should have been able to perform this task. Similarly, lack of motivation should not have been a problem: ample verbal reinforcement was provided to ensure attention and effort on this task, and the subjects seemed to perceive the task as fun to do.

A more likely explanation of the results is that these TMR children possessed inadequate memory and information-processing abilities for motor schema formation. The data did not consistently indicate learning on the tasks practiced. In fact, these TMRs apparently could not remember or perform the same task after a relatively brief rest break, as evidenced by the decrement in performance levels during Trial Block 4. Since there was only scattered evidence that these subjects learned the car-pushing task, the failure to find group differences in transfer task performances is not surprising. My conjecture is that these subjects were either unable to remember task requirements or unable to discern the relationship between response specifications and movement outcomes. The presumed inability to remember task requirements or to develop a schema for this task may be due to nonuse or ineffective use of memory strategies. Such an interpretation of these results would be consistent with the work of Brown (1974) and Flavell (1970; Flavell & Wellman, 1977) in verbal-learning research.

Although the results of this study are inconclusive with respect to motor schema formation by mentally retarded children, the results do suggest that the motor-learning behaviors of mentally retarded and young intellectually normal children may be a function of MA. Children of similar MA exhibited near-equal mean performance levels on the practice and transfer trials associated with the car-pushing task used in this study. This finding is consistent with Poretta's (1982) data on MA-matched EMR and nonretarded boys.

The finding of similar motor performance levels by subjects of similar MA is subject to limitations. Before such MA comparisons may be generalized to other populations and motor-learning situations, additional research needs to be conducted using children of various MAs and varying levels of retardation. A second limitation of this study concerns task selection. Several factors in addition to intelligence are believed to affect the motor performance of retardates, including physical growth and development (Bruininks, 1974; Rarick, 1973), motivation (Zigler, 1969), and experience. The fine motor car-pushing task used in my study was selected to permit the contribution of information-processing abilities to motor performance to be isolated from the contributions of these other factors as much as possible. However, when the tasks to be performed are gross motor in nature, or when these tasks must be performed in a different social or motivational context, equal MA comparisons may be inappropriate.

CONCLUSIONS

Although the results of this study are inconclusive with respect to motor schema formation by TMRs, the results do shed light on their motor-learning behaviors. It seems likely that the failure of these TMRs to develop motor schemata for the linear positioning task of this study was due to poor information-processing skills. In Schmidt's terms, these subjects seemed unable to remember task requirements or to discern the relationship between response specifications (target distance) and movement outcomes (force requirement). The information-processing deficits demonstrated by TMRs in this study are characteristic of those identified by verbal-learning researchers (Belmont & Butterfield, 1977; Brown, 1974; Flavell, 1970).

If retardates do indeed demonstrate similar problems in both verbal learning and motor learning, they may also benefit from similar remediation strategies. In verbal learning, researchers have helped improve the performance of retardates by training them to select and use effective information strategies for the task at hand (Belmont & Butterfield, 1977; Borkowski & Cavanaugh, 1979; Brown, 1975). If the motor-learning deficits demonstrated in my study are in fact due to poor information-processing skills, it may be possible to remedy these deficits in a similar manner. Instruction in the use of effective information-processing strategies may help TMRs to develop schemata and learn motor skills more efficiently. Further experimentation and observations are necessary to determine the validity of this hypothesis and to further elucidate the nature of motor schema learning by mentally retarded children.

REFERENCES

Baumeister, A., & Kellas, G. (1968). Distribution of reaction times of retardates and normals. *American Journal of Mental Deficiency, 72,* 715-718.

Belmont, J. M. (1978). Individual differences in memory: The cases of normal and retarded development. In M. Gruenbert & P. Morris (Eds.), *Aspects of memory* (pp. 153-185). London: Methuen.

Belmont, J. M., & Butterfield, E. C. (1971). Learning strategies as determinants of memory deficiencies. *Cognitive Psychology, 2,* 411-420.

Belmont, J. M., & Butterfield, E. C. (1977). The instructional approach to developmental cognitive research. In R. Kail & J. Hagen (Eds.), *Perspectives on the development of memory and cognition* (pp. 437-481). Hillsdale, NJ: Erlbaum.

Borkowski, J. G., & Cavanaugh, J. C. (1979). Maintenance and generalization of skills and strategies by the retarded. In N. R. Ellis (Ed.), *Handbook of mental deficiency: Psychological theory and research* (pp. 569-617). Hillsdale, NJ: Erlbaum.

Brown, A. L. (1974). The role of strategic behavior in retardate memory. In N. R. Ellis (Ed.), *International review of research in mental retardation* (Vol. 7, pp. 55-111). New York: Academic Press.

Brown, A. L. (1975). The development of memory: Knowing, knowing about knowing, and knowing how to know. In H. W. Reese (Ed.), *Advances in child development and behavior* (Vol 10, pp. 103-152). New York: Academic Press.

Brown, A.L., & Campione, J.C. (1978). Memory strategies in learning: Training children to study strategically. In H. Pick & H. Stevenson (Eds.), *Applications of basic research in psychology* (pp. 85-99). New York: Plenum Press.

Bruininks, R.H. (1974). Physical and motor development of retarded persons. In N.R. Ellis (Ed.), *International review of research in mental retardation* (Vol. 7, pp. 209-261). New York: Academic Press.

Bruner, J.S. (1973). Organization of early skilled action. *Child Development, 44,* 1-11.

Clark, J.E. (1978). Memory processes in the early acquisition of motor skills. In M.V. Ridenour (Ed.), *Motor development: Issues and applications* (pp. 99-112). Princeton, NJ: Princeton Book.

Dummer, G.M. (1978). *Information processing in the acquisition of motor skills by mentally retarded children.* Unpublished doctoral dissertation, University of California, Berkeley.

Dummer, G.M. (in press). Teacher training to enhance motor learning by mentally retarded individuals. In C. Sherill (Ed.), *Adapted physical education: Personnel preparation, trends, issues and new directions.* Springfield, IL: Thomas.

Dunn, J.M. (1978). Reliability of selected psychomotor measures with mentally retarded adult males. *Perceptual and Motor Skills, 46,* 295-301.

Eckert, H.M., & Eichorn, D.H. (1974). Construct standards in skilled action. *Child Development, 45,* 439-445.

Ellis, N.R. (1970). Memory processes in retardates and normals. In N.R. Ellis (Ed.), *International review of research in mental retardation* (Vol. 4, pp. 1-32). New York: Academic Press.

Flavell, J.H. (1970). Developmental studies of mediated memory. In H. Reese & L. Lipsitt (Eds.), *Advances in child development and behavior* (Vol. 5, pp. 181-211). New York: Academic Press.

Flavell, J.H., & Wellman, H.M. (1977). Metamemory. In R. Kail & J. Hagen (Eds.), *Perspectives on the development of memory and cognition* (pp. 3-33). Hillsdale, NJ: Erlbaum.

Francis, R.J., & Rarick, G.L. (1959). Motor characteristics of the mentally retarded. *American Journal of Mental Deficiency, 63,* 792-811.

Hogan, J.C., & Hogan, R. (1975). Organization of early skilled action: Some comments. *Child Development, 46,* 233-236.

Kelso, J.A.S., & Norman, P.E. (1978). Motor schema formation in children. *Developmental Psychology, 14,* 153-156.

Malpass, L.F. (1963). Motor skills in mental deficiency. In N.R. Ellis (Ed.), *Handbook of mental deficiency* (pp. 602-631). New York: McGraw-Hill.

Mann, L., Burger, R.M., & Proger, B.B. (1974). Physical education intervention with the exceptional child. In L. Mann & D. Sabatino (Eds.), *The second review of special education* (pp. 193-250). Philadelphia: J.S.E. Press.

Marascuilo, L.A., & McSweeney, M. (1977). *Nonparametric and distribution-free methods for the social sciences.* Monterey, CA: Brooks/Cole.

Marteniuk, R.G. (1976). *Information processing in motor skills.* New York: Holt, Rinehart & Winston.

McGown, C.M., Dobbins, A.D., & Rarick, G.L. (1973). Intra-individual variability of normal and educable mentally retarded children on a coincidence timing task. *Journal of Motor Behavior, 5,* 193–198.

Mercer, C.D., & Snell, M.E. (1977). *Learning theory research in mental retardation: Implications for teaching.* Columbus, OH: Merrill.

Poretta, D.L. (1982). Motor schema formation by EMR boys. *American Journal of Mental Deficiency, 87,* 164–172.

Rarick, G.L. (1973). Motor performance of mentally retarded children. In G.L. Rarick (Ed.), *Physical activity: Human growth and development* (pp. 227-256). New York: Academic Press.

Rarick, G.L., & Dobbins, D.A. (1972). *Basic components in the motor performance of educable mentally retarded children: Implications for curriculum development* (Contract No. OEG-9-70-2568-610). Washington, DC: U.S. Office of Education.

Rarick, G.L., & McQuillan, J.P. (1977). *Factor structure of motor abilities of trainable mentally retarded children* (Contract No. OEG-0-73-5170). Washington, DC: U.S. Office of Education.

Schmidt, R.A. (1975a). The schema basis for motor control. In W.W. Spirduso & J.D. King (Eds.), *Proceedings of the motor control symposium* (pp. 136–141). University of Texas, Austin.

Schmidt, R.A. (1975b). A schema theory of discrete motor learning. *Psychological Review, 82,* 225–260.

Schmidt, R.A., & Johnson, W.R. (1972). A note on response strategies in children with learning difficulties. *Research Quarterly, 43,* 509–513.

Spitz, H.H. (1966). The role of input organization in the learning and memory of mental retardates. In N.R. Ellis (Ed.), *International review of research in mental retardation* (Vol. 2, pp. 29–56). New York: Academic Press.

Sugden, D.A. (1978). Visual motor short term memory in educationally subnormal boys. *British Journal of Educational Psychology, 48,* 330–339.

Todor, J.I. (1974). Ability development and the use of strategies in motor learning. In M.G. Wade & R. Martens (Eds.), *Psychology of motor behavior and sport* (pp. 321-326). Urbana, IL: Human Kinetics.

Wade, M.G. (1976). Developmental motor learning. In J.F. Keogh & R.S. Hutton (Eds.), *Exercise and sport sciences reviews* (Vol. 4, pp. 375–394). Santa Barbara, CA: Journal Publishing Affiliates.

Wade, M.G., & Craig, T. (1970). Inter-trial response strategy of educable mentally handicapped children in learning time estimation. In G.S. Kenyon (Ed.), *Contemporary psychology of sport* (pp. 507-510). Chicago: Athletic Institute.

Zigler, E. (1969). Developmental versus difference theories of mental retardation and problem of motivation. *American Journal of Mental Deficiency, 73,* 536–556.

12

Motor Performance and Physical Fitness Status of Regular and Special Education Students

PHILIP L. REUSCHLEIN AND PAUL G. VOGEL
Michigan State University

The performance status of Michigan boys and girls entering fourth, seventh, and tenth grades was determined for selected fundamental motor skills, body management skills, and components of physical fitness. A stratified random sample of more than 1,500 regular education and 700 mainstreamed special education students was drawn from 117 schools representing 61 different school districts. Student performances on 17 test items were assessed in terms of both qualitative and quantitative standards. The overall performances of both the regular and special education students were lower at each grade level than the preset target attainment rate of 75% of all students meeting the stated performance standards for each test item. Performances of regular education students were higher than those of special education students at each grade level. Changes in performance expectations and/or changes in the delivery system for physical education instruction are needed in Michigan schools.

The Michigan Educational Assessment Program (MEAP) is responsible for measuring the extent to which Michigan students have mastered specified basic skills. Since 1969, MEAP has provided information to the governor, legislature, State Board of Education, citizens, district personnel, teachers, parents, students, and interested others on the status and progress of Michigan essential skills education.

Each fall all entering fourth-, seventh-, and tenth-grade students are tested on selected essential reading and mathematics skills. MEAP also measures attainment of objectives in other skill areas. Each year a stratified random sample of schools is drawn and one or two additional subject areas are assessed. Physical education was assessed for the first time in the fall of 1981.

Knowledge of the performance status of children provides school personnel with insight into the results of their efforts to promote the achievement of skills judged essential to schoolchildren. It also provides the baseline from which characteristics of the instructional context and the delivery systems associated with varying levels of achievement can be studied. Although the data are limited to Michigan children, the specification of both qualitative and quantitative performance standards and a general description of the way in which physical education services are delivered in Michigan provide educators in other states with the information necessary to determine the degree to which the results are generalizable to other populations of interest.

Assessments of the qualitative standards of performance of special and regular education students in addition to assessments of quantitative standards of performance distinguish this study from other descriptive studies of motor performance. There are many studies that provide quantitative standards of performance for children by age and gender. Although data from these studies are useful, they do not appropriately represent the extent to which children have learned the elements of qualitative performance commonly advocated by motor development specialists. The purpose of this study, therefore, is to describe the qualitative and quantitative performances of entering fourth-, seventh-, and tenth-grade regular and special education children on fundamental motor skills, body management skills, and components of physical fitness selected by experts as appropriate, important, and attainable by at least 75% of the students in Michigan's public schools.

METHOD

Sample

Fifteen schools were randomly selected from each of six population strata which were based on geographical area (tri-county Detroit, southern lower peninsula, northern lower peninsula, and upper peninsula) and community type (urban, suburban, and rural). The six strata were identified as (a) Tri-County Detroit Urban, (b) Tri-County Detroit Suburban, (c) Southern Lower Peninsula Urban, (d) Southern Lower Peninsula Suburban, (e) Southern Lower Peninsula Rural, and (f) Northern Lower Peninsula and Upper Peninsula.

Eighteen regular education students and up to 18 special education students, depending on availability, were selected from each of three grade levels (Grades 4, 7, and 10) in each of the schools identified in the sample. The total enrollment at each of these grade levels was separated into two lists, regular education students and special education students. Systematic sampling (e.g., every other student) was used to select the appropriate number of students from these separate class rolls of the randomly selected schools. Because some of the schools initially selected for the sample had only a few eligible special education students, additional schools were selected to increase the number of special education students included in the sample. These additional schools were chosen from the same districts as the schools initially selected to minimize variation among districts. Only special education students were selected from these additional schools. In total, a stratified random sample of over 1,500 regular education and 700 mainstreamed special education students was drawn from 117 schools representing 61 different school districts.

The special education students mainstreamed in physical education were identified as those who (a) were found eligible for special education programs and services by the Individual Educational Planning Committee, (b) had an approved Individual Education Plan, and (c) received any part of his or her instruction in a regular classroom and in special education programs or services.

The distribution of handicapping conditions in this sample of mainstreamed special education students was determined from the special education statistics for 1980-1983 that included the head count of special education students served in the regular classroom. These data were reported in a memorandum from the Special Education Service Area of the Michigan Department of Education (E.L. Birch, personal communication, May 5, 1983). The following types of handicapping conditions were found in these approximate percentages: mildly mentally impaired—12%, emotionally impaired—14%, learning disabled—41%, sensory impaired—2%, physically and otherwise health impaired—2%, and speech and language impaired—28%.

Test Battery

Seventeen essential skills in the areas of fundamental movement, body management, and physical fitness were selected to be tested as part of MEAP. Not all of these skills were tested at each grade level. Table 1 lists the specific skills selected for assessment at each grade level.

These test items were selected by a panel of experts who represented regular education and special education, physical educators and classroom teachers, university personnel, administrators, and the Michigan Department of Education staff. The essential skills selected were those judged appropriate for inclusion in the physical education programs of Michigan schools and also included in the state's *Essential Performance Objectives for Physical Education in Michigan* (Michigan Department of Education, 1981).

Each test item contained either qualitative and/or quantitative performance standards. Qualitative standards refer to those elements of performance advocated by motor development specialists that are

Table 1
Test Battery

Test Items	Grade 4	Grade 7	Grade 10
Fundamental Motor Skills			
Locomotion			
Run	X	X	
Hop	X	X	
Skip	X	X	
Body projection			
Horizontal jump	X	X	
Vertical jump	X	X	
Rhythm			
Even beat	X	X	
Object projection			
Overhead throw	X	X	
Forehand strike	X	X	
Object reception			
Catch	X	X	
Bounce	X	X	
Body Management Skills			
Body awareness			
Directions in space	X		
Body control			
Dynamic balance	X		
Posture			
Lifting/lowering		X	
Physical Fitness Components			
Flexibility			
Hip/trunk flexion	X	X	X
Strength			
Abdominal	X	X	X
Arm/shoulder	X	X	X
Endurance			
Cardio-respiratory	X	X	X

associated with good form or biomechanically correct technique. Quantitative standards refer to performance outcomes such as distance, time, frequency, or accuracy.

Examples of qualitative standards are the following components of a mature throwing pattern which were assessed in this study: (a) side orientation with the weight on the rear leg to initiate the throw, (b) near complete extension of the throwing arm to initiate the throw, (c) weight transfer to the foot opposite the throwing arm, (d) marked hip and spine rotation during throwing motion, (e) follow-through well beyond the ball release and in line with the target, and (f) flowing movement (not mechanical or awkward).

Examples of quantitative standards are the following distance and accuracy requirements listed in the throwing tests for Grades 4 and 7: (a) throw a softball at least 40 ft two out of three times (Grade 4) and (b) throw a softball 40 ft and hit a target 6 ft in diameter placed 1 ft off the ground two out of three times (Grade 7).

The standards judged appropriate for each skill at each grade level were stated in objective form and are included in the Appendix. The panel of experts determined that these standards were the criteria that would operationalize the concept of essential abilities for entering fourth-, seventh-, and tenth-grade students in Michigan. The standards were judged to be appropriate, important, and attainable by at least 75% of the students in Michigan's public schools.

Although the standards were set for Michigan children by Michigan educators, they are not uniquely applicable to Michigan. The qualitative standards, particularly, are generalizable to children living in any state since they are elements of performance that define skilled or unskilled performance. As such, they form the basis for systematic instruction and quantitative performance at a level that is consistent with the innate ability levels of individual children. The quantitative standards represent one state's interpretation of appropriate performance levels and the degree to which those standards should be achieved. When the results of this study are compared with the quantitative standards stated in the Appendix, they provide useful estimates of what may be expected in other states that have delivery systems similar to Michigan's system.

Data Collection

A team of 26 people was recruited from the six geographic areas to be tested. In a 2-day workshop, these people were trained to mastery in administering the test battery. A testing manual (MEAP, 1981a), a training manual (MEAP, 1981c), and training films (MEAP, 1981b) were used in the workshop sessions. The testing manual contained the following information for each test item: (a) statement of the associated performance objective, (b) description of the test item, (c) test equipment and materials needed, (d) testing station diagram, (e) instructions for demonstrating the test, (f) verbal instructions to be given to the students for practice trials, (g) directions for administering the test to students, (h) scoring instructions, and (i) score sheet.

The workshop leaders demonstrated the set-up, administration, and scoring of the complete test battery. Then the workshop attendees formed groups and administered all test items to each other and practiced the scoring of each test item. The workshop leaders critiqued these practice sessions.

The training films were used in conjunction with the training manual. The training manual contained a written description of the performance objectives and the qualitative performance standards. Stick figures also were used to help illustrate key features of the qualitative standards. The films consisted of one slow-motion view and two regular-speed views of performances that met the specified standards, one regular-speed view of a performance that did not meet the standards, and three self-testing views of variable performances at regular speed for each test item. For each skill, a second and third series of three self-testing views at regular speed were available for practice as needed.

In the training sessions the workshop leaders guided the testers through the written materials and the associated films. After the self-testing views were shown and the correct answers were given for each skill, discrepancies in the scoring of each skill were discussed. The additional practice views were used until the raters scored the performances correctly and/or understood their mistakes through subsequent discussion. Then the testers were given a final test with a series of three views of variable performances at regular speed for each test item. The workshop staff compared the obtained ratings to the criterion assessment established by repeated slow-motion analysis of each film clip by a motor development specialist. If the raters scored each skill at 80% accuracy or higher, they were considered competent to administer the tests. If they fell below the 80% accuracy criterion for the rating of any skill, they were retrained and retested. Different films were used for the training sessions, the testing sessions, and the retesting sessions. This procedure resulted in a composite accuracy score (objectivity score), calculated across testers and items, that was slightly over 90%.

At the end of the training session, each tester was given the equipment needed for conducting the tests. Instructions for contacting their assigned schools, making arrangements for the testing sessions, and returning the test results were described in detail in the testing manual. Specifically, the testers received the names of the District Coordinators who had been identified by MEAP personnel after the districts had been randomly selected. The testers then contacted their District Coordinators, who in turn selected and contacted School Coordinators in all of the schools that had been randomly selected. The School Coordinators were instructed to obtain the class lists from which the test administrators would systematically select the students, to reserve the appropriate facilities for testing, and to select teachers or teacher aides to assist the tester. The state provided reimbursement for the cost of any substitute teachers needed for the release of the appropriate teachers to assist in the test administration. The testers and the School Coordinators then scheduled the testing periods within the specified time frame of September 14-October 9. The students were tested in groups of six for ease and accuracy of test administration. After the tests were administered and the score sheets completed, the results were returned for analysis to MEAP, Michigan Department of Education.

RESULTS

The data were gathered in the fall of 1981 and analyzed by MEAP personnel. An interpretive report of these data was written by the Michigan Department of Education (1982b). The established standards represent what the panel of experts would accept as evidence of the achievement of essential skills, thus the results are presented as the percentage of students achieving the standards.

The results cannot be compared directly across grades because the test battery differed by grade level. The students in Grade 10 were tested only on the four physical fitness items. The students in Grades 4 and 7 were tested on the same physical fitness components and fundamental motor skills, but with changes in the qualitative and quantitative standards of each item judged appropriate for their advancing ability. These changes are noted in the standards found in the Appendix. The body management skills which were tested at Grades 4 and 7 differed in order to test appropriate skills. Directions in space and dynamic balance were tested in Grade 4 and the skills of lifting and lowering were tested in Grade 7.

The overall performances of all students were lower at each grade level than the target attainment rate of 75%, but the overall performances of the regular education students were higher than those of the special education students at each grade level. Specifically, the average rates for regular education and special education students, respectively, were 55.1% and 42.1% in Grade 4, 49.2% and 38.7% in Grade 7, and 37.2% and 30.5% in Grade 10.

Grade 4

Of the 16 performance objectives that were tested at Grade 4, the regular education students had attainment rates of 75% or better on only three objectives (Table 2): run (83.6%), skip (90.7%), and directions in space (95.4%). The special education students had attainment rates of 75% or better in only two areas, skip (79%) and

Table 2
Percentage of Grade 4 Students Achieving the Performance Standards

Performance Objective	Regular Education Students	Special Education Students
Fundamental Motor Skills		
Locomotion		
Run	83.6	58.4
Hop	60.1	37.0
Skip	90.7	79.0
Body projection		
Horizontal jump	43.0	35.2
Vertical jump	42.7	19.0
Rhythm		
Even beat	63.8	39.4
Object projection		
Overhead throw	47.4	48.6
Forehand strike	57.7	57.3
Object reception		
Catch	51.1	59.0
Bounce	63.4	50.5
Body Management Skills		
Body awareness		
Directions in space	95.4	75.2
Body control		
Dynamic balance	40.9	18.2
Physical Fitness Components		
Flexibility		
Hip/trunk flexion	64.7	50.5
Strength		
Abdominal	32.2	18.6
Arm/shoulder	38.4	25.7
Endurance		
Cardio-respiratory	7.1	2.3
Overall	55.1	42.1

directions in space (75.2%). Poor attainment rates were recorded by the special education students in the vertical jump (19.0%), balance (18.2%), and sit-ups (18.6%). Both the regular and special education students scored poorly on the endurance test (7.1% and 2.3%, respectively).

Grade 7

Students in the seventh grade had to meet both Grade 4 and Grade 7 standards to be scored as achieving the objective. This included maintaining the qualitative components of the skill where specified, and reaching the quantitative performance standards. Regular education students had attainment rates of 75% or better in only 3 of the 15 objectives tested at Grade 7 (Table 3): the 100-yd run with four turns in 40 s (99.3%), the skip (80.5%), and movement to an even beat (91.1%). The special education students in Grade 7 had no attainment rates of 75% or better. Only the 100-yd run (73.4%) approached this level of attainment. Poor attainment rates were recorded by the special education students in the 100-yd run with one turn (6.8%), vertical jump (12.6%), lifting/lowering (19.4%), endurance (14.7%), sit-ups (20.9%), and push-ups (19.8%). Poor attainment rates were recorded by the regular education students in the 100-yd run with one turn (13.5%), vertical jump (18.3%), and endurance (14.2%).

Grade 10

As shown in Table 4, the students scored the highest attainment rates in the flexibility test: 73.6% for regular education students and 66.9% for special education students. The scores for the three remaining fitness objectives were all below the 40% attainment level, with the scores for abdominal strength being lowest (5.3% for regular education students and 1.6% for special education students).

DISCUSSION

On the basis of the results of this study (less than 75% of the students achieving the stated criterion levels in most objectives tested), the following conclusions seem warranted:

1. Student achievement of selected skills and abilities commonly taught in physical education programs in Michigan does not occur at performance levels judged appropriate by experts for a large number of students classified as regular or special education students.
2. Changes in the delivery of physical education services and/or the performance expectations are needed before physical educators can claim that effective programs are available to the residents of Michigan.
3. Because qualitative elements of skilled performance are readily learned by children, it is often assumed that with exposure to physical education these skills are automatically achieved. The data from our study, obtained on a large sample of children

Table 3
Percentage of Grade 7 Students Achieving the Performance Standards

Performance Objective	Regular Education Students	Special Education Students
Fundamental Motor Skills		
Locomotion		
Run with one turn	13.5	6.8
Run with four turns	99.3	73.4
Hop	42.4	30.7
Skip	80.5	62.8
Body projection		
Horizontal jump	51.1	47.3
Vertical jump	18.3	12.6
Rhythm		
Even beat	91.1	69.1
Object projection		
Overhead throw	49.1	47.0
Forehand strike	31.9	30.9
Object reception		
Catch	69.3	64.3
Bounce	63.5	50.2
Body Management Skills		
Posture		
Lifting/lowering	34.4	19.4
Physical Fitness Components		
Flexibility		
Hip/trunk flexion	62.7	48.6
Strength		
Abdominal	39.2	20.9
Arm/shoulder	27.6	19.8
Endurance		
Cardio-respiratory	14.2	14.7
Overall	49.2	38.7

taught physical education within a delivery system not unlike many other states, indicate that this assumption is not supportable. Accordingly, existing quantitative standards of motor performance may be a significant underestimate of the performance capabilities of children.

A recent survey (83% return) conducted by the Michigan Department of Education (1982a) for the Attorney General's Office

Table 4
Percentage of Grade 10 Students Achieving the Performance Standards

Performance Objective	Regular Education Students	Special Education Students
Physical Fitness Components		
Flexibility		
Hip/trunk flexion	73.6	66.9
Strength		
Abdominal	5.3	1.6
Arm/shoulder	37.5	31.9
Endurance		
Cardio-respiratory	33.4	21.6
Overall	37.2	30.5

identified some interesting facts regarding the implementation of the physical education requirement in Michigan. Physical education is required in 71.4% (ninth grade) to 82.0% (fifth grade) of Grades 1-9. The schools also reported that content was being taught in curricular areas similar to those in which MEAP evaluated the students. The percentages of schools reporting the specified content at the various grade levels in this separate but related study are presented in Table 5. In spite of the fact that the skills reported in Table 5 were taught in most of the schools, low achievement rates were recorded by many schools in these skills.

Table 5
Percentage of Schools Teaching in the Specified Content Areas

Content Area	Grade Levels		
	1-3	4-6	7-9
Fundamental motor skills	79.1	79.3	n.a.
Fundamental movement skills	69.1	75.2	78.2
Body management skills	74.3	78.2	77.0
Physical fitness skills	71.1	80.9	89.8

Other findings from this Michigan Department of Education survey which might have had an adverse effect on the performance of the youngsters tested in this study are as follows:

1. Elementary school students receive very little instruction in the development of physical education skills (an average of 35.9 h/year in Grades 1-3 and an average of 48.7 h/year in Grades 4-6).

2. Less than half of the schools use physical education specialists at the elementary level.
3. Wide variances in program offerings exist, and a great deal of content is taught in a short period of time.
4. Although approximately 70% of the school districts reported having goals and objectives, only 35% use student assessment to evaluate their physical education program.
5. Only 9.8% of the local school districts have a physical education specialist who also is certified in special education of the handicapped.

The performance data obtained in this study and the brief description of the Michigan delivery system for physical education instruction provide a basis for the state, its professional groups, and local school districts to make refinements in their performance expectations and/or their delivery systems. The problem is that when objectives and performance standards are established by politically representative groups such as the State Department of Education, and universities, public schools, special education, the Michigan Association for Health, Physical Education, Recreation, and Dance, it becomes difficult to achieve unanimity. This problem is compounded by the fact that different groups were used to establish the objectives, to determine the appropriate standards, to develop the test battery, and to interpret the results. Each group expressed somewhat different opinions regarding what objectives to select for the test battery, what standards to use, and how to interpret the results. Consensus was achieved, however, and thus the expectations that selected experts held prior to the testing are indicated.

The final decision of whether or not to make modifications in the objectives and/or the instructional delivery system should reside with local school districts. If the objectives tested in this study are taught in the school districts, if the performance standards are accepted as appropriate, and if, nevertheless, the standards are not achieved in sufficient amounts, then the findings of this study suggest that there is a need to modify portions of the K-12 physical education delivery system. For example, on the basis of the poor performance in lifting/lowering (34.4% for regular education and 19.4% for special education students) one would suspect that school districts simply are not teaching the essentials of those skills, because the poor performance cannot be explained as the result of a difficult standard—the weight used was only 25 lb.

If, however, a standard is judged by local educators as inappropriate, then it may be entirely appropriate to alter that standard. When assessing the performances in the mile run for Grade

4, for example, one finds a very low attainment rate for this item (7.1% for regular education and 2.3% for special education students). In addition, an examination of the quantitative standard of 8 min, 30 s, suggests that the standard may have been too difficult to expect 75% of the children to attain it. Standards set too high may also explain the low attainment rates for seventh-grade students in the 100-yd run with one turn and the physical fitness items.

If any objective listed in this study is not valued sufficiently by a local school district to be included in its physical education program, and there is a sound rationale in support of that decision, then poor performance on that test item could be ignored. Furthermore, inclusion of the objective in the test battery should be questioned, with the ultimate decision to alter the test battery or alter the program with respect to the item in question based upon the strength of the rationale supporting the alternative positions. Similarly, if the standards of performance are judged inappropriate by a local school district, the same general process should be followed regarding whether to change the test battery or to change the local program standards.

In sum, the performance levels of Michigan's entering fourth-, seventh-, and tenth-grade regular and special education students on selected skills are well below the levels desired by Michigan educators, despite the fact that schools indicate that they provide instruction in the tested skill areas. Although there is some indication that the performance expectations on some of the skills tested are too high, there appears to be a greater indication that the delivery of physical education services needs to be improved significantly in many of the state's school districts.

REFERENCES

Michigan Department of Education (1981). *Essential performance objectives for physical education in Michigan.* Lansing, MI: State Board of Education.

Michigan Department of Education (1982a). *Current status of physical education in Michigan public schools.* Lansing, MI: State Board of Education.

Michigan Department of Education (1982b). *Physical education interpretive report.* Lansing, MI: State Board of Education.

Michigan Educational Assessment Program (1981a). *Assessment administration manual: Physical education.* Lansing, MI: State Board of Education.

Michigan Educational Assessment Program (1981b). *Physical education training films.* Lansing, MI: State Board of Education.

Michigan Educational Assessment Program (1981c). *Physical education training manual.* Lansing, MI: State Board of Education.

APPENDIX
Qualitative and Quantitative Test Standards

Run—Grade 4

Given a verbal request, a demonstration, and a trial run, the student will run 50 yards with 2 turns in 15 seconds, or less, while completing at least half of the run demonstrating the following performance standards: (a) knee of non-supporting leg bent at least 90° (from side view), (b) consistent period non-support, (c) foot placement near or on line (inside edge of foot touching an imaginary 5″ wide line), (d) heel-toe and/or toe-heel-toe placement (not flat-footed), (e) arms in direct opposition to legs with elbow bent, (f) arms not crossing midline, and (g) flowing movement (not mechanical or awkward).

Run—Grade 7

Given a verbal request, a demonstration, and a trial run, the student will maintain a Grade 4 pattern and run 100 yards demonstrating the following performance standards: (a) 16 seconds (100 yards with 1 turn) and (b) 40 seconds (100 yards with 4 turns).

Hop—Grade 4

Given a verbal request and a demonstration, the student will hop 8 out of 10 times on the right foot, and then on the left foot, in the following manner: (a) carriage of non-support leg near the midline, (b) thrust of non-support leg to the rear on each hop, (c) arms flexed and used primarily for balance, and (d) flowing movement (not mechanical or awkward).

Hop—Grade 7

Given a verbal request and demonstration, the student will maintain the Grade 4 pattern and hop at least 8 out of 10 beats in time to a fast, even beat on the right foot, and then on the left foot.

Skip—Grade 4

Given a verbal request and a demonstration, the student will skip 8 out of 10 times in the following manner: (a) repetition of the step and hop pattern on alternate feet, (b) period of non-support with each step-hop, and (c) flowing movement (not mechanical or awkward).

From Michigan Department of Education (1981). *Essential Performance Objectives for Physical Education in Michigan.* Lansing, MI: State Board of Education.

Skip—Grade 7

Given a verbal request and a demonstration, the student will maintain a Grade 4 pattern and skip 8 out of 10 times to a fast, uneven beat.

Horizontal Jump—Grade 4

Given a verbal request and a demonstration, the student will jump horizontally 2 out of 3 times demonstrating the following performance standards: (a) preparatory movement where arms reach a full extension behind the body at approximately the same time that the knees reach maximum flexion of a 90° angle (±10°), (b) forceful, forward, upward thrust of both arms and a full extension of the legs at takeoff, (c) takeoff angle of 55° (±5°), (d) simultaneous foot contact (at landing) ahead of the body's center of mass (point midway to back, behind navel), (e) thighs near parallel to the floor at touch-down, (f) arms extended forward during the landing, and (g) flowing movement (not mechanical or awkward).

Horizontal Jump—Grade 7

Given a verbal request, a demonstration, and a trial jump, the student will maintain a Grade 4 pattern and jump horizontally 2 out of 3 times, a distance equal to at least 2/3 of his/her standing body height.

Vertical Jump—Grade 4

Given a verbal request and a demonstration, the student will jump vertically 2 out of 3 times in the following manner: (a) preparatory movement with arms reaching to near full extension behind the body at approximately the same time that the knees reach maximum flexion of 90° (±10°), (b) forceful upward thrust of both arms coordinated with full extension of legs at takeoff, (c) balanced landing incorporating a trunk and knee flexion, (d) little horizontal displacement at landing (at least one foot landing within a 2 foot circle drawn around the takeoff spot), and (e) flowing movement (not mechanical or awkward).

Vertical Jump—Grade 7

Given a verbal request, a demonstration, and a trial jump, the student will maintain a Grade 4 pattern and, from a standing position, jump 2 out of 3 times to a height of at least 10″ above the student's maximum reach (measured with feet together, standing on the toes, with one arm extended above the head).

Even Beat—Grade 4

Given a verbal request, a demonstration, and 16 loud, slow, even "drum" beats, the student will demonstrate the ability to walk in time for 8 out of 16 consecutive beats.

Even Beat—Grade 7

Given a verbal request, a demonstration, and 16 loud, moderate tempo, even "drum" beats, the student will demonstrate the ability to walk in time for 8 out of 16 consecutive beats.

Overhand Throw—Grade 4

Given a verbal request and a demonstration, the student will throw a softball at least 40 feet, 2 out of 3 times, while demonstrating the following performance standards: (a) side orientation with the weight on the rear leg to initiate the throw, (b) near complete extension of the throwing arm to initiate the throw, (c) weight transfer to the foot opposite the thowing arm, (d) marked hip and spine rotation during throwing motion, (e) follow-through well beyond the ball release and in line with the target, and (f) flowing movement (not mechanical or awkward).

Overhand Throw—Grade 7

Given a verbal request, a demonstration, and a practice trial, the student will maintain in Grade 4 pattern and throw a softball at least 40 feet, 2 out of 3 times and hit a target 6 feet in diameter, placed 1 foot off the ground.

Forehand Strike—Grade 4

Given a verbal request, a demonstration, a paddle, and a tennis ball, the student will strike the ball 2 out of 3 times, demonstrating the following performance standards: (a) side orientation to direction of travel (side opposite the striking arm is forward), (b) hand behind shoulder prior to strike (preliminary motion), (c) initiation and maintenance of weight transfer to the foot opposite the striking arm, (d) hip and spine rotation during the swing and follow-through, (e) follow-through well beyond the point of contact, and (f) flowing movement (not mechanical or awkward).

Forehand Strike—Grade 7

Given a verbal request, a demonstration, a tennis ball tossed to a point within 10 feet of the student's original position, from at least 30 feet away, the student will move into position on cue from the ball's flight and strike the ball, while maintaining the Grade 4 pattern, propelling it to a target 20 feet wide, 10 feet high, and at least 30 feet away, 2 out of 3 times.

Catch—Grade 4

Given a verbal request, a demonstration, a practice trial, and a softball tossed softly to the student (between head and chest height), from a distance of 20 feet and with an arc of between 6 and 10 feet from the floor, the student will catch the ball 2 out of 3 times while demonstrating the following performance standards: (a) preparatory position with hands in front of the body and elbows flexed and near the sides, (b) arms moving forward to meet the ball, (c) only hands securing the ball, (d) arms retracting to absorb the force of the ball, and (e) flowing movement (not mechanical or awkward).

Catch—Grade 7

Given a verbal request, a demonstration, a practice trial, and a softball thrown between 20 and 30 feet high, from a distance of at least 45 feet to a point within 10 feet of the student's initial position, the student will move into position on cue from the ball's flight path and catch the softball, while maintaining in Grade 4 pattern, 2 out of 3 times.

Ball Bounce—Grade 4

Given a verbal request and a demonstration, the student will bounce an 8-10″ playground ball 10 consecutive bounces without a miss, in 2 out of 3 trials of 15 bounces, with the dominant hand while moving forward at least 20 feet and demonstrating the following performance standards: (a) hand contact with the ball at hip height, (b) ball contact with the fingers (not a slap), (c) ball contact with the floor in front of, or slightly outside of, the foot on the side of the arm bouncing the ball, and (d) flowing movement (not mechanical or awkward).

Ball Bounce—Grade 7

Given a verbal request, a demonstration, and a practice trial, the student will maintain a Grade 4 pattern and bounce a basketball around a specified obstacle course, 2 out of 3 times, while demonstrating the following performance standards: (a) move at moderate speed, (b) maintain control of the ball, and (c) change to outside hand on each turn.

Directions in Space—Grade 4 Only

Given a verbal request and a demonstration of one correct response (e.g., backward), the student will correctly move her/his body or body part 5 out of 6 times, in response to instructions: (a) sideways—left, (b) forward, (c) up, (d) sideways—right, (e) backward, and (f) down.

Given a verbal request, a set of special reference objects, and a demonstration of one correct response (e.g., beside), the student will appropriately position her/his body, 12 out of 14 times, in response to instructions: (a) in front of, (b) away from, (c) between, (d) behind, (e) toward, (f) beside, (g) near, (h) through, (i) over, (j) inside, (k) outside, (l) around, (m) under, and (n) far.

Dynamic Balance—Grade 4 Only

Given a verbal request and a demonstration, the student will walk at least 8 feet on a 1 1/2 inch walking beam (set 3 1/2 to 8 inches off the ground), 2 out of 3 times, while demonstrating the following performance standards: (a) eyes focused on the beam, (b) heel of the leading foot initiating contact with the toes on the trailing foot on each step, (c) arms raised and extended from sides, (d) alternate placement of one foot in front of the other, and (e) flowing movement (not mechanical or awkward).

Lifting and Lowering—Grade 7 Only

Given a verbal request and a demonstration, the student will lift and lower (using both hands) a 25 pound object placed on the floor, 2 out of 3 times, while demonstrating the following performance standards: (a) body positioned close to object throughout the lift/lower, (b) weight evenly distributed between feet, (c) simultaneous extension of the knees and hips, and (d) upper body (head, shoulders, back and hips) in parallel alignment with the lower leg during the lift.

Hip and Trunk Flexibility—Grade 4, 7, and 10

Given a verbal request, a demonstration, correction positioning (sitting on the floor, legs straight and the feet together in full contact with the wall), and a practice trial, the student will maintain a flexed position for at least 5 seconds while demonstrating the following performance standards: (a) legs straight (knees do not bend), and (b) at least one fingertip of each hand maintaining contact with the wall.

Abdominable Strength—Grade 4, 7, and 10

Given a verbal request and a demonstration with correct position (knees bent at 90°, feet flat on the floor), the student will perform sit-ups at the criterion level appropriate for the grade in the following manner: (a) arms folded across chest, (b) sit-up initiated by tucking chin and lifting trunk, (c) sit-up completed by having the mid to upper back perpendicular to floor, and (d) upper body lowered in a controlled return of the shoulder blades to the mat.

Grade	*Criterion Level* Number of sit-ups	Minutes
4	30	1
7	50	2
10	70	2

Shoulder Strength and Endurance—Grade 4, 7 and 10

Given a verbal request and a demonstration, the student will demonstrate the ability to perform a static push-up at the criterion level appropriate for the grade in the following manner: (a) prone position assumed parallel to the floor, hands directly under the shoulders, fingers pointed forward and toes tucked with feet together and (b) body lowered until elbows are flexed to 90° (±5°) and the position maintained.

Grade	Criterion level
4	15 seconds
7	30 seconds
10	45 seconds

Cardio-Respiratory Endurance—Grade 4, 7, and 10

Given a verbal request and an explanation of the task, the student will run the appropriate course at the criterion level specified below:

Grade	Distance	Time
4	1 mile (1760 yards)	8 min., 30 sec.
7	1 1/4 miles (2200 yards)	10 min., 15 sec.
10	1 1/2 miles (2640 yards)	12 min., 0 sec.

13

Examining Differentiation in Motor Proficiency Through Exploratory and Confirmatory Factor Analysis

GEOFFREY D. BROADHEAD
Louisiana State University, Baton Rouge

GEOFFREY M. MARUYAMA AND ROBERT H. BRUININKS
University of Minnesota, Minneapolis

Differentiation of motor proficiency through childhood was examined by exploratory and confirmatory factor analysis techniques. Data (N = 863) obtained during the standardization of the 14-item Short Form of the Bruininks-Oseretsky test were divided by sex and into four age groups (4–16 years). Exploratory factor analysis techniques showed that the matrices were nonsingular and therefore amenable to confirmatory factor analysis. The results suggested differentiation with age, because the first factor accounted for almost 40% of the variance for the youngest samples, but only 20% for the older groups. Subsequently, confirmatory factor analyses were used to fit the data on an a priori factor structure which viewed each of the eight subtests as conceptually distinct but correlated. The conclusions of the exploratory analyses were supported. For each of the younger samples, items within the eight subtests were consistent with one another, and each subtest was significantly correlated with all the other subtests. For older children, many of the correlations between subtests were nonsignificant, and items within subtests often were not consistent with one another. These findings point to greater differentiation between and within subtests for these subjects.

The structure and nature of motor abilities in children and young adults has been of interest to motor development researchers for many years. From the factor analytic work of Cumbee (1954), Larson (1941), Hempel and Fleishman (1955), and Rarick (1937), gross motor abilities were described using terms such as agility, balance, endurance, flexibility, speed, and strength. Other studies by Carpenter (1941), Clausen (1966), Fleishman and Ellison (1962), and Vandenburg (1964) have described fine motor abilities with terms

Partial support was provided by a Spencer Foundation Fellowship to Dr. Maruyama from the National Academy of Education.

such as control precision, hand-eye coordination, manual dexterity, and speed of response. Based upon these and other studies, one might well assume that an accurate picture of the development of gross and fine motor proficiency has accumulated. Unfortunately, however, such is not the case, because studies vary on a number of dimensions that make cross-study conclusions difficult. For example, there are marked differences between studies in age and intellectual functioning of the samples; the studies have sampled children from across the whole school age range and from different levels of intellectual functioning. Furthermore, different studies have employed tasks that vary both in the number and range of measures and in complexity. Hence it is not yet possible to describe a clear, logical developmental pattern of motor abilities for any well-defined group.

In studying motor proficiency, one must certainly take into account individual differences, because a limit to understanding the nature of motor abilities is the complex array of variables that affect them. Motor proficiency is affected by genetic factors, by factors of the social-cultural matrix, by growth and maturation, by body size and composition, and by the chance to be physically active in formal and informal settings. Thus, individual variability must necessarily be large. Nevertheless, based upon prior research and theory, it seems that there ought to be definite developmental patterns to psychomotor skills that would appear despite individual differences, and that would account for appreciable variability in motor proficiency.

In summarizing many of his own studies in which a number of influences were examined, Fleishman (1964) reported the existence of 11 fine and 9 gross motor abilities in young adult samples. Fleishman viewed these abilities as separating during infancy from verbal abilities, with new motor abilities emerging with age. Some of them, like flexibility or strength, become branched or differentiated into several subabilities (see also Cratty, 1979; Rarick & Dobbins, 1972). Even collectively, however, these disparate studies and ideas cannot be interpreted as establishing the existence of motor ability differentiation, for no single study demonstrates differentiation across the childhood years.

If age differences in the structure of motor abilities are shown to exist, it seems likely that they are accounted for at least partially through developmental changes. But few studies have examined with the same motor tasks more than a single chronological age group. Studies with normal children (Broadhead & Bruininks, 1983b; Peterson, Reuschlein, & Seefeldt, 1974) and with handicapped children (Broadhead, 1975; Rarick, 1968; Rarick & Dobbins, 1972;

Rarick & McQuillan, 1977) described quite similar findings when comparing the structure of motor abilities of two and three, usually collapsed, age groups. Thus, even the stages of development of motor abilities through childhood are only partially understood.

Using data from the Short Form of the Bruininks-Oseretsky Test of Motor Proficiency (Bruininks, 1978), Broadhead and Bruininks (1983a) examined the consistency of a factor structure across 10 age groups of boys and girls, aged 4 1/2-14 1/2 years. In that study the particular factor analytic methodology of Rarick and Dobbins (1972) and the strategy for interpreting the results in terms of comparable common and specific factors (Harris & Harris, 1971) were followed. Although overall the number of factors extracted was between four and six, the higher number of specific rather than common factors for the older age groups was thought to point to increased differentiation in the structure of motor abilities with age.

USE OF EXPLORATORY VERSUS CONFIRMATORY FACTOR ANALYSIS

Without exception, though to varying degrees, the previously cited factor studies used what have been called exploratory analytic methods to examine the interrelationships among variables. As will be explained more fully later, commonly used factor analytic techniques should be called exploratory factor analysis, because they are not able to control the nature of the factors that emerge. Thus, they cannot directly compare solutions across different populations. The most theoretical approach seems to be that used by Rarick and Dobbins (1972) and Rarick and McQuillan (1977), who attempted to blend exploration with hypothesis testing by selecting variables according to a preconceived comprehensive framework of motor ability structure. Nevertheless, this work also used exploratory factor analysis techniques, which preclude direct testing of hypotheses about factor structure.

There are three basic problems with exploratory factor analysis techniques.[1] First, and most fundamental, is that a researcher cannot specify the variables that load on each factor, because exploratory factor analysis extracts the largest sources of common variance, whatever those sources might be (e.g., the largest source of common variance could be a response set of subjects). It is therefore highly unlikely that the solution would display the factor structure that the researcher designed, even if that structure was in fact as plausible as the obtained solution. Second, the solution obtained from

[1]The discussion of exploratory and confirmatory factor analysis is intended to provide only a rudimentary introduction. Further readings might include Kenny (1979) or Mulaik (1975).

exploratory factor analysis is only one of an infinite number of "best solutions" (i.e., solutions that recreate the observed data as well as possible); exploratory factor analysis does not yield a unique best solution. (The issue of rotation becomes important to mention, because rotation changes from one solution to another that is mathematically equivalent). Thus, failure to find a hypothesized factor structure in general does not disprove the plausibility of that structure. Third, as it is commonly used, exploratory factor analysis presents orthogonal (uncorrelated) rather than oblique (correlated) factors. When a researcher believes the factors that underlie the measures are conceptually distinct but related, orthogonal factor analysis is inappropriate. Unfortunately, oblique exploratory factor analysis is also not advisable to use, because only when there is a unique solution (which, as already noted, is not true to exploratory factor analysis) is it possible to estimate factor loadings and factor correlations independently of one another.[2]

To summarize, although exploratory techniques have helped develop hypotheses about the factor structure of motor abilities, those techniques are not designed for testing theoretical conceptualizations about underlying factor structures, because researchers cannot control the solution that emerges. The solution obtained is one of an infinite number of possible solutions, each of which is empirically nondistinguishable from the others with respect to the observed data. Therefore, given that it is unlikely that exploratory factor analysis techniques would yield a hypothesized factor structure for any single population, it is clearly not the methodology to use to test for consistency and change in a hypothesized factor structure across age groups. Exploratory factor analysis techniques should be used only to provide information about plausible structures which can be used to develop hypotheses, which can later be supported or disproved using other methodologies. The type of methodology to be used to accomplish this latter task is one that empirically restricts the relationship among the variables.

The appropriate methodology to use is called confirmatory factor analysis. This blends hypothesis testing with the logic of factors analysis, and avoids all three of the problems with exploratory techniques, provided certain restrictions are followed. These restrictions require specifying a priori a number of relations to be fixed, most commonly to zero, which allows a unique solution to be obtained. By imposing restrictions drawn from theoretical considerations, the researcher should be estimating only the

[2]To illustrate, imagine that you know that $A \times B \times C = 0.6$. Given this, B could take on an infinite number of values as long as A and C were changed so that the product of the three remains 0.6. Said differently, there is no unique solution for B.

parameters that are substantively interesting. That is, plausibility of a hypothesized factor structure is assessed by a priori selecting a number of factors, determining which measures are related to each factor and which factors are interrelated with other factors, and specifying any residual covariation (relations among uniqueness, due to things like common method variance). Parameters of no substantive interest (i.e., that are not theoretically predicted) are not estimated, but are set at zero. Because the solution is unique, confidence intervals can be calculated for each parameter that is estimated; thus, the significance of all factor loadings, relations among factors, and residuals (uniqueness) can be estimated. The overall fit of the model to the data is assessed by a chi-square goodness-of-fit test, with a nonsignificant chi-square statistic indicating that the model adequately fits observed data.

In summary, confirmatory factor analysis avoids many of the problems that make exploratory factor analysis inappropriate for testing theory. Because a researcher can test plausibility of a hypothesized factor structure through confirmatory factor analysis, that approach is the one that should be used in examining whether motor proficiency does become more differentiated with increasing age.[3] Furthermore, it can be used to examine whether a hypothesized factor structure is reasonable for any age group.

The purpose, then, of this study is to examine a hypothesized structure of motor abilities across several age groups, using confirmatory factor analysis techniques (Joreskog & Sorbom, 1978). The data analyzed are those collected while developing the Bruininks-Oseretsky Test of Motor Proficiency (Bruininks, 1978).

METHOD

Subjects

Subjects were 863 nonhandicapped children between the ages of 3 1/2 and 16. They were divided into four groups each of boys and girls, based upon their ages. The age groups were (a) 3 1/2–6 1/2, (b) older than 6 1/2 but not older than 9, (c) older than 9 but not older than 11 1/2, and (d) older than 11 1/2 but not older than 16. For boys, the respective sample sizes were 103, 111, 111, and 107; for girls they were 99, 103, 117, and 112. (We went beyond the original

[3]The best test of the differentiation hypothesis would involve repeatedly testing a sample of children at different ages. Such an approach would avoid potential problems linked to individual differences. In this instance, however, we do not believe that the results of such testing would diverge appreciably from the present design, which compares children of different ages tested at a single point in time. It is difficult to imagine how any "cohort" explanation could account for differentiation with age or that subject selection biases would lead to problems.

standardization sample—ages between 4 1/2 and 14 1/2—to keep sample sizes around 100 for each subsample.)

Data Analysis

Initially, principal factors exploratory factor analytic techniques with iterations were used to analyze the raw score responses from the 14-item, eight-subtest, Short Form Bruininks-Oseretsky test (Table 1). These analyses were conducted to ensure that the matrices were nonsingular and therefore amenable to confirmatory factor analysis, and to provide an initial look at the differentiation of factor structure of boys and girls for the four age groups. This initial look was assessed by the size of the first factor's eigenvalue and the number of factors with eigenvalues greater than 1.0.

Table 1
Motor Proficiency Subtests and Short Form Items

Subtest 1.	Running Speed and Agility
Item a.	Running speed and agility
Subtest 2.	Balance
Item a.	Standing on preferred leg on balance beam
Item b.	Walking forward heel-to-toe on balance beam
Subtest 3.	Bilateral Coordination
Item a.	Tapping feet alternately while making circles with fingers
Item b.	Jumping up and clapping hands
Subtest 4.	Strength
Item a.	Standing broad jump
Subtest 5.	Upper-limb Coordination
Item a.	Catching a tossed ball with both hands
Item b.	Throwing a ball at a target with preferred hand
Subtest 6.	Response Speed
Item a.	Response speed
Subtest 7.	Visual-motor Control
Item a.	Drawing a line through a straight path with preferred hand
Item b.	Copying a circle with preferred hand
Item c.	Copying overlapping pencils with preferred hand
Subtest 8.	Upper-limb Speed and Dexterity
Item a.	Sorting shape cards with preferred hand
Item b.	Making dots in circles with preferred hand

Subsequently, the confirmatory factor analyses (using the computer program LISREL, Joreskog & Sorbom, 1978) fitted the data to an a priori factor structure which viewed each of the eight subtests of the Bruininks-Oseretsky test as conceptually distinct. By the confirmatory approach, each of the eight factors was defined by the items from a single subtest (Figure 1).

Figure 1. Illustration of an a priori factor structure for the Short Form Bruininks-Oseretsky test.

		Factor							
Subtest	*Item*	*1*	*2*	*3*	*4*	*5*	*6*	*7*	*8*
1	1	1.0	0	0	0	0	0	0	0
2	2	0	λ_1	0	0	0	0	0	0
2	7	0	λ_2	0	0	0	0	0	0
3	1	0	0	λ_3	0	0	0	0	0
3	6	0	0	λ_4	0	0	0	0	0
4	1	0	0	0	1.0	0	0	0	0
5	3	0	0	0	0	λ_5	0	0	0
5	5	0	0	0	0	λ_6	0	0	0
6	1	0	0	0	0	0	1.0	0	0
7	3	0	0	0	0	0	0	λ_7	0
7	5	0	0	0	0	0	0	λ_8	0
7	8	0	0	0	0	0	0	λ_9	0
8	3	0	0	0	0	0	0	0	λ_{10}
8	7	0	0	0	0	0	0	0	λ_{11}

Figure 1 displays the factor pattern matrix for the hypothesized factor structure. Note that there are eight factors, each corresponding to a subtest. The nonzero entries in the factor pattern matrix (ones and lambdas) represent the relations of measures with factors. For those three factors that have only a single measure, the factor was defined as equal to the measure, thus the loadings of 1.0. For the other five factors, each factor was defined by a weighted combination of the measures. The weights can be thought of as reliabilities on each common factor. Note that this method of estimation defines factors consistent with theoretical predictions. That is, factors and subtests have a one-to-one correspondence. For a fuller description of how to use the methodology of the confirmatory factor analysis, see Maruyama and McGarvey (1980) or Kenny (1979).

RESULTS

The findings of the exploratory factor analyses indicated that the confirmatory analyses were possible and also were consistent with the notion of increased differentiation with age. As can be seen from Table 2, the first unrotated factor accounted for approximately 40% of the variance for the youngest samples of boys and girls, but only 20%

Table 2
Factor Analysis, Principal Factors with Iterations (and Commonality Estimates on Diagonal) Loadings on First Unrotated Factor

		Age							
		3½ ≤ 6½		>6½ ≤ 9		>9 ≤ 11½		>11½ ≤ 16	
Subtest	Item	Boys	Girls	Boys	Girls	Boys	Girls	Boys	Girls
1	1	-.67	-.79	-.63	-.65	-.58	-.58	-.52	-.63
2	2	.64	.55	.25	.38	.48	.53	.41	.02
2	7	.73	.67	.47	.29	.35	.52	.14	.33
3	1	.41	.29	.24	.33	.26	.11	.06	.27
3	6	.59	.55	.63	.45	.30	.46	.43	.58
4	1	.73	.83	.71	.54	.69	.43	.68	.65
5	3	.57	.52	.50	.53	.25	.23	.08	.27
5	5	.51	.36	.52	.29	.37	.18	.37	.37
6	1	.57	.55	.45	.38	.35	.39	.31	.46
7	3	-.58	-.67	-.46	-.46	-.20	-.12	.02	-.12
7	5	.47	.48	.23	-.08	.01	.07	.29	.02
7	8	.41	.37	.49	.41	.03	.29	.16	.18
8	3	.57	.64	.63	.53	.57	.44	.76	.42
8	7	.65	.81	.61	.57	.55	.33	.59	.46
Eigenvalue		5.35	5.55	3.34	4.23	2.83	2.54	2.80	2.71
% variance accounted for		38.2	39.6	23.9	30.2	20.2	18.2	20.2	19.4
N		103	99	103	111	111	117	107	112
Determinant		.007	.004	.037	.074	.147	.218	.095	.162
No. of factors with eigenvalue > 1		3	3	3	4	6	5	5	6

for the older groups. Furthermore, the loadings of measures on the first unrotated factor were all substantial for the youngest samples, but were much less so for the older samples. Note also that the number of factors with eigenvalues greater than 1.0 increased with age, as did the value of the determinant (which provides information about how highly interrelated the elements of the correlation matrix are). All of these types of information argue for increased differentiation with age.

The factor structure yielded by the confirmatory factor analyses appears in Table 3. The non-1.0 values are estimates of the lambdas shown in Figure 1. The 1.0 loadings appear for subtests having a single measure (Subtests 1, 4, and 6). Because those three factors are measured only by a single item, internal consistency for those scales cannot be assessed. For the other five subtests, the values in Table 3 can be thought of as reliabilities of items (for their common factor). Thus, Table 3 provides further information suggestive of differentiation of factor structure, because the number of nonsignificant loadings increased markedly. Note, for example, that for the oldest age group, only Subtest 8 displayed internal consistency (i.e., had significant loadings for both items) for both boys and girls. Thus, there appears to be substantial differentiation within subtests.

Table 4 displays all significant correlations between subtests for each of the eight samples. These correlations, which came from the confirmatory factor analysis solutions, provide further evidence that there is differentiation across subtests. For the youngest age group, every correlation between two subtests was significant, whereas for the older samples substantial numbers of correlations were nonsignificant. Although the data seem consistent with other findings, there were problems in fitting the data to the a priori factor structure. Those problems, which occurred for subtests on which there were no significant factor loadings, resulted in a number of "out of range" estimates (e.g., correlations greater than 1.0). This finding is not surprising; if a factor is not well defined, it could hardly be expected to show predicted and consistent relations with other factors. Furthermore, none of these "out of range" estimates was significant.

Given the obvious discrepancies in findings across populations, we did not attempt to proceed further by simultaneously estimating factor structures across populations and comparing covariance structures directly. In addition, we did not focus on covariances, which would yield coefficients that could be directly compared across populations (which correlations could not). Because the solutions for the different age groups are so obviously discrepant, testing equivalence of coefficients would not add appreciably to the present findings.

Table 3
Confirmatory Factor Pattern Matrices From Factor Analyses of Sex and Age Groups: Each Subtest Set Up as a Separate Factor

		Age							
		3½ ≤ 6½		>6½ ≤ 9		>9 ≤ 11½		>11½ ≤ 16	
Subtest	Item	Boys	Girls	Boys	Girls	Boys	Girls	Boys	Girls
1	1[a]	1.0	1.0	1.0	1.0	1.0	1.0	1.0	1.0
2	2	.69*	.65*	.35*	.58*	.76*	.77*	.86*	.21
2	7	.87*	.81*	.95*	.42*	.45*	.55*	.12	.76*
3	1	.43*	.31*	.27*	.48*	.32*	.16	.06	.36*
3	6	.76*	.86*	.69*	.59*	.71*	.53	3.17	.76*
4	1[a]	1.0	1.0	1.0	1.0	1.0	1.0	1.0	1.0
5	3	.66*	.71*	.58*	.61*	.29*	.05	.02	.38*
5	5	.62*	.50*	.61*	.24*	.58*	.03	.07	.85*
6	1[a]	1.0	1.0	1.0	1.0	1.0	1.0	1.0	1.0
7	3	-.65*	-.82*	-.43*	-.22	.07	-.15	.08	.01
7	5	.61*	.57*	.27*	-.13	.02	.10	.79*	.06
7	8	.42*	.39*	.50*	.22	.00	.55	.32*	3.32
8	3	.63*	.66*	.68*	.53*	.61*	.50*	.70*	.71*
8	7	.70*	.85*	.65*	.70*	.54*	.35*	.67*	.51*
n		103	99	103	111	111	117	107	112
Goodness of fit $\chi^2(55)$		62.86	53.05	57.96	71.72	41.90	49.73	69.37	40.79

Note. χ^2 All are nonsignificant.
[a] Loading fixed to 1.0.
*$p < .05$.

Table 4
Correlations of Subtests (Factors) From Confirmatory Factor Analyses, Significant ($p < .05$) Coefficients Only

Correlation of Subtests	Age: 3½ < 6½ Boys	3½ < 6½ Girls	>6½ ≤ 9 Boys	>6½ ≤ 9 Girls	>9 ≤ 11½ Boys	>9 ≤ 11½ Girls	>11½ ≤ 16 Boys	>11½ ≤ 16 Girls
1 w/ 2	-54	-60	—	—	—	-31	—	—
1 w/ 3	-52	-59	-68	-42	—	—	—	-29
1 w/ 4	-64	-68	-56	-55	-47	-39	-47	-51
1 w/ 5	-54	-65	-59	-67	—	—	—	-41
1 w/ 6	-38	-45	-27	-28	—	—	—	-28
1 w/ 7	-41	-58	-53	—	—	—	—	—
1 w/ 8	-69	-79	-50	-42	-44	-45	-43	-32
2 w/ 3	73	50	42	71	—	—	—	—
2 w/ 4	57	74	34	32	44	—	—	—
2 w/ 5	63	52	50	—	—	—	—	—
2 w/ 6	51	41	26	36	—	27	—	—
2 w/ 7	78	65	—	—	—	—	—	—
2 w/ 8	67	79	45	42	56	50	—	—
3 w/ 4	59	57	60	—	31	—	—	35
3 w/ 5	56	56	72	59	—	—	—	—
3 w/ 6	55	38	35	—	—	—	—	34
3 w/ 7	38	43	88	—	—	—	—	—
3 w/ 8	73	60	81	56	46	—	—	—
4 w/ 5	64	55	55	43	41	—	—	—
4 w/ 6	36	46	28	27	24	19	20	31
4 w/ 7	59	67	64	—	—	—	—	—
4 w/ 8	67	80	66	32	65	44	61	42
5 w/ 6	55	51	30	37	—	—	—	—
5 w/ 7	70	42	86	—	—	—	—	—
5 w/ 8	77	65	74	85	76	—	—	—
6 w/ 7	48	58	52	—	—	—	—	—
6 w/ 8	51	46	50	31	46	48	36	32
7 w/ 8	83	85	92	—	—	—	—	—

Note. Leading decimals on correlations were omitted.

DISCUSSION

Given the changes in factor structure across age groups, it seems clear that the factor structure of motor abilities shows increased differentiation as children develop. This differentiation occurs both within and across subtests of the Bruininks-Oseretsky test. Although in this study there were many instances in which the items defining various subtests did not define single dimensions, it remains to be determined whether this finding would be repeated for other batteries of test items. Thus, it seems reasonable to proceed further by examining in more detail the nature of the factors involved in motor development. Such analyses would require a more elaborate set of measures of motor skills than were available in the present study.

It should be remembered that we used cross-sectional data in this study; longitudinal data would provide greater insights into the questions of differentiation of motor abilities with time. However, the use of these conceptual and statistical techniques to examine motor proficiency as a function of the sex or level of intellect of the subjects, as well as of age, seems appropriate.

REFERENCES

Broadhead, G.D. (1975). Factors of gross motor performance in special education. *Journal of Biosocial Science, 7,* 57–65.

Broadhead, G.D., & Bruininks, R.H. (1983a). Development of motor proficiency factors through childhood. *Physical Educator, 40,* 16–19.

Broadhead, G.D., & Bruininks, R.H. (1983b). Factor structure consistency in the Bruininks-Oseretsky test—Short Form. *Rehabilitation Literature, 44,* 13–18.

Bruininks, R.H. (1978). *The Bruininks-Oseretsky Test of Motor Proficiency, Examiner's Manual.* Circle Pines, MN: American Guidance Service.

Carpenter, A. (1941). An analysis of the relationships of the factors of velocity, strength, and dead weight to athletic performance. *Research Quarterly, 12,* 34–39.

Clausen, J. (1966). *Ability structure and subgroups in mental retardation.* Washington, DC: Spartan Books.

Cratty, B.J. (1979). *Perceptual and motor development in infants and young children.* Englewood Cliffs, NJ: Prentice-Hall.

Cumbee, F.Z. (1954). A factorial analysis of motor coordination. *Research Quarterly, 25,* 412–428.

Fleishman, E.A. (1964). *The structure and measurement of physical fitness.* Englewood Cliffs, NJ: Prentice-Hall.

Fleishman, E.A., & Ellison, G.D. (1962). A factor analysis of fine manipulative performance. *Journal of Applied Psychology, 46,* 96–105.

Harris, M.L., & Harris, C.W. (1971). A factors analytic interpretation strategy. *Educational and Psychological Measurement, 31,* 589–606.

Hempel, W.E., Jr., & Fleishman, E.A. (1955). A factor analysis of physical proficiency and manipulative skill. *Journal of Applied Psychology, 39,* 12–16.

Joreskog, K.G., & Sorbom. D. (1978). *LISREL IV: Estimation of linear structural equation systems by maximum likelihood methods.* Chicago: National Educational Resources.

Kenny, D.A. (1979). *Correlation and causality.* New York: Wiley & Sons.

Larson, L.A. (1941). A factor analysis of motor ability variables and tests for college men. *Research Quarterly, 12,* 499–517.

Maruyama, G., & McGarvey, B. (1980). Evaluating causal models: An application of maximum-likelihood analysis of structural equations. *Psychological Bulletin, 87,* 502–512.

Mulaik, S. (1975). Confirmatory factor analysis. In D.J. Amick & H.J. Walberg (Eds.), *Introductory multivariate analysis* (pp. 170-207). Berkeley, CA: McCutchan.

Peterson, K.L., Reuschlein, P.L., & Seefeldt, V. (1974). *Factor analyses of motor performance of kindergarten, first and second grade children: A tentative solution.* East Lansing: Michigan State University, Department of Physical Education.

Rarick, G.L. (1937). An analysis of the speed factor in simple athletic activities. *Research Quarterly, 8,* 89-105.

Rarick, G.L. (1968). The factor structure of motor abilities of educable mentally retarded children. In G.A. Jervis (Ed.), *Expanding concepts in mental retardation.* (pp. 238-246) Springfield, IL: Thomas.

Rarick, G.L., & Dobbins, D.A. (1972). *Basic components in the motor performance of educable mentally retarded children: Implications for curriculum development* (Report to the United States Office of Education). Berkeley: University of California, Department of Physical Education.

Rarick, G.L., & McQuillan, J.P. (1977). *The factor structure of motor abilities of trainable mentally retarded children: Implications for curriculum development* (Report to the United States Office of Education). Berkeley: University of California, Department of Physical Education.

Vandenburg, S.G. (1964). Factor analytic study of the Lincoln-Oseretsky test of motor proficiency. *Perceptual and Motor Skills, 19*, 23-41.

14-17

Reviews of Research Presented at the 16th Gatlinburg Conference on Mental Retardation and Developmental Disabilities

14

Motor Skill Acquisition and Mental Retardation: Overview of Traditional and Current Orientations

K.M. NEWELL
University of Illinois, Urbana-Champaign

This paper overviews the major contributions and limitations of the physical fitness and information-processing orientations to the study of skill acquisition in mentally retarded persons. The strengths and weaknesses of these two orientations are in some respects complementary. An operational framework distinguishing between coordination, control, and skill is briefly outlined as a functional basis to promote links between the concepts of intelligence, cognition, and action.

The study of the motor skills of mentally retarded persons has generated only sporadic scholarly interest over the years. This is hardly surprising given that the motor skill acquisition area itself is a relatively minor area within experimental psychology and, on a more general note, that inquiry into the behavior of subpopulation groups tends to lag behind developments in the respective theoretical areas of psychology. It is as if many elements of psychology are pursued independently of people and real phenomena, to the extent that the recent revitalization of these concerns has, ironically, required the introduction of the label "ecological psychology."

This paper provides an overview of the primary approaches that have been taken in the study of skill acquisition in mentally retarded persons. The major contributions and limitations of each orientation are examined to provide a springboard for the ensuing discussion of the significance of the study of actions rather than isolated movements. Subsequently, the distinction between the three concepts of coordination, control, and skill is made as a precursor of a functional orientation for understanding constraints to the acquisition of skill in the mentally retarded. It is anticipated that this functional framework will provide a better basis upon which to

This work was supported in part by the National Science Foundation Award DAR 80-16287. Peter A. Hancock provided helpful comments on an earlier version of the manuscript.

promote links between the concepts of intelligence, cognition, and action.

TRADITIONAL ORIENTATIONS

There have been two principal orientations to the study of movement skills in the mentally retarded: what I call here a physical fitness approach and an information-processing approach. These have to some degree followed theoretical frameworks adopted in the motor development and skill acquisition domains, respectively. These orientations are not mutually exclusive but hold sufficient distinction to be characterized as an identifiable body of literature, with prescribed tasks and observational tactics.

Physical Fitness Approach

The traditional issue in the physical fitness approach has been the categorization of physical parameters associated with movement that may distinguish between individuals who have been characterized as mentally retarded and those not so designated. This examination of physical parameters is appealing because the construct validity of the measures holds intuitive appeal (i.e., face validity), thus providing a readily acceptable approach to the description of the motor performance of mentally retarded individuals. The individual subject parameters recorded in this orientation often include height, weight, strength, and body composition measures. Furthermore, performance outcome scores are traditionally obtained on such fundamental motor skills as running, jumping, and throwing. In these skills, optimal performance is reflected by the maximization of a physical parameter (e.g., distance thrown). Bruininks (1974) and Rarick (1973) synthesized the findings of studies indicating that mentally retarded children and adults usually score lower on these performance tasks than their nonretarded peers and tend to have poorer physiques than is average for their respective ages.

The physical parameters of the organism from a variety of levels of analysis do constrain the movements which individuals may generate in support of action (Newell, 1984). However, the studies conducted under the physical fitness banner have not focused on the concepts of either action or cognition and, in effect, have left the physical parameters as mere descriptors of subpopulations and their motor performance.

The theoretical framework most often alluded to in the physical fitness orientation to the motor performance differences between mentally and nonmentally retarded persons (e.g., Rarick, 1973) is the ability concept (Fleishman & Bartlett, 1969). This approach is consonant with general orientations to the construct of intelligence. However, in terms of motor performance, the ability concept has proved to be no more than an alternate performance description at the same level of analysis as outcome scores. In addition, outside of the contribution to individual differences, the ability framework fails to even attempt to provide a basis for studying the *acquisition* of skill in mentally retarded persons.

In summary, the physical fitness orientation has made relatively little contribution to our understanding of mental retardation and the impact of retardation on cognition and action. One obvious limitation is that the mentally retarded are generally less active than nonretarded individuals, and this alone contributes to many of the performance differences typically reported in studies with a physical fitness orientation to motor skill acquisition and mental retardation. Thus, the legacy of this approach is the quantitative assessment of observable physical parameters of mentally retarded individuals and their performance on what are considered to be primarily phylogenetic skills.

Information-Processing Approach

In sharp contrast to the physical fitness approach to the study of motor skills in the mentally retarded is the information-processing approach. This orientation has followed the traditional information-processing framework of experimental psychology (e.g., Broadbent, 1965) and its subsequent developments in an attempt to understand where in the information-processing continuum, from stimulus input to response output, resides the source of limitation(s) to the motor performance of mentally retarded persons. A common experimental technique in this orientation is the use of a pressure time measure, such as reaction time (RT), to index the time course of information transmission in the organism and the complexity of various so-called mental operations (transformations) that are presumed to occur. Baumeister and Kellas (1968) provided an early synthesis of the studies that support the general finding that the RT of retarded persons is consistently slower and more variable than the RT of their peer nonretarded group.

This early work on RT was rather global and, in effect, a necessary preliminary in the approach to an understanding of the parameters that provide limitations to the information processing of mentally retarded persons. Recently, a number of RT investigations have attempted to establish more directly the relative contribution of various mental operations to the RT difference in mentally retarded and nonretarded persons. Nettelbeck and colleagues (e.g., Nettelbeck, 1979; Nettelbeck & Brewer, 1981) have focused on stimulus input and stimulus-response operations; Wade, Newell, and colleagues (e.g., Newell, Wade, & Kelly, 1979; Wade, Newell, & Wallace, 1978) have examined response output parameters and their influence on the time to organize response initiation. A review of these complementary approaches may be found in Wade, Hoover, and Newell (in press). In general, performance decrements in mentally retarded persons are observed in all designated stages of information transmission, which reflects the notion that the information-processing approach has, in effect, been no more than another description of mentally retarded persons' motor performance. This is despite claims to the contrary in terms of the theoretical motivation for the shift to the information-processing approach and post hoc claims on the basis of specific empirical findings from experiments.

The information-processing framework has been the guiding theoretical backdrop either explicitly or implicitly for much of the research on the motor performance of retarded persons during the last decade, as indeed it has been to the motor-learning domain in general (Newell, 1981). As such, the work conducted under this banner is open to the general criticisms that have been advanced about the information-processing framework per se (e.g., Neisser, 1976). In addition, and of more specific concern to the consideration of skill acquisition in the mentally retarded, is the realization that a very small range of motor skills have been utilized for analysis (often a key press or a simple unidimensional movement) and that problems of learning have been eliminated by the motor performance orientation.

This latter trend exists despite the demonstration by training studies that retarded persons may reduce RT (e.g., Hoover, Wade, & Newell, 1981) and improve performance on a number of different motor tasks (Wade & Gold, 1978). In some instances these performance capabilities can extend within the bounds of the normative performance of their nonretarded peers. Indeed, the findings from training studies undermine some of the strong structural interpretations of performance differences often promoted by information-processing considerations and biological interpretations of the IQ relationship to RT (e.g., Jensen, 1980; Jensen & Munro, 1979). Broader arguments for the significance of recent training studies for both theoretical and practical consideration of the acquisition of motor skills in the mentally retarded are outlined in Wade et al. (in press).

Summary

The rather brief outline I have given of the physical fitness and information-processing orientations should be adequate to document the major contributions and limitations provided by each of these approaches to understanding the sources of constraint to the motor skill acquisition of the mentally retarded. Of more importance, however, is the realization that the strengths and weaknesses of these two orientations are in some respects complementary. The physical fitness approach has focused on ecologically relevant skills but from a position divorced of a guiding theoretical framework. In contrast, the information-processing framework has provided a machinelike theoretical backdrop to examine the performance limitations of mentally retarded persons on isolated movements devoid of an ecologically relevant contextual setting. Some degree of complementarity is perhaps inevitable, given the fact that many researchers adopted the information-processing framework because it appeared to go beyond mere description of motor performance and the legacy of the physical fitness orientation.

Both orientations have failed to develop any theoretical framework to the *acquisition* of motor skills by individuals designated as mentally retarded. This criticism applies to both the development of our understanding of the process of motor learning per se and the development of insights into the strategies instructors might employ to facilitate the rate of learning and the ultimate level of performance generated by mentally retarded persons. What seems to be lacking is a theoretical perspective from which to consider the acquisition of motor skills in the broad range of everyday activities that people engage in. This omission is, of course, pertinent to the understanding of skilled action of both mentally and nonmentally retarded individuals.

CURRENT ORIENTATIONS

Although the preceding review may at first glance appear rather critical of the progress to date regarding our understanding of the motor skill acquisition of mentally retarded persons, a broader perspective suggests that this is not really the case. Progress in any field of scientific endeavor is typically reflected in the efforts of the square root of the number of researchers in that field (e.g., Lotka, 1926). In light of this, the overall outcome from the two traditional orientations is probably a reflection of a more productive and focused scientific output than is usually the norm in a given domain.

It should not pass unnoticed either that researchers in this area typically use one of two approaches, regardless of the theoretical orientation. On the one hand, there has been a group of psychologists who are primarily interested in retardation per se, independent as it were of a focus to specific tasks and activities. In this approach motor skills are utilized without respect to the consideration of task characteristics and how they interact with, and provide constraints to, the performance in the activity at hand. A motor task is selected primarily on its availability and/or tradition as if a motor skill is a motor skill, to paraphrase that hackneyed phrase. On the other hand, there has been a group of researchers from psychology, special education, and kinesiology who focus on the motor task and simply use a sample of mentally retarded individuals to infer population differences. In this approach, the characterization of the individual is shallow and the assessment of retardation is left to performance on an IQ test. In short, regardless of orientation there has not been a concerted effort to integrate concepts such as intelligence, cognition, and action. There have been attempts to bridge to some degree the first two concepts with respect to problems of comprehension (e.g., Campione & Brown, 1978) but not human action.

CONSIDERATIONS FOR CHANGING ORIENTATIONS

In the remainder of this paper I will discuss some considerations that might be usefully introduced into the study of the motor skills of mentally retarded persons. The intention is not to lay out a theory of motor skills, but rather to introduce some background considerations from a functional perspective to problems of action. Furthermore, these functional considerations hold the advantage of cutting across different theoretical orientations. Many of the points raised are not new to the motor skills domain but tend to be forgotten factors, as reflected in a perusal of the current literature on both mentally retarded and nonretarded persons. The focus is on concepts of action rather than intelligence or retardation.

Actions Not Movements

Movement may be characterized as being a necessary but not sufficient condition for action (Newell, 1978). Movements can be measured rather precisely through the space-time measures of kinematics, but this measurement category is not the criterion for action. Actions are usually identified by the goal of the activity, although the pattern of movement kinematics (relative motion) may also define the action at hand. Much of the motor skills literature has focused on the quantitative details of the absolute motion of movement kinematics in contrast to the more qualitative criteria of actions. Although the details of movement provide useful descriptors of motor performance, they have not been placed into a functional framework to provide guiding insights into the organization of movement in action. For example, in accuracy tasks mentally retarded individuals prove to be less accurate in terms of movement spatial or temporal outcome (e.g., Wade et al., 1978), but the relevance of these kinds of findings to the broader concept of action is not apparent. In effect, both mentally retarded and nonretarded individuals have been so constrained in motor performance tasks that the issue of whether the subject is engaging in the appropriate action is not at stake.

Coordination, Control, and Skill

A related concern to the action/movement distinction is the recognition of the impact that a limited range of motor tasks has had upon our understanding of motor skill acquisition. This limitation is prevalent in the literature dealing with the mentally retarded as well as the literature on the nonretarded. An obvious consequence is that studies of skill acquisition have predominantly occurred on tasks where only one degree of freedom need be controlled to meet the goal of the task (Bernstein, 1967). The key press RT procedure and linear positioning tasks are reflections of this limitation. One important outcome of this precondition is that by definition problems of coordination have been eliminated from the analysis of skill.

The terms "coordination," "control," and "skill" are prevalent in the motor-learning domain, but typically there has been no useful distinction advanced between these concepts. In fact, these terms are often used synonymously. In outlining a broad-ranging basis to the study of motor skills, Kugler, Kelso, and Turvey (1980) provided a framework for a meaningful distinction between the terms. In the following section I briefly outline their approach and elaborate on it by providing a basis for operationalizing the distinctions advanced.

Coordination is the function that constrains the potentially free variables into a behavioral unit: F (A. B. C. . . . . N). The description of the variables in this function is, of course, one of the fundamental unknowns in the theory of action. Probably every variable from cells to kinematics has at one time or another been postulated as the appropriate language for the function. Unraveling the nature of this function represents one of the most important questions in the development of a theory of action.

Control is the process by which values are assigned to the variables in the function; that is, the values parameterize the function.

Skill requires that the optimal value be assigned to the controlled variables.

These distinctions are useful in theorizing about action, although to date we are no closer to understanding the language of the coordination function. It is appropriate, however, to develop concepts about the behavioral unit (or activity) independent (for now) of gains regarding the language of the coordination function. Indeed, activities may be understood by an operationalization of the terms "coordination," "control," and "skill" through insights from the visual perception of biological motion (Cutting & Proffitt, 1982; Johansson, Van Hofsten, & Jansson, 1980).

Briefly, recent work in the visual perception of biological motion has implicated the priority of relative motion over absolute motion. It appears that it is the relative motion of the body and limbs that affords the perception of labeling a given activity (Cutting & Proffitt, 1982; Johansson et al., 1980). In other words, the natural nominal categorization of activities is determined by the perception of relative motions. Although the data supporting this proposition are limited, it may be postulated that each physical activity is defined by a unique set of relative motions. Some evidence toward this view has been provided by Hoenkamp (1978), who has shown that the ratio between the time that the lower leg takes to swing forward and its corresponding return motion determines the labeling of human gaits (walking, running, skating, limping). It is possible then to elaborate and propose that coordination for a given activity is defined by a unique set of relative motions, whereas control is reflected by the scaling of the given relative motions.

Thus, relative and absolute motion help define operationally from a behavioral perspective the distinction between coordination and control. This distinction becomes very important in the acquisition of tasks requiring the constraint of more than a single degree of freedom. Moreover, the distinction may more usefully reflect organizational properties of the neuromuscular system than extant attempts at task categorization.

It should be apparent from my analysis that the literature dealing with the motor skill acquisition of mentally retarded persons has confined itself to the study of motor control. Wade's paper on timing and Horgan's on memory (both in this volume), which deal with two principal research areas in the motor performance of retarded persons, reflect this proposition. Thus, consonant with the action/movement distinction, the acquisition of the appropriate pattern of coordination in the mentally retarded has not been a concern.

By the same token, the study of skill has been conspicuous by its absence in that a one-shot laboratory-learning session is nowhere near enough practice to approach the optimal parameterization of the coordination function. Thus, we have not taken advantage of Guthrie's (1935) helpful definition of skill as "the ability to bring about some predetermined outcome with maximum certainty and *minimum outlay of time and energy* [italics added]" (p. 162). In summary, the study of skill acquisition has confined itself to the study of control within the hierarchical triumvirate of coordination, control, and skill.

REFERENCES

Baumeister, A. A., & Kellas, G. (1968). Reaction time and mental retardation. In N.R. Ellis (Ed.), *International review of research in mental retardation* (Vol. 3, pp. 163-193). New York: Academic Press.

Bernstein, N. (1967). *The co-ordination and regulation of movements.* New York: Pergamon Press.

Broadbent, D.E. (1965). Information processing in the nervous system. *Science, 150,* 457-462.

Bruininks, R.H. (1974). Physical and motor development of retarded persons. In N.R. Ellis (Ed.), *International review of research in mental retardation* (Vol. 7, pp. 209-261). New York: Academic Press.

Campione, J.C., & Brown, A.L. (1978). Toward a theory of intelligence: Contributions from research with retarded children. *Intelligence, 2,* 279-304.

Cutting, J.F., & Proffitt, D.R. (1982). The minimum principle and the perception of absolute, common and relative motions. *Cognitive Psychology, 14,* 211-246.

Fleishman, E. A., & Bartlett, C. J. (1969). Human abilities. *Annual Review of Psychology, 20,* 349-380.

Guthrie, E.R. (1935). *The psychology of learning.* New York: Harper.

Hoenkamp, E. (1978). Perceptual cues that determine the labelling of human gait. *Journal of Human Movement Studies, 4,* 59-69.

Hoover, J.H., Wade, M.G., & Newell, K.M. (1981). Training moderately and severely retarded adults to improve reaction and movement times. *American Journal of Mental Deficiency, 85,* 389-395.

Jensen, A.R. (1980). *Bias in mental deficiency.* New York: Free Press.

Jensen, A.R., & Munro, E. (1979). Reaction time, movement time and intelligence. *Intelligence, 3,* 121-126.

Johansson, G., Von Hofsten, C., & Jansson, E. (1980). Event perception. *Annual Review of Psychology, 31,* 27-63.

Kugler, P.N., Kelso, J.A.S., & Turvey, M.T. (1980). On the concept of coordinative structures as dissipative structures: 1. Theoretical lines of convergence. In G.E. Stelmach & J. Requin (Eds.), *Tutorials in motor behavior* (pp. 3-47). Amsterdam: North Holland.

Lotka, A.J. (1926). The frequency distribution of scientific productivity. *Journal of the Washington Academy of Science, 16,* 317-323.

Neisser, U. (1976). *Cognition and reality.* San Francisco: W.H. Freeman.

Nettelback, T. (1979). Skill and mental retardation. In W.T. Singleton (Ed.), *The study of real skills: Vol. 2. Compliance and excellence* (pp. 63-81). Baltimore: University Park Press.

Nettelback, T., & Brewer, N. (1981). Studies of mild mental retardation and timed performance. In N.R. Ellis (Ed.), *International review of research in mental retardation* (Vol. 15, pp. 61-106). New York: Academic Press.

Newell, K.M. (1978). Some issues on action plans. In G.E. Stelmach (Ed.), *Information processing in motor control and learning* (pp. 41-54). New York: Academic Press.

Newell, K.M. (1981). Skill learning. In D.H. Holding (Ed.), *Human skills* (pp. 203-226). New York: Wiley & Sons.

Newell, K.M. (1984). Physical constraints to the development of motor skills. In J.R. Thomas (Ed.), *Motor development during preschool and elementary years* (pp. 105-120). Minneapolis: Burgess.

Newell, K.M., Wade, M.G., & Kelly, T.M. (1979). Temporal anticipation of response initiation in retarded persons. *American Journal of Mental Deficiency, 84,* 289-296.

Rarick, G.L. (1973). Motor performance of mentally retarded children. In G.L. Rarick (Ed.), *Physical activity: Human growth and development* (pp. 225-256). New York: Academic Press.

Wade, M.G., & Gold, M.W. (1978). Removing some of the limitations of mentally retarded workers by improving job design. *Human Factors, 20,* 339-348.

Wade, M.G., Hoover, J.H., & Newell K.M. (in press). Training and trainability in motor skills performance of mentally retarded persons. In J. Hogg & P.J. Mittler (Eds.), *Advances in mental handicap research* (Vol. 2). New York: Wiley & Sons.

Wade, M.G., Newell, K.M., & Wallace, S.A. (1978). Decision time and movement time as a function of response complexity in the motor performance of retarded persons. *American Journal of Mental Deficiency, 83,* 135-144.

15

Issues in Memory for Movement With Mentally Retarded Children

JAMES S. HORGAN
University of Illinois, Chicago

Much attention has been devoted to the study of short-term memory in the mentally retarded for verbal and visual information. Although not commanding the same level of attention, interest in the study of memory for movement cues has increased. This research has been directed toward the characterization of factors (cognitive and motor) that serve to distinguish the mentally retarded from the nonretarded child. One issue addressed in this paper involves a discussion of a procedural flaw which bears upon the valid representation of movement in arm-positioning tasks. Also presented is a brief report on research being conducted in the area of mnemonic instruction, and its usefulness in improving motor memory in the mentally retarded.

An issue of scientific interest in the area of mental retardation is the retarded child's short-term memory for movement-related cues. The conceptual framework of studies dealing with this issue has been developed from the memory research conducted in the verbal and visual domains (Brown, 1974; Butterfield & Belmont, 1971; Flavell, Friedrichs, & Hoyt, 1970; Spitz, 1973). The study of short-term motor memory has been centered on the memory for movement in linear positioning tasks, (Barclay, 1979; Kelso, 1975, 1977; Laabs, 1973; Roy, 1977). These tasks are designed to determine the accuracy of memory for a previous movement. Unfortunately, very few investigations have focused on memory for movement of mentally retarded persons. Those completed have been conducted by investigators who apparently had limited interest in the continuous application of this line of inquiry to studies in mental retardation (Kelso, Goodman, Stamm, & Hayes, 1979; Reid, 1980a, 1980b; Sugden, 1978). As a result, the findings of a few investigations have raised a number of interesting questions that have not been extensively pursued.

This work was supported in part by a National Institute of Health Biomedical Research Grant (SO-7RR07158).

Systematic research efforts, which will help to clarify and define the structure and function of memory in the mentally retarded, are essential to further understanding of the developmental motor and cognitive processes that influence behavior.

The fact that scientific progress in motor behavior and mental retardation has lagged well behind research with nonretarded persons is a factor of great concern. Consequently, that which is not yet known about motor memory, i.e., cognitive representation of movement, in mental retardation parallels the lag in motor development that has been demonstrated between mildly mentally retarded and nonretarded children. It is for this reason that this line of inquiry is important to the field of motor behavior in general. The limited number of investigations conducted to date with the mentally retarded have only provided the conceptual boundaries, while leaving a myriad of unanswered questions that are most difficult to address from a procedural standpoint. However, their answers lie closest to the central mechanisms responsible for behavior and, hence, would provide a more definitive characterization of the factors responsible for the divergence in behavior between the retarded and nonretarded.

Because the majority of the existing research in motor memory and mental retardation has been carried out utilizing arm-positioning tasks, the discussion to follow will be limited to these.

MEMORY RESEARCH WITH ARM-POSITIONING TASKS

A specific procedural flaw is highlighted in this section which has a direct bearing on the validity of previous findings in memory research employing arm-positioning (linear) tasks. Movement of a human limb invariably occurs through an arc of a circle, and the observed linear displacement is a translation from an angular source of movement (Horgan & Horgan, 1982). Without consideration of or correction for individual anatomical differences, the linear representation at the distal extent of a limb relative to its criterion is likely to be inherently biased. Thus, it seems illogical to presume that such a measure could accurately represent the spatial elements contributing to an inherently angular movement. Stelmach, Kelso, and Wallace (1975) made reference to "anatomical characteristics such as arm length" when they expressed their concern about the validity of movement-yoked designs employing linear positioning tasks. To illustrate this problem and to offer a solution we proposed the model shown in Figure 1 (Horgan & Horgan, 1982).

When a limb is maintained rigid (lever), the movement at the end of the lever is directly proportional to its distance from its fulcrum (joint about which movement occurs) for any given angular

Figure 1. Rationale and formulation of the angular transformation protocol. *(A)* Lever length differences: equal linear with differential angular displacement. *(B)* Resolution of angular movement from linear values. (From "Measurement Bias in Representation of Accuracy of Movement on Linear Positioning Tasks" by J.S. Horgan and J. Horgan, 1982, *Perceptual and Motor Skills, 55,* p. 973. Reprinted by permission.)

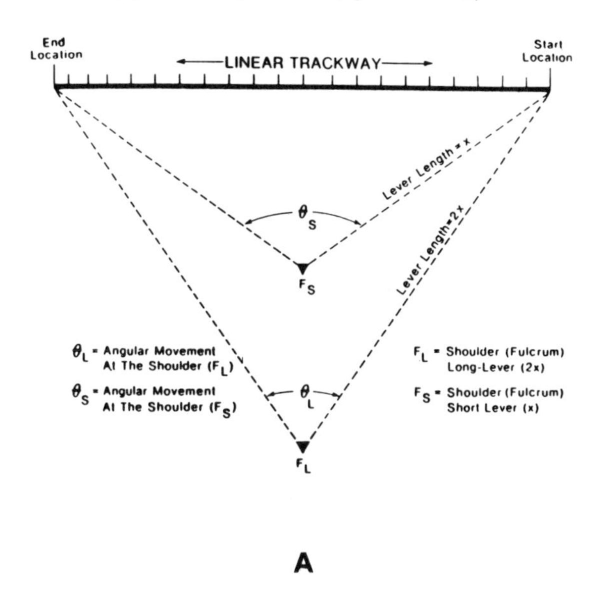

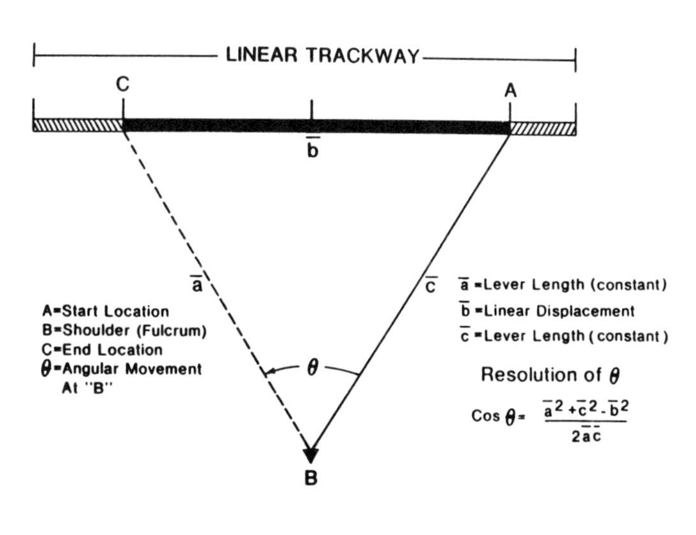

B

displacement. For example, one of the levers illustrated in Figure 1*A* is twice as long as the other. Given the exact linear displacement at the ends of each lever, the results would represent marked differences in the respective angular displacements. This means that the *actual* movement (angular) required to achieve linear parity would be quite different. These differences can vary in extent but the result is, nonetheless, a misrepresentation of the movement magnitude when using the linear metric as a dependent measure. A relatively simple way to resolve this problem is illustrated in Figure 1*B*. With one additional measurement (the distance from each subject's shoulder joint [fulcrum] to the center of the hand), the law of cosines may be applied. The lever itself forms two sides (lengths) of an isosceles triangle and the linear displacement provides the length of the third side. From these known values it is a very simple proposition to calculate the angular value (direct transformation) which logically represents the angular movement (actual) of the human limb.

This model has been tested in several experiments (Horgan, 1983a, 1983b; Horgan & Horgan, 1982) which compared various age and intellectual levels with interesting contrasts resulting when data were reported in both their linear and angular form. The results of these experiments are reviewed in this paper for two reasons: (1) to illustrate the experimental evolution of the angular protocol and (2) to demonstrate the application of this protocol in a specific area of memory research in mental retardation.

In the first investigation (Horgan & Horgan, 1982) different age groups of nonretarded subjects were utilized. Sixty male subjects were randomly selected within three age ranges; 7–9 years ($\overline{X} = 8$ years, 6 months); 10–12 years ($\overline{X} = 11$ years, 1 month); and 14–16 years ($\overline{X} = 15$ years, 3 months). The experimental task required the reproduction of preselected movements on an arm-positioning task. Each subject performed 25 trials across five retention conditions. Absolute error in both its linear and angular form was used as the dependent measure in a 3 (Groups) $\times$ 5 (Retention Conditions) $\times$ 5 (Trials) factorial with repeated measures on the last factor. The data analyzed in its linear form (Figure 2*A*) yielded a significant main effect for groups (age), with the two older age groups more accurate in movement reproduction ($p < .01$) than the youngest group. Do these results represent developmental differences or merely an anatomical artifact?

Figure 2*B* represents the same data transformed into its angular form using the procedure described. Although a group main effect was once again isolated ($p < .05$), only the eldest and the youngest groups were found to differ significantly. We believe this finding resulted from an upward correction (decrease in accuracy when lever length was taken into account) in the movement error of the longer-

Figure 2. Contrast of data represented "raw" and after transformation. *(A)* Mean absolute error in a linear form. *(B)* Mean absolute error in an angular form: 1 = immediate recall; 2 = unfilled; 3 = interpolated mental activity; 4 = overt rehearsal; 5 = overt rehearsal with interpolated mental activity. (From "Measurement Bias in Representation of Accuracy of Movement on Linear Positioning Tasks" by J.S. Horgan and J. Horgan, 1982, *Perceptual and Motor Skills, 55*, pp. 977, 979. Reprinted by permission.)

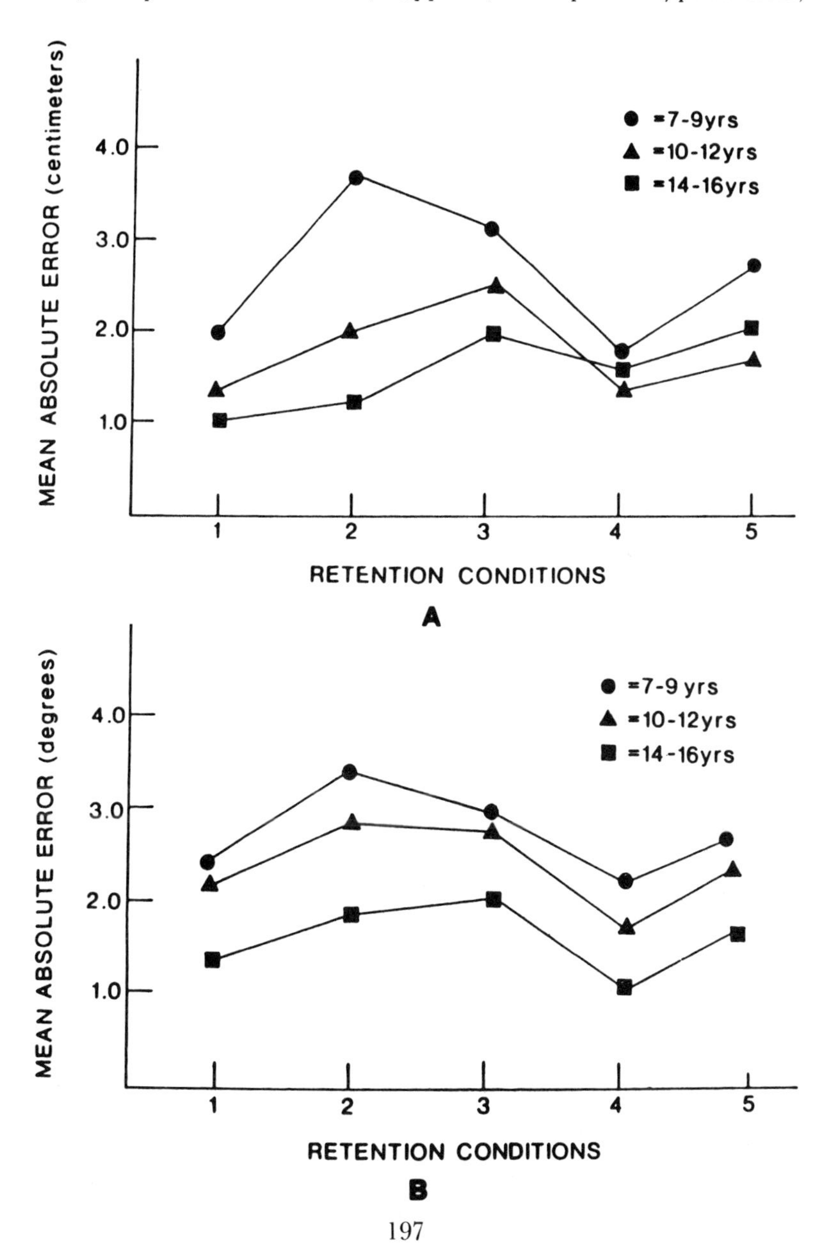

levered subjects, coupled with a downward correction (increase in accuracy) in the shorter-levered subjects. The use of the angular metric appeared to negate an inherent advantage possessed by the longer-levered subjects in the linear analyses. However, this upward and downward shifting was not of sufficient magnitude to overcome the difference between the two age group extremes. From these results it was argued that the angular protocol affords one more precision in formulating developmental explanations for the differences obtained.

Figure 3 illustrates the same phenomenon described in the previous study with subjects of divergent intellect (Horgan, 1983a). In this investigation, 100 mentally retarded (IQ $\overline{X} = 65$; age $\overline{X} = 15$ years, 8 months) and 100 nonretarded children (age $\overline{X} = 11$ years, 3 months) comprised the study groups. Again, the arm-positioning task was employed in the examination of memory for movement cues. The experimental design of this investigation was quite similar to that of the previous study. The statistical design was a 2 (Groups) $\times$ 5 (Retention Conditions) $\times$ 5 (Trials) factorial with repeated measures for trials.

There is a striking contrast between Figures 3*A* and 3*B* that is in all probability based upon the choice of the dependent measure used to represent movement. This choice, of course, is whether to represent the movement executed in its raw linear or transformed angular form. In its linear form (Figure 3*A*), there was a significant main effect for groups ($p < .01$) and retention conditions ($p < .01$) favoring the nonretarded in accuracy of recall. The data analyzed in its angular form (Figure 3*B*), however, did not yield a main effect for groups ($p < .07$), with the plots virtually superimposed. The main effect for retention conditions was significant ($p < .05$), with differences isolated between the immediate recall and unfilled retention condition.

These results at first seem to contradict those reported earlier. It was theorized in the previous study (Horgan & Horgan, 1982) that there was a "longer lever advantage (accuracy)—and a short lever disadvantage" responsible for the upward and downward shifting in the three age groups of nonretarded subjects. However, in a re-examination of the data characteristics in both investigations (Horgan, 1983b; Horgan & Horgan, 1982), it was found that all four of the nonretarded groups in both studies consistently "overshot" their movement criterion at 80%, 87%, and 88% in the first study and 82% in the second study. The mentally retarded subjects just as consistently "undershot" the criterion at 83% in the second study. Hence, it was further theorized that a long lever undershooting the criterion results in an overall downward shift (increased accuracy) in

Figure 3. Comparison of movement accuracy between mentally retarded and nonretarded children before and after data transform. *(A)* Mean absolute error in a linear form. *(B)* Mean absolute error in angular form: 1 = immediate recall; 2 = unfilled; 3 = interpolated mental activity; 4 = overt rehearsal; 5 = overt rehearsal with interpolated mental activity. (From "Measurement Bias in Memory for Movement by Mentally Retarded and Nonretarded Children" by J.S. Horgan, 1983, *Perceptual and Motor Skills, 56,* pp. 667-668. Reprinted by permission.)

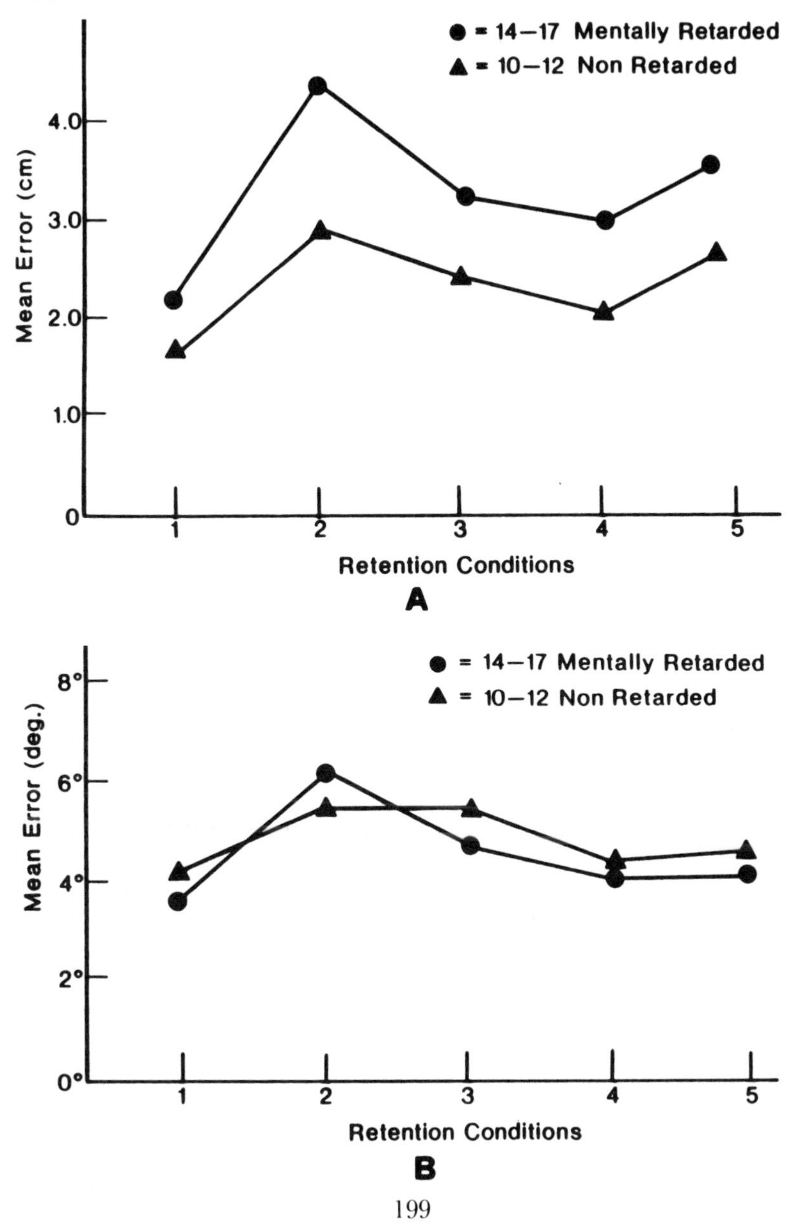

angular error relative to a shorter lever overshooting. The fundamental question that emerges is which metric (linear or angular) is the most precise representation of the spatial components that serve to characterize human movement? We have argued that the angular representation is the most logical choice.

STRATEGY TRAINING AND MOTOR MEMORY OF THE MENTALLY RETARDED

In mental retardation, covert rehearsal for the retention of movement cues has been explored on a limited basis. For example, Sugden (1978) studied the effect of covert rehearsal with mentally retarded and nonretarded children. A visual-motor positioning task was employed in a short-term memory (motor) paradigm. Sugden found that the mentally retarded subjects did not spontaneously adopt a rehearsal (mnemonic) strategy and were, therefore, significantly less accurate than nonretarded subjects in movement (constrained) recall. Kelso et al. (1979) reported findings contrary to Sugden's in that their retarded subjects seemed capable of covertly rehearsing (apparently spontaneously) kinesthetic cues for up to 7 s after preselecting a criterion movement. Reid (1980a) countered the conclusion of Kelso et al. by suggesting that they "unwittingly" provided instruction in the use of a mnemonic strategy (i.e., rehearsal) by directing the subjects to "remember the spot" when preselecting movements. If this was true, then Sugden's conclusion may be accurate. Reid (1980a) examined this equivocation by manipulating instruction in the use of mnemonic rehearsal strategy with mentally retarded subjects. His findings were consistent with those of Sugden. He found that the retarded did not spontaneously adopt a mnemonic to covertly rehearse movement cues. However, when subjects were prompted through instruction in the use of a strategy to recall movement, accuracy of recall was superior to the retarded subjects who did not receive instruction. Unfortunately, Reid did not use a nonretarded sample in this investigation, so cross-categorical comparisons could not be made. From these findings, it appears that the issue of spontaneity in adopting mnemonic strategies (an executive process) for the recall of movement cues is fundamental to understanding the memory structure of the mentally retarded.

I am now conducting several investigations using the angular metric to represent movement and accuracy of recall in arm-positioning tasks. In the most recent of these investigations (Horgan, 1983b), the effects of formal instruction in the use of a mnemonic strategy (rehearsal) were examined. Subjects in this study were 80 mentally retarded (IQ $\overline{X} = 68$; age $\overline{X} = 15$ years, 2 months) and 80 nonretarded (age $\overline{X} = 10$ years, 10 months) male and female children. Movement location and movement extent cues were manipulated in two experiments to characterize divergent behaviors between study groups. Forty mentally retarded and 40 nonretarded subjects were used in each experiment. Half of each of these groups were then randomly designated to receive instruction in the use of a rehearsal strategy; their respective counterparts served as controls, receiving no instruction. Three retention conditions were employed in this study: (1) immediate recall, (2) a 15-s unfilled interval, and (3) a 15-s interval filled with mental activity (backward counting). All subjects performed 12 trials within each of the retention conditions which were then blocked in groups of 3. The angular representation of total error, as described by Henry (1974), was used as the dependent measure in a 4 (Groups) × 3 (Retention Conditions) × 4 (Trial Blocks) factorial with repeated measures on the latter factor. This procedure remained constant across both experiments.

In the first experiment (Figure 4*A*), movement location cues were maintained reliable and extent cues were controlled across retention conditions. A main effect for groups ($p < .01$) and retention conditions ($p < .01$) with interaction ($p < .05$) was significant. The mentally retarded group, performing without benefit of instruction in the use of a mnemonic, was significantly less accurate overall than the other groups. There were no differences between the mentally retarded instruction group and the two nonretarded groups, which supports the notion that improvements in movement accuracy can be made by the mentally retarded that are equal to those of their nonretarded counterparts. A qualifier for this last finding, however, is that the retarded *must* be made aware of effective means to assist them in coding, processing, and retaining movement information. This finding is consistent with those of Sugden (1978) and Reid (1980a).

In the second experiment (Figure 4*B*), the same procedures as in Experiment 1 were used, except movement extent cues were maintained reliable and location cues were controlled. A main effect for groups ($p < .01$) and retention conditions ($p < .01$) with interaction ($p < .01$) was again significant. The mentally retarded group in the no-instruction condition was significantly less accurate than all remaining groups. However, the most important finding from this experiment was the fact that in the analysis of simple effects, the retarded group receiving instruction in the use of a mnemonic was the only group to demonstrate a significant decrement in performance accuracy from the unfilled to the filled retention condition ($p < .05$). This has customarily been accepted as a proof that "processing" of movement-related cues has been interrupted by

Figure 4. Comparison of movement accuracy between mentally retarded and nonretarded children for different movement cues. *(A)* Mean total error for movement location. *(B)* Mean total error for movement extent: 1 = immediate recall; 2 = unfilled; 3 = interpolated. (From "Mnemonic Strategy Instruction in Coding Processing and Recall of Movement Related Cues by the Mentally Retarded" by J.S. Horgan, 1983, *Perceptual and Motor Skills, 57,* pp. 553, 555. Reprinted by permission.)

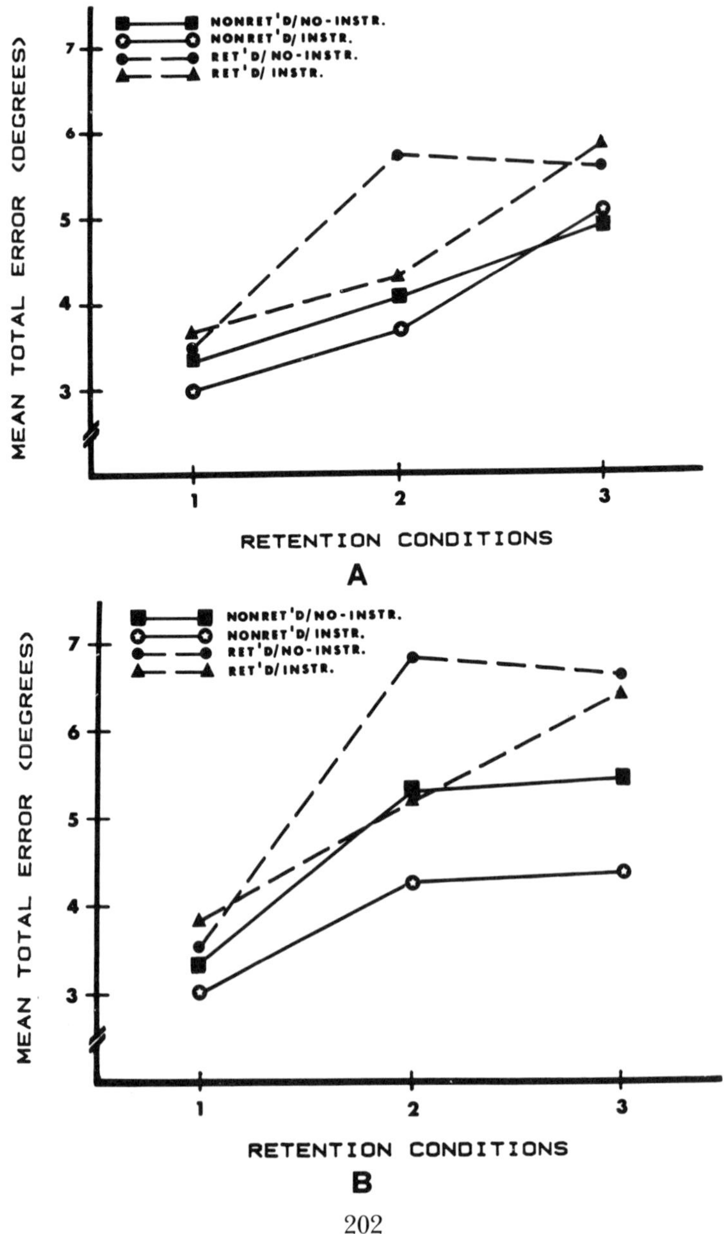

diverting attention of the processor from the primary task. This is an interesting finding because data reported with the nonretarded is replete with evidence that movement extent cues are not amenable to deeper levels of processing, hence they should be unaffected by interpolated activity (Keele & Ellis, 1972; Roy, 1977). So with a degree of cautious speculation, this factor may be but one index for discriminating between the mentally retarded and the nonretarded relative to functional memory processes.

CONCLUDING REMARKS

The problems created by differences in arms lengths when using the traditional linear metric extend beyond the spatial components to which this paper has been limited. The procedural issue discussed is of great import to a valid, independent characterization of the behavior of the mentally retarded. It is also crucial to an accurate representation of the differences observed between the retarded and nonretarded.

With regard to research in motor memory and mental retardation, the future holds considerable promise. For the mentally retarded in particular, memory has such a pervasive influence on general intellectual function that a basic understanding of memory as it operates in the retarded is a logical requisite in defining the structure and limits of the intellect. I believe that continuous inquiry, centering on the role of the executive in the organization and control of movement, will have a significant impact on the existing knowledge base. The mentally retarded child's ability to organize an effective means to recognize and attend to relevant information available in motor tasks should be of prime interest to investigators. The reason for this is that the majority of the evidence in the motor (Horgan, 1983b; Reid, 1980a) and cognitive domains (Brown, 1974; Ellis, 1970) supports the notion that the short-term memory deficit in the mentally retarded is not due to a faulty storage mechanism. In the absence of structural deficits, it seems reasonable to assume that memory deficiencies may be due to their inability to internally organize an effective strategy to retain movement information. This seems to be characteristic of both the intellectually immature (young nonretarded) and the mentally retarded, but it is not consistent with the findings in the nonretarded literature when mature subjects are used. Therefore, the locus of control for retarded persons' adoption of effective organizational strategies for movement retention information is fundamental to the understanding of the role played by the executive. The inability of the mentally retarded to spontaneously adopt a method of organizing what is to be remembered is clearly a meta-memorial deficit. I believe that this deficiency in the spontaneous ability to derive meaningful involvement of executive processes is the key to distinguishing the retarded from the nonretarded and that specific contributing factors will be isolated in a focus upon meta-memorial issues.

REFERENCES

Barclay, C. R. (1979). The executive control of mnemonic activity. *Journal of Experimental Child Psychology, 27,* 262-276.

Brown, A. L. (1974). The role of strategic behavior in retardate memory. In N. R. Ellis (Ed.), *International review of research in mental retardation* (Vol. 7, pp. 55-111). New York: Academic Press.

Butterfield, E. C., & Belmont, J. M. (1971). Relationship of storage and retrieval strategies as short-term memory processes. *Journal of Experimental Psychology, 89,* 319-328.

Ellis, N. R. (1970). Memory-processes in retardate and normals. In N. R. Ellis (Ed.), *International review of research in mental retardation* (Vol. 4, pp. 1-32). New York: Academic Press.

Flavell, J. H., Friedrichs, A. G., & Hoyt, J. D. (1970). Developmental changes in memorization processes. *Cognitive Psychology 1,* 324-340.

Henry, F. M. (1974). Variable and constant performance errors within a group of individuals. *Journal of Motor Behavior, 6,* 149-154.

Horgan, J.S. (1983a). Measurement bias in memory for movement by mentally retarded and nonretarded children. *Perceptual and Motor Skills, 56,* 663-670.

Horgan, J. S. (1983b). Mnemonic strategy instruction in coding, processing and recall of movement related cues by the mentally retarded. *Perceptual and Motor Skills, 57,* 547-557.

Horgan, J. S., & Horgan, J. (1982). Measurement bias in representation of accuracy of movement on linear positioning tasks. *Perceptual and Motor Skills, 55,* 971-981.

Keele, S., & Ellis, J. (1972). Memory characteristics of kinesthetic information. *Journal of Motor Behavior, 4,* 127-134.

Kelso, J. A. S. (1975). Central and peripheral information in motor control. In W. W. Spirduso & J. King (Eds.), *Proceedings of motor control symposium* (pp. 130-135). Austin: University of Texas Press.

Kelso, J. A. S. (1977). Planning and efferent components in the coding of movement. *Journal of Motor Behavior, 4,* 127-134.

Kelso, J. A. S., Goodman, D., Stamm, C. L., & Hayes, C. (1979). Movement coding and memory in retarded children. *American Journal of Mental Deficiency, 83,* 601-611.

Laabs, G. (1973). Retention characteristics of different cues in motor short-term memory. *Journal of Experimental Psychology, 100,* 168-177.

Reid, G. (1980a). The effects of memory strategy instruction in the short-term motor memory of the mentally retarded. *Journal of Motor Behavior, 12,* 221-227.

Reid, G. (1980b). Overt and covert rehearsal in short-term motor memory of mentally retarded and nonretarded persons. *American Journal of Mental Deficiency, 85,* 69-77.

Roy, E. R. (1977). Spatial cues in memory for movement. *Journal of Motor Behavior, 9,* 151-156.

Spitz, H. (1973). Consolidating fact into the schematized learning and memory of educable retardates. In N. R. Ellis (Ed.), *International review of research in mental retardation* (Vol. 6, pp. 149-166). New York: Academic Press.

Stelmach, G. E., Kelso, S., & Wallace, S. A. (1975). Preselection in short-term memory. *Journal of Experimental Psychology: Human Learning and Memory, 1,* 745-755.

Sugden, D. A. (1978). Visual motor short term memory in educationally subnormal boys. *British Journal of Educational Psychology, 48,* 330-339.

16

Timing and Precision as Variables in the Motor Performance of the Moderately Mentally Handicapped

MICHAEL G. WADE
Southern Illinois University

Knowing when to initiate a movement is no doubt as important as knowing how to do so. Thus, timing and precision are of utmost importance when observing skill performance. This report deals with the various factors of timing, taking into account the extent to which timing and precision are essential ingredients to consider in skill performance of the mentally handicapped.

There can be little doubt to any of us who have observed skillful behavior that timing and precision are perhaps the most important ingredients when skill performance is observed. In a hierarchical structure of skill components that fulfill the necessary and sufficient conditions, it is clear that knowing *when* to initiate a movement is at least as important as knowing *how*—although, of course, both the *how* and the *when* must be known to the performer.

The traditional research paradigm for investigating timing as it relates to the performance of the mentally handicapped has been with reaction time (RT) studies. Recently, there has been an upsurge of empirical interest in the cognitive elements that control motor behavior of such persons. This has stemmed primarily from the work of the Australian group (Nettelbeck, Kirby, Lally, and Brewer) and our laboratory (myself, Newell, and co-workers). The research thrust of the Australians has focused on the relative contributions of perceptual elements; we have investigated those elements mediated by the complexity of the response required. What has resulted from the work so far is that one cannot clearly label the perceptual elements or the response elements as completely explaining the nature of the performance. In addition to the traditional RT studies, some work has been reported on the dynamic aspects of timing behavior for the mentally handicapped (Wade, 1980; Wade, Newell, & Hoover, 1982).

This paper focuses on two areas from our research program: (1)

This research was supported in part by funds from Project HD05951 awarded by the National Institute for Child Health and Human Development.

temporal anticipation and response initiation as they relate to discrete movements which vary in complexity, and (2) anticipation that involves coincident timing behavior, which may be defined as how the subject responds to the special environmental demands for predicting motion and also timing the arrival of a moving target to a specified location.

In an early paper (Wade, Newell, & Wallace, 1978), we demonstrated that mentally retarded persons may have a facility to preprogram elements of a response prior to the signal for the response initiation. This inference was based upon findings that parameters of the response difficulty elevated RT only in the choice paradigm—presumably because in the simple RT situation elements of the response could to some extent be preprogrammed.

Learning to predict the arrival of a stimulus in the environment so that a response may be prepared in advance of the stimulus is termed *perceptual anticipation*. There are basically two components of perceptual anticipation, one spatial and a second temporal. Research has focused primarily on the temporal parameters. The ability to anticipate seems crucial to the successful performance of everyday motor skills for all of us, because merely reacting to a stimulus causes intolerable lags in response initiation and control.

REACTION TIME AND MOVEMENT TIME

For some time, it has been known that normal adults may learn to anticipate the temporal arrival of a stimulus in a simple RT paradigm. In fact, RT data are collected, utilizing random foreperiods between warning and start signals, to eliminate or minimize this possibility. Similarly, in more complex discrete and continuous responses, the advantage gained from a fixed foreperiod between the warning and start signal is clear for normal populations.

Baumeister and Hawkins (1966) and Terrell and Ellis (1964) showed that retarded persons may anticipate the temporal arrival of a signal, but the tasks used in these experiments were simple, requiring little or no precision. Tasks requiring a reasonable degree of speed and precision may have a different outcome. Two experiments (Newell, Wade, & Kelly, 1979) addressed this question and focused on the temporal anticipation to a signal, requiring initiation of a discrete aiming movement in a Fitts' law paradigm. The apparatus was a 16-cm × 42-cm rectangular plate on which were located three target holes 7.62, 15.24, and 30.44 cm from the starting position. Circular copper disks could be inserted into the target holes in the apparatus. The target disks were of three diameters—64, 127, and 2.54 cm—affording nine possible combinations of distance and target size. Of interest here was whether or not retarded persons could spontaneously reduce response latency as a result of switching from a variable to a fixed foreperiod, and whether practice would facilitate anticipation. Of further concern was the extent to which anticipation interacted with the difficulty of the movement and/or the length of the foreperiod.

Subjects were given usually 10 practice trials before each test period, although the first time in the testing protocol they were given as many trials as were necessary to indicate that they understood and could perform the task. There were 5 testing days. Subjects were presented on each day with nine target (width-amplitude) combinations. Data were collected for 10 successful trials (hits) for every combination. The order of the nine conditions was randomized for each subject on each day. Knowledge of results was withheld during the experimental sessions, and subjects were not informed about their performance relative to that of other subjects. Error rates were kept within the range tolerated by Fitts and Peterson (1964)—10%—and, in fact, the number of targets missed over the random and fixed foreperiod conditions was low (3.98% and 3.33%, respectively). For all practice trials and experimental trials on Days 1 and 2, the interval between the auditory warning signal and the starting line was randomized between 1 and 4 s. The foreperiod was held constant for the experimental trials on Days 3–5, when half the subjects performed a task following a 1-s warning interval and the other half performed a task following a 3-s warning interval.

The data illustrated on the left side of Figure 1 show no beneficial anticipations for the fixed interval. In fact, the distribution of RTs for the random and fixed intervals was essentially the same. The RT frequency distribution complements the average RTs in showing no differential response initiation time to a fixed versus a random warning interval. Movement time (MT) in this experiment decreased as target size increased and increased as movement amplitude increased.

Failing to demonstrate temporal anticipation in the first experiment ran contrary to data from Braumeister and Hawkins (1966) and Terrell and Ellis (1964). These studies employed a simple cue press response, which reduced programming demands with respect to response selection and preparation. Thus, it may be that the temporal anticipation ability of retarded persons is a direct function of the complexity of the response, and this hypothesis was examined in the second of the two experiments reported (Newell et al., 1979). Subjects were asked to raise the stylus from the stop position on the aluminum plate as rapidly as possible after the onset of the starting signal. This eliminated many of the response requirements of the aiming movement used in Experiment 1. Procedures were the same,

Figure 1. Percentage frequency of reaction times for Experiment 1 *(left)* and Experiment 2 *(right)*. (From "Temporal Anticipation of Response Initiation in Retarded Persons" by K.M. Newell, M.G. Wade, and T.M. Kelly, 1979, *American Journal of Mental Deficiency, 84,* p. 293. Reprinted by permission.)

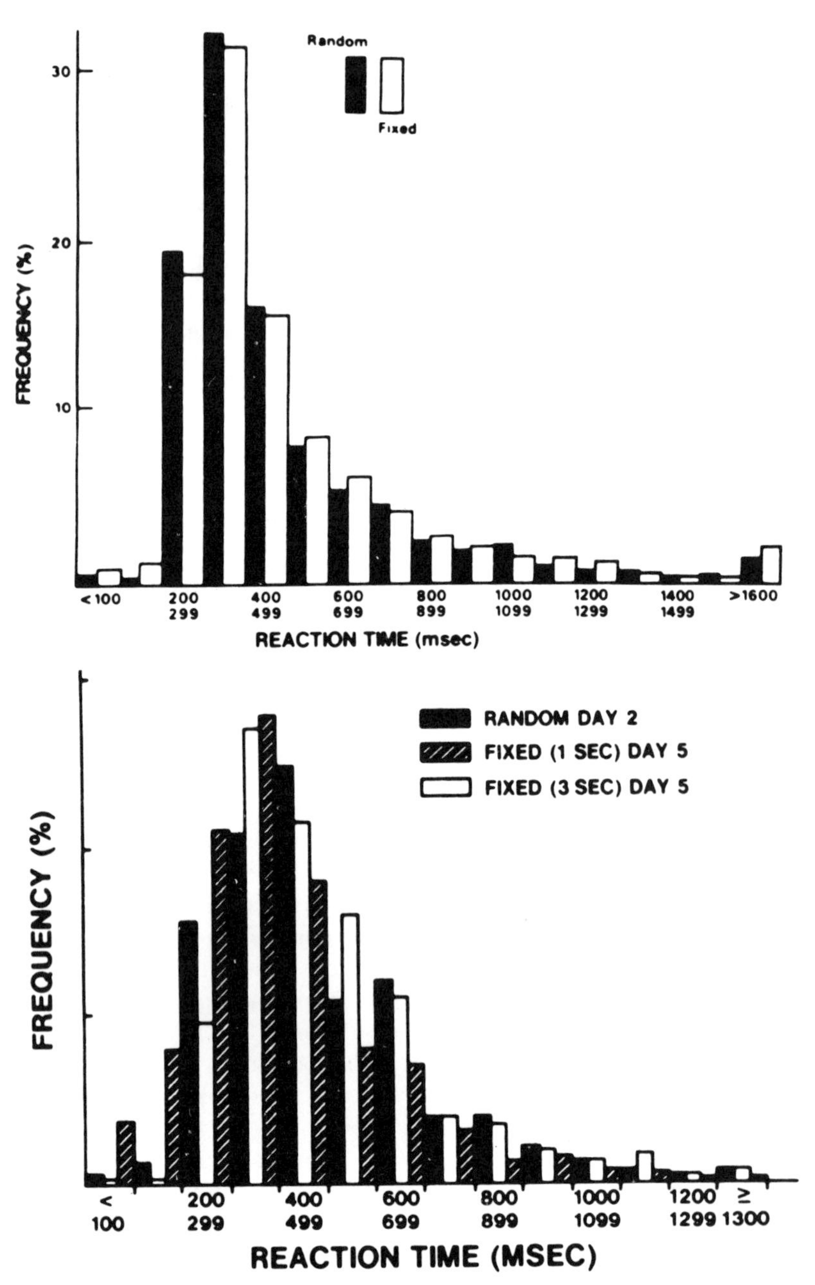

with the exception that the subjects has 90 trials of the stylus-raise task on each of the 5 days of testing.

As the right side of Figure 1 illustrates, the RTs were lower than those reported in Experiment 1, which is a direct reflection of the reduction of response difficulty in Experiment 2. The RT frequency distribution shown in the figure illustrates well the interaction between the fixed foreperiod and days. The interaction was produced by no significant difference between the fixed foreperiod conditions on Day 3, but by Day 5 the 1-s fixed foreperiod group had significantly reduced their mean RT in comparison with the 3-s foreperiod condition (464 ms down to 400 m for the 3-s fixed). The 1-s fixed foreperiod group on Day 5 exhibited considerably more RTs between 100 and 200 ms, and this may be contrasted with the 1-s fixed group in the first experiment (see Figure 1).

The key finding from these two experiments was that the ability of retarded persons to anticipate the fixed foreperiod for the initiation of discrete movements clearly interacted with the complexity of the response. When precision was demanded relative to spatial and temporal criteria, as in Experiment 1, no beneficial anticipation occurred. When response details were minimal, temporal anticipation resulted from a short 1-s fixed foreperiod interval. The retarded group did not demonstrate any significant degree of beneficial or perfect anticipations typically shown by the normal populations, whereby latencies were reduced to the region of 100 ms or even less. In other words, the retarded group showed no evidence of perceptual anticipation (Poulton, 1957) in an aiming response over 3 days of practice.

A contributing factor to a retarded person's failure to temporarily anticipate the arrival of a warning signal may be poor attentional capacity (Brown, 1974; Fisher & Zeaman, 1973). In fact, explanations of poor foreperiod effects with normal persons have been attributed to attentional effects (Adams, 1966), or what has been considered a general readiness to response. It appears, then, that attentional deficits may hinder the ability to time-keep and predict temporal intervals; alternatively, attentional deficits may only magnify the basic inability of the mentally handicapped to time-keep and preprogram responses. Given more appropriate training, retarded persons might successfully anticipate the temporal duration of the response warning interval and, as a consequence, reduce response latencies. Verbal cues have been successful with normal subjects, but whether this strategy would work with retarded populations is open to speculation.

It was just such speculation that motivated a further series of two experiments (Hoover, Wade, & Newell, 1981) which sought to determine the susceptibility to specific training procedures, in line with the ideas of the late Marc Gold. Given that our previous work had shown that moderately retarded persons were capable of preprogramming responses when the precision of the response requirements are held to a minimum, we applied a "Gold-influenced task analysis" by reducing the task into what Gold and Pomerantz (1977) referred to as teachable units. The main objective in the first experiment was to determine whether specific training procedures would lower RT and MT, or both, and whether such improvements in performance would prove to be stable over time. The apparatus used was similar to that used in the Newell et al. (1979) experiments. Only the center target of the three, which was 1.27 cm in diameter, was used, and this combined with the amplitude yielded an index of difficulty of 4.58 (Fitts, 1954). Subjects ($n = 11$; $\bar{X}$ IQ = 41; $\bar{X}$ age = 32 years) were given sufficient practice to demonstrate that they understood the task and were able to perform it. Immediately following the practice session, subjects were given 50 baseline trials.

The starting light was preceded by a warning tone, with the interval between the tone and the response signal being a randomly predetermined period of 1, 2, 3, or 4 s. The subjects were instructed to emphasize speed and accuracy, and a 10% error rate was tolerated. During the training phase of the experiment, subjects were taught to improve initial RT, speed of movement, and accuracy.. The trainer employed many different methods, individualized to the extent possible for each subject. Typically, training techniques included nonverbal prompts and verbal feedback which categorized trials (e.g., "good," "that was fast," "you hit the target"). All prompts and feedback were completely faded by the end of each experimental session. Each session consisted of a series of trials, during which the trainer employed as many of the techniques as were appropriate. Training was followed by 80 test trials. During these daily test trials, the trainer withdrew from the situation, and the only communication with the subjects was in the form of encouragement. Data were collected for 13 training days (Days 2–14) over 3 workweeks. At completion of the training phase, another set of data was collected under baseline conditions (Day 15) and approximately 5 months later (Day 16).

Figure 2 illustrates no significant decrease between the first and last days of training for RT (644 to 711 ms); The decrease across the 13-day training period was not significant. RT was highly variable across the 13 days of training. However, the training data for MT suggest a clear training effect across the 13 days. The average MT on the first day of training was 821 ms; by the last day of training (Day 14) it was reduced to 539 ms. Data in Experiment 1 suggest that RT is not

Figure 2. Mean reaction time and movement time as a function of training in Experiment 1. Days 1 and 15 were baseline; days 2 through 14 were training. (From "Training Moderately and Severely Mentally Retarded Adults to Improve Reaction and Movement Times" by J.H. Hoover, M.G. Wade, and K.M. Newell, 1981, *American Journal of Mental Deficiency, 85,* p. 393. Reprinted by permission.)

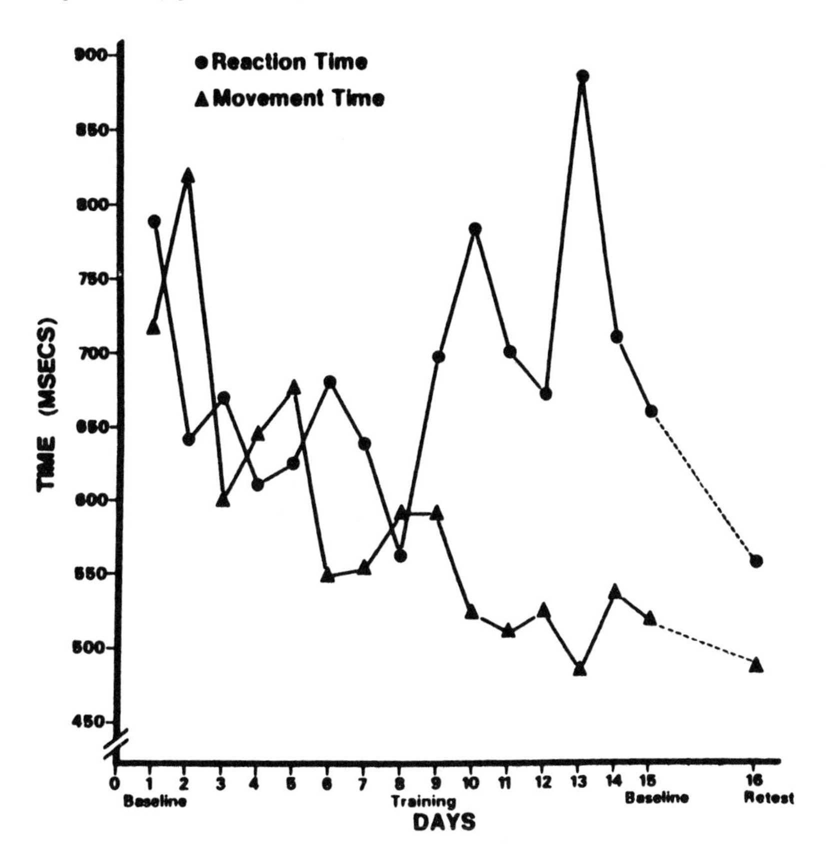

susceptible to training, but that MT shows considerable reduction as a result of training.

Data from a second experiment were collected to determine whether or not the contingent feedback reinforced subjects for a rapid and accurate movement, rather than a quick initiation of the movement. Because reinforcement effects tend to control the behavior most temporally proxemic to it, any change in RT resulting from the first experiment might be inconclusive due to the subsequent requirements of the discrete response. Thus, Experiment 2 examined the effects of training and contingency feedback on RT in the absence of demanding response requirements. Subjects ($n = 8$; $\overline{X}$ IQ $= 45$; $\overline{X}$

age = 36.8 years) were randomly assigned to two groups, each containing one woman and three men. The apparatus was identical to that described in Experiment 1 except that, instead of a hand-held stylus, a standard telegraph key set at a 0.23 cm gap extended directly from the stimulus light. When the telegraph key was released from a closed position, the RT and false starts were recorded; thus the task was a simple RT activity. On Day 1, subjects were given a demonstration and were then given 80 trials.

Following every 20 trials, subjects were reminded to lift their index fingers as quickly as possible and keep their eyes on the light. On Day 2, the key press operation was demonstrated to each subject. The experimenter first performed the task alone and then manually guided the subjects through the operation, using verbal instructions and prompting. Subjects were again reminded to watch the light and move their fingers as rapidly as possible. To reduce the number of false starts, the experimenter, following each false start, verbally reminded the subject, "Don't lift your finger until the light comes on." Other than this, no feedback was provided to the control group. On Days 2-10, experimental subjects were provided with feedback in the form of chips delivered electromechanically in a tray, in front of them, following trials that were at least 10% faster than their previous day's median score. All subjects were given 80 trials per day. Day 1 represented baseline and Days 2-6 consecutive workdays during the first week of testing; and Days 7-10 were workdays of the following week. All subjects were paid at the end of the experiment their hourly workshop rate, independent of the monies earned during the experimental sessions.

The data illustrated in Figure 3 show a significant reduction in RT by the experimental group receiving feedback, suggesting that in the absence of precise spatial and temporal response requirements subjects are trying to reduce RT. A significant decrease in the variability of scores and a reduction in the number of extreme and aberrant RT scores accompanied the reduction in average RT scores. Furthermore, a speed accuracy trade-off might be expected to occur, insofar as subjects were being encouraged to produce ever-faster responses. As can be seen in the lower section of Figure 3, this was not the case. In fact, error rates decreased over days, yielding a significant reduction in false starts.

Researchers have argued that RT and MT are essentially independent in the nonretarded (Marteniuk, 1976) and in the handicapped (Jensen & Munro, 1979). Although our data do not suggest any contrary explanation, it should be recognized that in many respects RT and MT reflect a continual process in response production. This is buttressed by the fact that recent RT analysis of

Figure 3. Mean reaction time and error rate as a function of feedback and control conditions in Experiment 2. (From "Training Moderately and Severely Mentally Retarded Adults to Improve Reaction and Movement Times" by J.H. Hoover, M.G. Wade, and K.M. Newell, 1981, *American Journal of Mental Deficiency, 85,* p. 393. Reprinted by permission.)

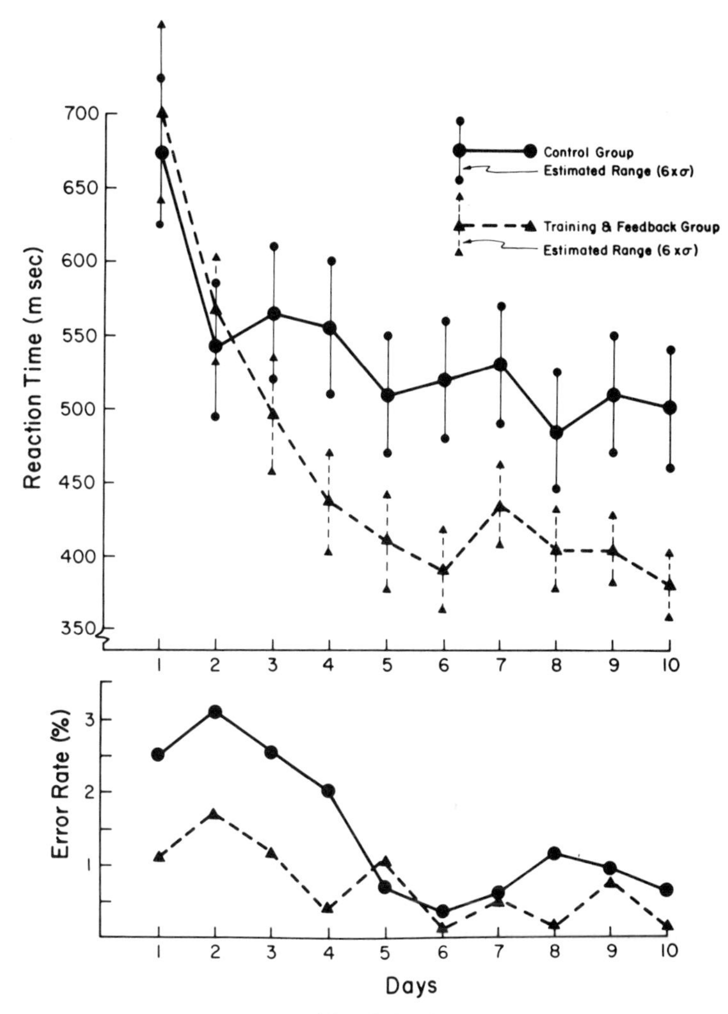

response programming has utilized the latency as an indicant of the features that might be programmed in the response. An interesting feature of this strategy is that it rests on the assumption that RT and MT are not independent (Kerr, 1978). Thus, although our data suggest that independence of RT and MT seems conceptually more reasonable, it is important to examine both theoretically and practically the mutual relationship between these two parameters, with a view toward developing a unified perspective on both the development of actual skills and the manner in which the mentally handicapped may be trained to improve their performance.

ANTICIPATORY TIMING BEHAVIOR

The second issue of timing is timing behavior that is reflected by motion prediction and the ability to perform coincident timing acts, which involve interception of targets moving through space. The two experiments reported here (Wade, et al., 1982) are an extension of my earlier work (Wade, 1980) in which subjects made perceptual judgments of a coincident timing task and also made an overt motor response to a moving object at a coincident point. Before training mentally handicapped individuals on tasks requiring linear prediction of motion, it is necessary to understand the response parameters that largely determine performance. These two experiments were, therefore, designed to establish some boundary conditions for retarded individuals' performance on motion prediction tasks.

The first experiment was essentially perceptual, requiring subjects to predict the arrival of a moving target at a predetermined point by a key press response. The second experiment required the subjects to respond with a higher degree of response complexity by propelling a doughnut-shaped missile along a horizontal rod to intercept a moving target. Our earlier work demonstrated that response complexity interacts with the decision processes involved in initiating discrete movements, and this was an additional concern in these experiments. The apparatus was a trackway moving from right to left. On the trackway was a target which crossed photocells at the beginning and endpoint to determine, via differential logic, the early and late timing errors. Screens could be placed over the trackway to mask portions of the trackway as desired. The apparatus is fully described elsewhere (Wade, 1980; Wade et al., 1982).

Subjects ($n = 10$; $\overline{X}$ IQ $= 40$; $\overline{X}$ age $= 25$ years) performed under nine conditions in Experiment 1, consisting of a matrix formed by crossing all combinations of three target velocities with three preview conditions. This produced equal exposure times on the diagonal of the matrix. The equal exposure conditions acted as a control to tease out the relative contributions of preview duration and target velocity. Training was carried out during practice trials on the first 2 days of the experiment, and then 80 trials were recorded for each condition. Subjects performed three conditions per day, resting approximately 3 min between each condition as the experimenter recalibrated the target speed and the preview distances. The experimenter said either "hit" or "good shot" after each response that met the preset criterion.

If absolute temporal error was under 100, 50, or 33 ms respectively for the three target speeds, the response was called a hit. These combinations provided approximately equal spatial error boundaries for the three target speeds. If subjects made five responses in a row that were misses in the same direction (early or late), the experimenter provided feedback in the form of a direct statement, such as "you're shooting too early" or "you're shooting too late." If the subject missed in one direction for 10 consecutive trials, the experiment was halted and the subject retrained. This, in fact, was a rare occurrence; it happened only twice, each time with a different subject.

Figure 4 illustrates the results of the first experiment, which primarily involved perceptual judgments using a key press. The top half of the figure shows the constant error and shows that subjects tended to respond slightly late when the exposure distance was small (30.5 cm) and progressively earlier as the preview distance increased to 91.5 cm. These effects were significant. Constant error changes of the target speed were not significant.

The lower half of the graph shows the variable error scores and shows that as target velocity increased, so did the variability of the subject's responses. This might be expected with this particular population. There was a significant response exposure by target velocity interaction, the performance differences being most evident at the highest velocity, where error increased as a function of degree of exposure.

Although the diagonal of the velocity by preview (3×3) matrix produced constant exposure times, errors were largest under conditions of maximum velocity and preview, suggesting that subjects' response decisions were influenced by information other than mere exposure time.

The second experiment repeated the first experiment except that, instead of a key press response at the coincident point, subjects were asked to propel a missile to intercept the moving target. In the original design, all subjects were to perform under the nine conditions produced; however, some target speed/exposure combinations proved impossible for subjects to perform owing to the difficulty of some conditions of the task, and thus yielded no data.

The data that were collected are illustrated in Figure 5. The missing data points are from conditions in which subjects were unable to perform. The top half of the figure shows the constant error scores, and there was no significant difference between the six conditions analyzed. There was, however, a trend for all three conditions involving the 30.5-cm target velocity to produce errors that were "late," whereas the target velocity conditions for the 61-cm

Figure 4. Mean scores for effects of preview distance and target velocity for Experiment 1. (From "Coincident Timing Behavior of Young Mentally Retarded Workers Under Varying Conditions of Target Velocity and Exposure" by M.G. Wade, K.M. Newell, and J.H. Hoover, 1982, *American Journal of Mental Deficiency, 86,* p. 645. Reprinted by permission.)

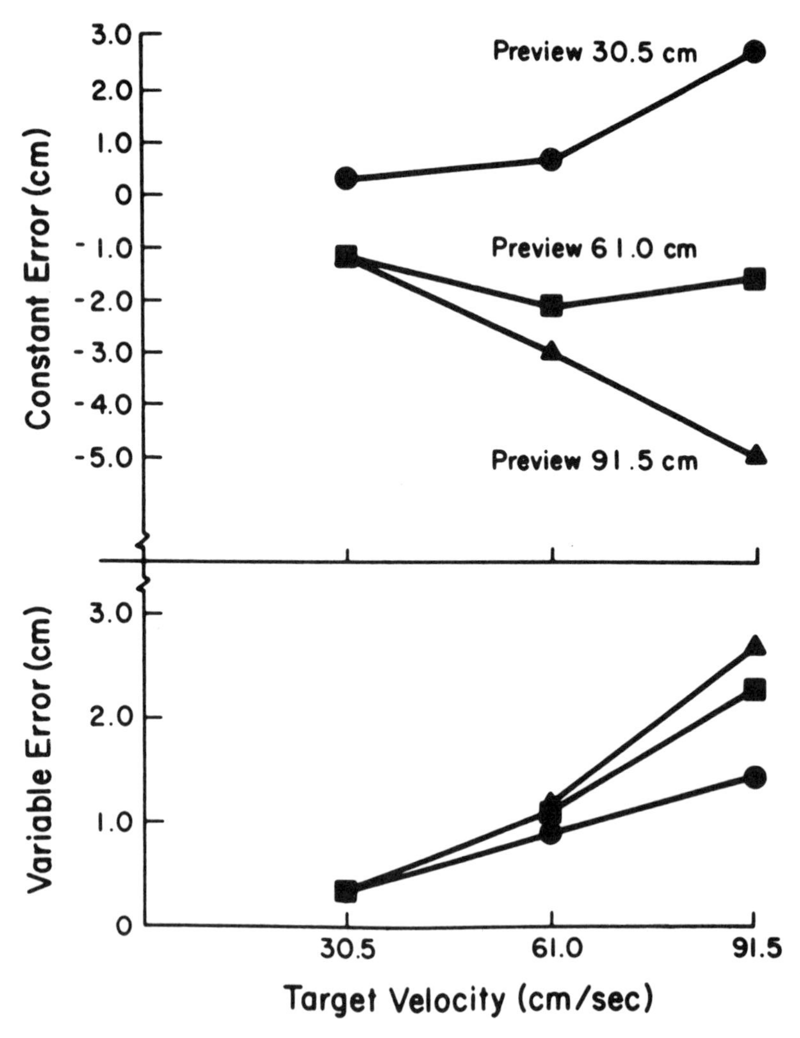

and 91.5-cm preview produced early errors. The lower half of the graph shows the variable errors, which were significantly different across conditions. A combination of the largest preview and fastest target velocity produced the highest mean variable error score, and the 30.5-cm preview combined with the 30.5-cm/s target velocity yielded the lowest mean score.

Figure 5. Mean scores for effects of preview distance and target velocity for Experiment 2. (From "Coincident Timing Behavior of Young Mentally Retarded Workers Under Varying Conditions of Target Velocity and Exposure" by M.G. Wade, K.M. Newell, and J.H. Hoover, 1982, *American Journal of Mental Deficiency, 86,* p. 647. Reprinted by permission.)

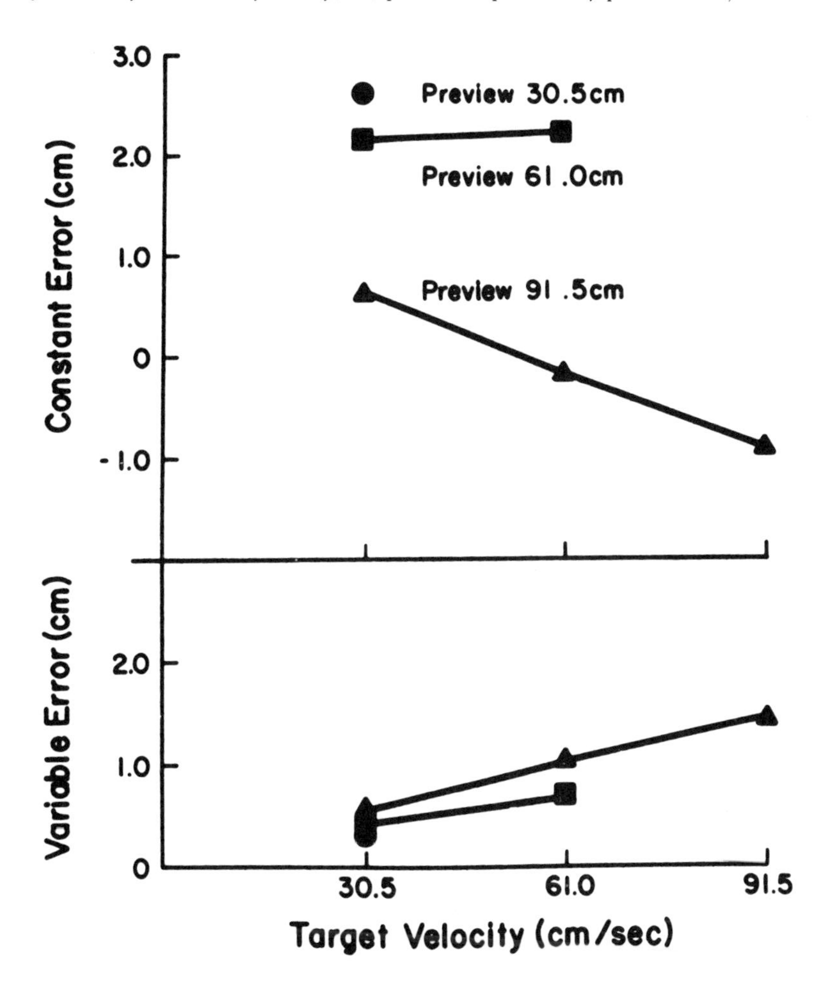

The data in Experiment 1 suggested an optimal condition under which subjects were required to make motion prediction judgments, and this, in the absence of complex motor response, might approach 30.5 cm, irrespective of the target velocity. A closer analysis of the constant errors for the first experiment suggested that slow responding and the inability to inhibit responses in the 61-cm and 91.5-cm exposure conditions together produced both the late responses of the 30.5-cm exposure and the early responses of the 61-cm and 91.5-cm exposures. This is corroborated by the variable error data in Figure 4.

The three constant exposure conditions suggested that the high preview/high velocity combination, although temporally consistent with the low preview/low velocity and medium velocity conditions, generated a more dramatic rate of change in the optic array, which produced larger errors. This argues in part for a more dynamic interpretation of motion prediction responses, which requires a sensitivity to the dynamics (mass and force) of the display, rather than the kinematics (velocity and acceleration). This is speculative in nature, but such ideas should not be discounted if the underlying components of temporal anticipation are to be fully understood.

SUMMARY

The three research studies (Hoover et al., 1981; Newell et al., 1979; Wade et al., 1982) that I have discussed together provide some insights into the acquisition and performance of motor skills requiring timing behavior on the part of the respondent. When the responding subject is mentally handicapped in the moderate range (such as the subjects used in these studies), the level of performance is sensitive to the complexity level of the required task response.

"Timing" is clearly an important component of skilled behavior, and it is possible to provide empirical evidence of poor timing behavior. The controversy still rages, however, as to whether there exists a timing mechanism in the system, or whether accurate timing somehow falls out of the other components of skilled behavior. In other words, is accurate timing an inherent characteristic of skilled behavior, devoid of its own infrastructure? The larger question then relates more to a need to determine the variables that constitute complex motor skills. Skills requiring fast, accurate movements to both stationary and moving targets fall under the "complexity" banner, and it is information of this nature that will make a significant contribution to the area of motor development.

REFERENCES

Adams, J. A. (1966). Some mechanisms of motor responding: An examination of attention. In E. A. Bilodeau (Ed.), *Acquisition of skill* (pp. 75-93). New York: Academic Press.

Baumeister, A. A., & Hawkins, W. F. (1966). Variations of the preparatory interval in relation to the reaction times. *American Journal of Mental Deficiency, 70,* 689-694.

Brown, A. L. (1974). The role of strategic behavior in retardate memory. In N. R. Ellis (Ed.), *International review of research in mental retardation* (Vol. 7, pp. 55-111) New York: Academic Press.

Fisher, M. A., & Zeaman, D. (1973). An attention-retention theory of retardate discrimination learning. In N.R. Ellis (Ed.), *International review of research in mental retardation* (Vol. 6, pp. 45-62). New York: Academic Press.

Fitts, P.M. (1954). The information capacity of the human motor system in controlling the amplitude of movement. *Journal of Experimental Psychology, 47,* 381-391.

Fitts, P.M., & Peterson, J.R. (1964). Information capacity of discrete motor responses. *Journal of Experimental Psychology, 67,* 103-112.

Gold, M.W., and Pomerantz, D.J. (1977). Issues in pre-locational training. In M. Snell (Ed.), *Teaching the moderately, severely and profoundly retarded* (pp. 52-75). Columbus, OH: Merrill.

Hoover, J.H., Wade, M.G., & Newell, K.M. (1981). Training moderately and severely mentally retarded adults to improve reaction and movement times. *American Journal of Mental Deficiency, 85,* 389-395.

Jensen, A.R., & Munro, E. (1979). Reaction time and movement time and intelligence. *Intelligence, 3,* 121-126.

Kerr, B. (1978). Task factors that influence selection and preparation for voluntary movements. In G.E. Stelmach (Ed.), *Information processing in motor control and learning* (pp. 55-69). New York: Academic Press.

Marteniuk, R.G. (1976). *Information processing in motor skills.* New York: Holt, Rinehart & Winston.

Newell, K.M., Wade, M.G., & Kelly, T.M. (1979). Temporal anticipation of response initiation in retarded persons. *American Journal of Mental Deficiency, 84,* 289-296.

Poulton, E.C. (1957). On prediction in skilled movements. *Psychological Bulletin, 54,* 467-478.

Terrell, C., & Ellis, N.R. (1964). Reaction time in normal and defective subjects following varied warning conditions. *Journal of Abnormal and Social Psychology, 69,* 449-452.

Wade, M.G. (1980). Coincidence anticipation of young, normal and handicapped children. *Journal of Motor Behavior, 12,* 103-112.

Wade, M.G., Newell, K.M., & Hoover, J.H. (1982). Coincident timing behavior of young mentally retarded workers under varying conditions of target velocity and exposure. *American Journal of Mental Deficiency, 86,* 643-649.

Wade, M.G., Newell, K.M., & Wallace, S.A. (1978). Decision time and movement time as a function of response complexity in retarded persons. *American Journal of Mental Deficiency, 83,* 135-144.

17

Coordination, Control, and Skill in the Mentally Handicapped: Commentary on Reviews of Research

CRAIG A. WRISBERG
University of Tennessee, Knoxville

Responses to the remarks made in Chapters 14–16 are given. Due to the large heterogeneity of behavior in mentally handicapped populations, more flexibility may be needed in developing theoretical frameworks designed to describe that behavior. Newell's call for increased theoretical attention to the notion of coordination is applauded; however, impaired coordination will probably represent only one of a variety of factors contributing to performance decrements for most mentally handicapped people. In response to Wade's paper, recent evidence is discussed which suggests that while the quality of performance of mentally retarded subjects may be lower than that of nonretarded subjects, both populations may respond in similar ways to various experimental manipulations. Horgan's discussion of memory processes is supplemented by the suggestion, first made by Belmont (1978), that memory development be viewed in terms of the refinement of self-programming skills. Finally, the prediction is made that future experimental paradigms will be characterized by both quantitative and qualitative measures of movement performance.

First, I would like to thank Mike Wade and the other contributors for this opportunity to respond to their remarks concerning recent conceptualizations and findings on the coordination, control, and motor skill of mentally handicapped people.

My academic background is in the area of motor learning and control and the majority of my research has represented an attempt to identify mechanisms underlying the anticipation and timing capabilities of nonretarded persons as well as to determine factors that limit those persons' ability to process, store, and utilize movement-related information. Owing primarily to the interests of several doctoral students, I have become involved in the assessment of the receptor anticipation performance of mildly retarded adults. Perhaps the most striking aspect of my initial research endeavor with this population has been an increased awareness of the large heterogeneity of variance in their performance, both within and between individual subjects. This, I am certain, is nothing new to the experienced investigator of mentally handicapped behavior, but it was quite a jolt to one accustomed to groups of subjects that demonstrate considerably more homogeneity in baseline performance. As a result of this experience I feel that I more clearly recognize the challenge that faces researchers in the field of mental retardation: specifically, to develop more precise theoretical frameworks which promote the identification of the important factors that might limit the performance of mentally retarded people yet retain their flexibility to handle the enormous individual differences inherent in this population.

I would now like to respond to each of the review papers in this volume. Karl Newell has provided an excellent conceptual framework by distinguishing between the terms "coordination," "control," and "skill." I concur with his observation that the notion of coordination has received insufficient theoretical attention in the literature on mental retardation. A recent exception is the work of Davis and Kelso (1982), in which the coordination of movements in Down's syndrome subjects was investigated. These researchers found that muscles that act to flex and extend the index finger about the metacarpophalangeal joint were constrained to act as a unit in both nonretarded and Down's syndrome subjects. However, for the latter group there appeared to exist a deficiency in the setting of damping and stiffness parameters for those muscles. Thus, it was concluded that while torque by joint angle functions are invariant characteristics of the muscle-joint system of both nonretarded and Down's syndrome subjects, the specification of stiffness as well as the damping chararacteristic is different for the two groups. Consonant with Newell's recommendation that coordination be observed in more real-life situations, it should be pointed out that some modification of Davis and Kelso's model may be necessary upon the investigation of movements involving simultaneous action by a variety of muscle-joint systems. Nevertheless, research strategies such as theirs appear to be of the type that will provide much-needed answers to questions about the mechanisms of coordination in mentally retarded people.

I was also intrigued by Newell's suggestion that coordination be expressed in terms of functions that serve to constrain variables within behavioral units, particularly with respect to patterns of relative motion. This approach certainly deserves experimental attention, and I anticipate that it will be utilized by a number of researchers investigating the coordination of mentally handicapped people in the near future. However, I feel that our enthusiasm for describing the invariant properties of motor coordination should continue to be tempered by a recognition of the possibility that the knowledge of such properties may not guarantee more accurate diagnosis of the factors that limit the performance of any single mentally retarded person. This is particularly important because it appears that decrements in the perceptual-motor performance of such populations are often due to deficits in a *variety* of areas (e.g., inefficient memory processes, inappropriate arousal levels, misdirected attention, deficiency in the setting of muscle damping and stiffness parameters) rather than in any single area.

Wade and Horgan have addressed additional areas where deficiencies in the perceptual-motor performance of mentally retarded subjects might be seen. Wade reported the results of a series of studies with a task that involved either a button press or the projection of a small doughnut-shaped object down a steel rod toward a target. In both response situations, subjects were attempting to "time" the arrival of a moving visual stimulus at the target point. Wade's finding of early anticipations in the button press situation and late anticipations in the doughnut-push condition suggests that the increased response complexity of the latter movement added to the time it took subjects to initiate their movements. Additional measures such as the time of initiation of the doughnut-push and the speed with which it traveled might have further illuminated the nature of retarded subjects' response strategies in that situation.

We recently found that while the overall quality of coincidence anticipation performance was lower (i.e., higher absolute errors, more-negative algebraic errors, greater within-subject variability) in retarded than in nonretarded adults, both groups responded similarly to error feedback and stimulus velocity manipulations (Wrisberg, Martin, & Wren, 1983). Specifically, the performance of both retarded and nonretarded groups improved with feedback regarding their timing errors when the stimulus velocity was slower (3 mph) but not when it was faster (7 mph). Moreover, increased within-subject variability occurred for both groups as the velocity of the stimulus increased. Thus, Wade, Newell, and Hoover's (1982) speculation that the dynamics of a more rapidly changing optical array (i.e., faster stimulus velocity) may limit the accuracy and consistency of visual perception in retarded persons apparently holds for the visual perception of nonretarded subjects as well. However, additional work in real-life situations that includes the measurement of a variety of response components (e.g., initiation time, movement time, movement velocity, temporal-spatial movement pattern) is necessary to more definitively assess the perceptual, motor, and situational factors having potential to limit performance in dynamic, open-skill settings.

Another factor with the potential to limit the perceptual-motor performance of mentally handicapped people may be an inefficient memory for movement-related information. Horgan reported the results of some of his work on short-term memory for movement-related information in mentally retarded individuals. Once again, the task used was of the artificial, laboratory-variety type (i.e., blindfolded angular positioning), which may be essential for the development of initial principles that describe the memory limitations of retarded people but must eventually be replaced by tasks that call for the storage, processing, and use of movement-related information in more natural settings. Another potentially fruitful direction for memory research with retarded persons has been suggested by Belmont (1978). He points out that individual differences in memory are quite pronounced in both retarded and nonretarded populations. For example, an average "forgetting curve" for a given group of people may often account for less than half of the variability in the forgetting curves of individual subjects. This suggests that work is needed to identify those aspects of memory that contribute to such dramatic individual differences.

One ability which Belmont has proposed limits the memory performance of retarded people is that concerned with self-programming skills (i.e., the understanding of, and diligence and adeptness at, management of one's own memory control processes). Indeed, he argues that one way memory development might be viewed is in terms of the development of self-programming skills. It appears that both retarded and normal children's memory deficiencies are largely due to their undeveloped self-programming skills (Belmont & Butterfield, 1977). Furthermore, it has been demonstrated that retarded people benefit from instructions regarding how to rehearse certain categories of verbal material (Butterfield, Wambold, & Belmont, 1973). Preliminary work by Reid (1980) has indicated that such instructional aids may also promote the rehearsal, storage, and retrieval of movement-related information by retarded subjects. However, further work is needed to assess the generalizability of acquired self-programming skills to a variety of movement situations.

My impression of the state of the art of motor behavior assessment is that we are on the verge of making some significant inroads into the identification of factors that limit the perceptual-motor performance of both handicapped and nonhandicapped people. I expect that several experimental paradigms discussed in this volume will be among those that will be used to elucidate both the invariant and variant parameters of purposeful motor activity. I further anticipate that the majority of future investigations will include both quantitative (e.g., movement velocity) and qualitative (e.g., film assessment of relative motion) measures of movement performance, and I look forward to the results of these studies.

REFERENCES

Belmont, J. M. (1978). Individual differences in memory: The cases of normal and retarded development. In M. M. Gruneberg & P. Morris (Eds.), *Aspects of memory* (pp. 153-185). London: Metheun.

Belmont, J. M., & Butterfield, E. C. (1977). The instructional approach to developmental cognitive research. In R. Kail & J. Hagen (Eds.), *Perspectives on the development of memory and cognition* (pp. 437-481). Hillsdale, NJ: Erlbaum.

Butterfield, E. C., Wambold, C., & Belmont, J. M. (1973). On the theory and practice of improving short-term memory. *American Journal of Mental Deficiency, 77,* 654-669.

Davis, W. E., & Kelso, J. A. S. (1982). Analysis of invariant characteristics in the motor control of Down's syndrome and normal subjects. *Journal of Motor Behavior, 14,* 194-212.

Reid, G. (1980). The effects of memory strategy instruction in the short-term motor memory of the mentally retarded. *Journal of Motor Behavior, 12,* 221-227.

Wade, M.G., Newell, K.M., & Hoover, J.H. (1982). Coincident timing behavior in young mentally retarded workers under varying conditions of target velocity and exposure. *American Journal of Mental Deficiency, 86,* 643-649.

Wrisberg, C. A., Martin, J. H., & Wren, C. A. (1983). Receptor anticipation of retarded and nonretarded adults. *American Journal of Mental Deficiency, 87,* 627-633.

Index